Ir

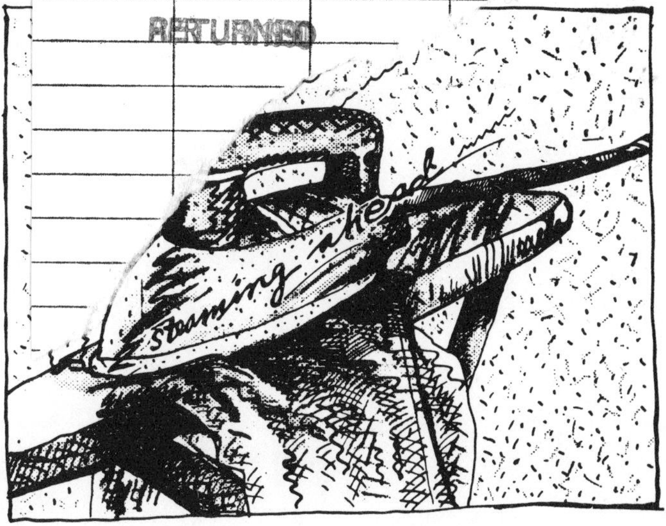

The four women who have worked collectively on compiling this book, Hannah Kanter, Sarah Lefanu, Shaila Shah and Carole Spedding, share amongst them a variety of contemporary feminist politics. They are all currently active in the women's liberation movement in Britain.

HANNAH KANTER, SARAH LEFANU,
SHAILA SHAH and CAROLE SPEDDING, editors

Sweeping Statements

Writings from the Women's Liberation Movement 1981–83

 The Women's Press

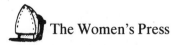

First published by The Women's Press Limited 1984
A member of the Namara Group
124 Shoreditch High Street, London E1 6JE

British Library Cataloguing in Publication Data

Sweeping statements.
   1. Women—Social conditions
   I. Kanter, Hannah
   305.4'2   HQ1154

   ISBN 0-7043-3930-7

Typeset by MC Typeset, Chatham, Kent
Printed in Great Britain by Nene Litho
and bound by Woolnough Bookbinding
both of Wellingborough, Northants

Contents

3 Racism

4 No Nukes

5 Up Against the State

6 Sex and Sexuality

7 Our Bodies

8 Challenges

Preface

Sweeping Statements, we hope, continues a tradition of radical collections from the women's liberation movement (WLM) that includes *Conditions of Illusion*, *The Body Politic* and *No Turning Back*. In this collection, we have selected pieces from feminist publications nationally, concentrating on local and internal journals, to show the range of political issues that feminists have been active around during the past three years.

We read as widely as we could, and from that enormous amount of material we have selected personal accounts, press releases, letters, debating pieces, conference papers and self-criticisms of the WLM. The inequality in size of the various sections does, we feel, reflect the major areas of recent debate.

We have tried to contact all the writers who appear in this book, but inevitably we have failed with some. We have not reprinted, without permission, anything that first appeared in a women-only publication but have, in a very few cases, reprinted some pieces which appeared in easily available publications even when we did not manage to obtain permission of the author.

We trust that those women will understand that we felt their words important enough to reproduce and we thank all the women who replied promptly to our requests for newsletters and journals and who gave permission for their articles to appear. We are only sorry that, for reasons of space, we could not include more.

1 Violence against Women

Introduction

Of all the concerns of feminists in the past two years, violence against women is the area where a clearly defined analysis has been developed, and, as in the peace movement, women have undertaken direct – and often illegal – action in protest. The analysis that pornography is a form of violence against women has derived from the work of American radical feminists. Criticism of the position has been fragmented and concerned with issues of representation and determination – what the status of these images is, how they come to mean certain things, and exactly how we talk about their effects.

Important theoretical work in this country first came from the revolutionary feminist tendency – a group of women who had previously often been discredited as the extremists of the movement. Soon, a national network of Women Against Violence Against Women (WAVAW) developed, and out of their work, and that of all women working against violence against women, have come many concrete gains. There have been several conferences, including those in Leeds, in Oxford and in Edinburgh, the last on the sexual abuse of girls;[1] the Incest Survivors group has been set up; as well as the publicity that 'Angry Women' have gained by their direct action against sex shops and 'video nasties', pressure from feminists here and in the States had a lot to do with the proposed film about Peter Sutcliffe, the Yorkshire rapist, being dropped; many Rape Crisis Centres and other interested women submitted recommendations to the Criminal Law Revision Committee, considering changes to the Sexual Offences (Amendment) Act 1967; the trades union movement has begun to take notice of the problem of sexual harassment at work, thanks to the efforts of women trades unionists.

Twenty-five per cent of all violent crime continues to be domestic, and there are now 150 Women's Aid refuges in the United Kingdom, including a few Asian women's refuges, set up to offer the particular support and services they need. An episode of the *Police* television series briefly aroused public outcry about police treatment of women reporting rapes, and individual judgments created a stir – for example, Judge Bertrand Richards (Ipswich, 1982), who stated that a woman was guilty of 'contributory negligence' because she was hitch-hiking at night when a man offered her a lift and raped her. However, in spite of issuing new guidelines to the police, women continue to be very badly treated and disbelieved when reporting crimes of sexual violence. The police advise women to stay at home to avoid rape, reinforcing the myth that rape only happens in dark alleys, and imposing a curfew on women while men have the freedom of the streets. There are now twenty-six rape crisis centres in the United Kingdom.

Police harassment of prostitutes has also been challenged; in autumn 1982 the English Collective of Prostitutes occupied a church in Kings Cross, London, an area where many prostitutes work, in protest. A group of women in Stockwell, London, have set up a collectively run, late-night lift service for women, and other efforts to provide safe transport for women include the Labyris taxi service.

It is notable, however, that WAVAW, although potentially a mass campaign, has failed to mobilise large numbers of women. And despite the wealth of analysis it offers, the particularly racist aspect of the use of black women in pornography, and of violence against black women, has been largely ignored. This section, we hope, reflects direct action, current analysis and personal experience, and commemorates some of the countless women who continue to be the casualties of male violence – Pat Malone, Mary Bristow and the Maw sisters.

Note

1. Other important papers on violence against women can be found in *Sexual Violence Against Women*, Onlywomen Press, 1984.

ANON

Incest – A Personal Account

First published in *Leeds Women's Liberation Newsletter*,
July 1982

The following article was written for Leeds Rape Crisis
Centre and as I think it's important that incest survivors speak out
about what incest is, I've decided to put it in this newsletter. I am
writing this under a pseudonym because I am frightened of making
myself too vulnerable. In the original version, the personal account
was followed by counselling hints – these have been left out.

My Father

He was very definitely the authority figure in the house. All of us,
including my mother, were quite frightened of him. There are three
children in my family. I have two younger sisters and I am definite
that he never sexually abused any of the others, although he did
subject all of us to similar sorts of ridicule, making us feel
unconfident in our ability to do or accomplish anything.

My relationship with my father was always fraught. I was the
apple of his eye in many ways, being quite stroppy and rebellious. I
still don't understand why he decided to pick on me, although it
might have simply been the way the bedrooms were organised in
our home, which meant that nobody could hear what was going on
in my bedroom. Also, because my sisters shared a bedroom, he
probably wouldn't have got away with it so easily.

I started my periods very early – I was about ten or eleven. At the
same time, I developed quite large breasts. My father was delighted
at this, but insisted that I carry on wearing very schoolgirly-type
clothes. It was a bit like men's schoolgirl fantasies. There were
always quite a few of his friends at the house. He used to tease me
all the time about having large breasts in front of his friends. I felt
embarrassed and dirty. The feeling of being dirty was made worse
by the fact that there was always loads of porn in the house –
Playboy, *Mayfair*, etc. I always felt that I had an image to aspire to,

3

i.e. I was supposed to look like the women in the porn mags, and my father was continually taunting me because I didn't.

My father started coming to my room at night when I was about twelve or thirteen years old. The first time it happened, I woke up with a start because there was someone sitting astride me, across my legs, and I couldn't turn over. It was quite dark, except for the street light coming in through the windows, and I was absolutely terrified. It felt so unreal. The sort of things he used to do to me were biting, scratching, squeezing, masturbating against me, trying to get me to masturbate him, verbal and physical abuse. He had a horror of menstrual blood, and was particularly cruel towards me if he found out that I was bleeding. He thought women's cunts were smelly, gaping wounds – he even convinced me of that, because I never ever touched my own.

These night-time visits were always accompanied by threats not to tell my mother, because she'd hate me and disown me. I was always pretty close to my mother up until this point, but afterwards, for a long, long time, I avoided her because I had such a horrible secret. I was terrified that she'd find out and not love me any more. It was even more tricky, because my mother used to make a lot of our clothes, and at the times when I had bites and scratches on my body, I had to run and hide somewhere so as not to have to take my clothes off when she wanted to measure me for dressmaking, in case she saw the marks and guessed where they came from. I used to feel like some sort of split personality – I used to cover up my fear and depression with a 'life and soul of the party' act. I once ran away from home to get away from my father – the police brought me back. My father didn't ask me why I had run away, he didn't have to, he knew. My mother was really confused by it. At that point, if she'd pushed me, I probably would have told her, because I was desperate. But she didn't. I think she put it down to my hormonal changes at puberty, and my natural, rebellious streak.

From this time onwards in my life, and especially when I was living at home, I never felt safe. I couldn't even go to bed at night, because sleep was so interrupted and I was chronically insecure. I had tried to put a chair under the door handle to prevent my father opening the door, but there was a step down into my room and the back of the chair didn't touch the handle. There had been a key to my room, but it disappeared a couple of nights before my father first started to make his night visits. Everything was in flux, nothing was safe. I used to fight sleep at night, staying awake as long as I possibly could. In the morning I was exhausted, bleary-eyed from crying and nervous exhaustion. I truanted from school, skipped every lesson I could – I waged a one-woman battle against school, which represented for me at the time the other major authority figure, and the only one I could fight back against. I think it was also a way of getting at my father, because he was so concerned that all his kids should do well academically.

Most kids have somewhere they can go for privacy – you have things you can call your own, however silly and slight they may seem. I had nothing – presents were given and taken back immediately. My bedroom wasn't safe, letters were opened 'by accident', phone calls were listened to – every minute of the day and night he wanted to know where I was going, who I was seeing, what I had done. To be more than two minutes late back meant punishment and interrogation. I always felt like I had no identity of my own, except that which my father allowed me to have. I certainly had no self-respect and never thought about myself. The prospect was too frightening. I think this is why I can remember very little about my adolescence. In fact, I never really started thinking about myself and who I was until I hit the women's movement head on (fanfare of trumpets) and more especially once I became a lesbian, because at that point I had to totally rethink my fucked-up sexuality, what I wanted, how to learn to take and not just give. Most people might take these for granted. I just never thought of thinking about myself. I had been convinced for years that I was a dirty, evil, worthless person, who had done dirty, evil things with her own father.

Emotionally, I distrusted everybody. The lesson that my father had taught me was that caring and vulnerability were punishable offences. I became totally self-sufficient emotionally. I never asked for help, never admitted to being weak or depressed or insecure, because it meant admitting vulnerability and my father was always just around the corner. I shut everybody out from what was turmoil inside and carried on as if nothing was happening. At one time I had been a very physically affectionate young woman. I became terrified of being touched, recoiled from it – being touched meant you had to give something in return and I distrusted everyone who said they loved me because trust had been so violently abused. I find it hard to trust still – take let-downs very badly, and it takes a long time to build up any sort of trust in relationships. Your father is supposed to be your male protector, the first man you know. You should (or are supposed to) love him and respect him. With my father, all these things were turned topsy-turvy. It was ironic when I started to go to discos and youth clubs, that my mother would send my father to pick me up, so 'nothing would happen' to me. If only she had known. I grew up thinking that, in heterosexual sex, coercion was an acceptable part of that.

Most women I've spoken to seem to have this idea that there's some sort of brand on them, and that people can spot the 'victim'. It was like this for me too – always living in fear and trembling that someone would guess my guilty secret. I felt as if I must have some mark or other on me that would single me out from the other 'normal' people around. Some women I've talked with have an obsession with cleanliness, which is what I have. You have so little control over your life when you are a child, especially if you are being denied any personhood. Keeping everything clean and tidy and being almost obsessional about keeping your own body clean is the only way that you can be sure where everything is, and that what is there is spotless and beyond reproach.

Sanity is another thing I struggled with for years and years. I fought and struggled to understand what was happening to me with my father – I tried to look at it from all sides and ended up just thinking that I must be crazy. He just totally denied that there was anything wrong with what he was doing and so I thought it must be me who was mad. I felt so angry underneath all the guilt, but did not feel that I had any right to feel anything at all, let alone something as fierce as anger. In the end, I got scared stiff of being angry, because I thought that if I got really angry I would end up in a bin or something. At times, I was pretty suicidal too.

When you are being sexually abused by a father, especially if it started to happen at a very young age, it's as if you haven't had any childhood. There's no innocence, no straightforward good times. It's always tinged by the threat of what could come from your father at any minute. You feel guilt-stricken, in fear – there's nobody you can turn to even if you wanted to because of the fear of recriminations. I used to pray that somebody would ask me outright about what was going on – but they never did. But it's so important to break the silence.

HILARY, MANCHESTER

Have You Been Raped Then?

First published in *FAST*, no. 8, Summer 1982

In my experience, this is the first thing most people ask if you say you're involved with a rape crisis line. I have the 'correct' answer, of course, that all women have been sexually assaulted, we're all kept in fear by men's sexual violence, we're all threatened by men, we're all hurt and damaged by pornography and the objectification of women. And yet I usually feel a fraud. I *haven't* been raped, as the questioner would define it. I know that this is a false division, that patriarchy wants to put the poor 'rape victims' on one side of a line and make out that everyone on the other side of the line is treated just fine by men. I know that there's no way of quantifying or ranking the pain, fear, humiliation we feel at the horrendously varied forms of sexual torture that have been, and are, directed at us. I know that many of the most upset women I've talked to on the rape crisis line have received so-called 'minor' assaults only. The least useful thing we can do is to collude in the idea that some assaults are real assaults and the others don't count. And yet, despite many years as a feminist, and several at the rape crisis line, I still retain a lot of damaging, male-defined assumptions about the nature of the sexual abuse I myself have received. Typically, having been brought up to be a caring female, I find no difficulty whatever feeling outrage on behalf of other women. I have many times been moved to tears by a woman's account of what a man has done to her in the name of innocuous terms like 'rough sex', 'over-enthusiasm', 'harassment'. But the minute I feel challenged about my credentials for being in a rape crisis line I find myself going along with the cruddy ideas of a male-run society that expects all women not only to put up with daily expressions of hatred towards us, but then to deny its real nature. It's not as though I haven't talked about my experiences, it's not as though I haven't felt fear, hatred, humiliation. Maybe we need constantly to remember and share our feelings about what's happened to us even more than we do, since the power of men's woman-hating ideology is so strong.

Next time I'm asked if I've been raped I'll recall a few of the countless assaults – the Hell's Angel with a sheath-knife at my throat when I was thirteen (a 'joke') – the three or four men who exposed their pricks to me when I was a schoolgirl and alone, away from help – the guard in the railway carriage when I had missed my connection in a foreign country, telling me I *had* to stand on the seat and reach up to put my suitcase on the rack . . . – the five young men who grabbed me, took my glasses and thrust their hands up my skirt as I passed a fairground – the grabbing, pushing, forcing from young men insisting I must have 'wanted it' or I wouldn't have accepted a lift/come to the party/let them buy me a drink – the infiltrating into my most inner self of the violent, objectified images of women in books, films, posters, everywhere . . . that's a few of the things that have happened just in the first half of my life so far . . . need I go on? And even as I write it my major feeling is that I've got off lightly. The point is that, yes, I have, but those assaults were real, they *were* assaults, they hurt me mentally and physically and I'm going to continue working with my sisters to do everything we can to put an end to it.

Poking Your Nose In/Getting Involved

First published in *Revolutionary and Radical Feminist Newsletter*, no. 6, Spring 1981

Some months ago, Madhu from the Indian women's journal *Manushi*, visited Leeds, and some of us were very impressed by the way *Manushi* readers were going out to investigate the details of newspaper reports involving the harassment, rape or deaths of women, and then writing in to *Manushi*. It would be good, Madhu said, if women over here were more prepared to get involved like that. We agreed, but it's difficult to go knocking on strange doors – maybe it would be seen as crude curiosity or anyway nosey-parkering. On the other hand, there's a real possibility that women in such situations do need help, and we just might be able to give some of the support they need. Not long after this, there was just such a situation on our doorstep. What were we going to do about it?

The Maw sisters

We saw a small paragraph in the paper when Annette and Charlene Maw first appeared in the magistrates' court charged with the murder of their father. It said their lawyer was appealing for witnesses who could testify to Thomas Maw's drunken brutality to his family. We wanted to find out more about the case and if possible make contact with the family to offer practical help and support. We knew that in other cases where a husband or father had been killed by a wife or daughter, the women involved had often felt isolated, guilty and/or confused and outfaced by the legal situation, publicity, etc. We were hoping we'd be able to stop or lessen at least some of these hassles. The first thing was to find out where they lived. Luckily one of us discovered that a friend used to teach one of the sisters. This provided not just an address but a

9

contact. Annette's ex-teacher was concerned, too, so one of us went with her to visit Annette. She and her mother were a bit taken aback at first, then very pleased that someone had taken notice and was offering support. At that time they were, of course, worried, they faced a murder trial, but their lawyer and the police had given them the impression that they would probably get off with a non-custodial sentence. We were not so confident, but then we did not know much about the case. They were nearing the end of a seven-month wait for the trial and just wanted to get it over with, and start a new life afterwards. This was only a short first visit, but they were glad of the contact and we were relieved that we'd taken the risk of (we feared) having the door shut in our faces. Also it was clear that if they could not go quietly home after the trial but had to go to prison, it would be their mother, Beryl Maw, who would need our support most immediately.

The trial and after

As we expected at least a five-day murder trial, we had fixed a rota of women to attend. Only one of us was there the first morning but there should have been more of us. She made some contact with Beryl, Annette and Charlene, so that they knew there was someone friendly there. Annette and Charlene were offered the chance to plead guilty to manslaughter, which they did, and they got three years. Their lawyer said he always advises clients to plead guilty to manslaughter if the police offer that option, because a conviction for murder means a life sentence. (We feel, if the police think the charge should be manslaughter, they should allow you to stand trial for that, not charge you with murder in order to get you to plead guilty to manslaughter and so avoid a trial.) This change of plea meant that no jury ever heard the background to Tommy Maw's death. We were shocked by the verdict and at first did not know what to do. Then we went to Women's Aid and put out a joint press statement about the sentence. We didn't know the press were going to make a big story of the case, and thought we might have to put work into drawing attention to it. We also organised a picket of the court for a week's time.

We called the lawyer and found they were going to appeal and began drawing up petitions and collecting signatures. We expected the usual long delay between sentence and appeal, so we would be busy, we thought, campaigning and getting a massive petition together. As it happened, the press stories influenced public opinion and the appeal was only three weeks later.

Offering support

We visited Beryl Maw immediately after the trial. We felt critical of
the way the trial had been conducted and the conditions under
which all three women had given their statements to the police, e.g.
with no solicitors present; twelve hours with no food, no drink.

We had explained our interest and our visits by saying we were
friendly, concerned women. The basis on which we were relating to
Beryl was as friends who were concerned to offer help. This meant
she could talk to us without the constraint and carefulness she had
to exercise in front of the press, and talk through her reactions to
hate letters, etc. We'd not set ourselves up as experts in any field,
which meant that although we were critical of the legal advice she
had been given, we couldn't cross over into the alienating
professional tones of voice of legal experts. This obviously isn't a
division that we accept, but on the other hand, why should a woman
for whom we were comparative strangers take our word for it that
she should change her solicitor, change her barrister? We were hoist
by our own petard – if you present yourselves as friends, you may
not be seen as having any legal expertise. To press the point may
sound patronising, know-it-all, etc. And we still don't know how to
deal with this.

We have visited Beryl Maw regularly since then. She was glad, if
only for the chance to talk to someone who wasn't trying to get
something out of her. She was being hounded by the press, and was
persuaded to sign an exclusive contract with the *Daily Mail*. She
thought she was acting in her daughters' best interest, as they
promised coverage. As it happened, other papers gave just as much
coverage. And now she is tied by that contract, for which she was
paid peanuts: a few hundred pounds. She is forbidden to talk to any
other press, to go on TV, to give interviews even now, even to *Spare
Rib*. She cannot tell, in her own words, what life with Maw was like,
why she never left, even to a woman's magazine. We ourselves, in
this article, are gagged – we cannot write down things that Beryl has
told us that we think are crucial to anyone's understanding of the
case. It would appear that signing such an exclusive is *not* the best
thing to do, and if any of you ever know anyone in that situation,
pass this on! Beryl also regrets it.

We consulted Beryl about everything we were doing. For
example, we asked if it was OK by her to hold a picket of the appeal
court, so that she was not put in the position where she felt
powerless.

After the appeal failed

London women sent a telegram of support to Beryl at her hotel when she went down for the appeal. They organised a picket outside the Court of Appeal, and some women were inside the court as observers. At the appeal, the defending barrister, Gilbert Gray QC (of Lord Kagan fame) disassociated himself from the 'feminist rabble'. He also said that the suggestion that Tommy Maw's death was planned, a suggestion which came out of one of the girl's statements, should be discounted because: 'People in this socioeconomic bracket often talk with unbridled tongues.' The judges appeared sanctimoniously ignorant, and incapable of imagining life with Tommy Maw (unlike the hundreds of people, mostly women, who wrote letters of support to Beryl Maw). One of the judges said Beryl had the protection of the Domestic Violence Act, and anyway she could have escaped. The Court of Appeal's verdict, which reduced Charlene's sentence to six months, but left Annette's at three years, was met with total, stunned, dismayed silence from the sympathetic women in court. One woman who was there told us that the overwhelming fear was that being there as feminists was going to make it worse for Annette and Charlene. As the verdict was read she felt our total powerlessness in the face of this male-bonding charade; the defence barrister just putting on a show for the three male judges.

The verdict ignored the fact that when Annette killed her father she was fighting for her life. It concentrated instead on two things: first, that they should have called the police. This ignores the fact that they had called the police so many times before and the police had done nothing. Second, that after he was stabbed, the women initially said he had a knife. (Charlene, when she phoned the police, said: 'Come quick – me dad's taken a knife to our Annette!') This was recorded and used in evidence against the sisters. Later, in the police cells, they admitted the truth – that he had no knife, but was killing Annette with his bare hands. Perhaps they knew that only if he had a weapon would they be justified in fighting back with one, in the eyes of the law.

We wanted to protest the appeal judgment for the sake of the Maw sisters and all women who find themselves in the same position. Beryl Maw was persuaded to issue press statements asking for the campaign to cease.

She still needs support. We are able to help with practical things, like lifts to the prison, and give time and friendship. Charlene will be released, we hope, in March; she wasn't even able to keep her pregnancy private – someone rang the press and told them. Annette is in prison, even with possible remission, for quite a long time.

What have we done to help in the long run?

You can say we have not 'succeeded'. The sentences were not quashed. So what good did it do?

Beryl knew there were lots of women who cared – and has many times expressed her surprise, and sense of being strengthened by this. She has also, for the first time since she married, been able to go out and have a good time with women friends. So we've been able to help one woman a bit on an individual level. We've made a new friend, and learnt – what? There are difficulties in explaining who we are, and why we want to get involved. If you're not honest about your political views, you limit yourselves; you cut yourselves off from the resources of the WLM, you can be seen just as do-gooders wanting to feel a nice, warm, inner glow; if you do declare your political involvement, you run the risk of being seen as exploiters, band-waggoning on another woman's misery in order to make a political point. Beryl has said many times that she has felt manipulated and reduced simply to an object by the general press and by politicians; but not by us. But then we hesitated over some important areas, like all the legal stuff, which could have made a difference to the prison sentences. We now think that if we had introduced a feminist solicitor to Beryl, Annette and Charlene, they might for instance have taken up the *Daily Mail*'s offer to pay for a different barrister for the appeal hearing. We wonder whether in fact we did anything to close the gap between friendly emotional support (traditionally women's work) and the hard practical realities of legal procedure (the 'real' world in which men rule). Again, we don't accept the division, but how do we integrate both sets of skills and resources?

Any woman who has got involved like this, taken steps to support a woman without being asked, please write and tell us – did you face similar dilemmas? Do you think we could have handled things better? We need to pool our thoughts on this. How do we shift public opinion and the law, e.g. towards women's right to self-defence, without 'using' the very women who are suffering precisely because the law does not protect women?

In spite of our doubts, it's important to get involved. Campaigning for someone from a distance could make things worse for them, but making personal contact means you can check out your ideas with the woman concerned. So we would like to follow *Manushi*'s line and say: Do get involved – the worst that can happen is that you'll be told to go away. At best you will actually be of some use.

WENDY HOLLWAY

'I Just Wanted to Kill a Woman.' Why? The Ripper and Male Sexuality

First published in *Feminist Review*, no. 9, Autumn 1981.

The trial of Peter Sutcliffe, the 'Yorkshire Ripper', was dominated by attempted explanations of his motives. Through an examination of newspaper reports[1] of the trial, I want to try to uncover the assumptions made about Sutcliffe's sexuality and its relation to the women who were his victims. I want to show how the discourses – the frameworks within which explanations are sought – have the effect of distorting systematically (though not necessarily intentionally) the understanding of men's masculinity and its expression through their sexuality.

Sutcliffe's trial demonstrated men's collaboration with other men in the oppression of women. As the mouthpieces for legal, psychiatric and journalistic discourses, men collaborated in reproducing a view of the world which masks men's violence against women. This position will certainly be objected to on the grounds that Peter Sutcliffe was punished; that the law has done its duty. But women are not safe from men's violence just because one 'Ripper' has been locked up. The trial refused to recognise the way in which Sutcliffe's acts were an expression – albeit an extreme one – of the construction of an aggressive masculine sexuality and of women as its objects. This 'cover-up' exonerates men in general even when one man is found guilty. It is not necessary to argue that the men whose accounts I cite were doing this consciously or intentionally. The power of a discourse resides in its hegemony, in the way it passes as truth, and in the way its premises and logic are taken for granted. Yet, despite this, there were many indications of the explanations for Sutcliffe's actions, pointers which could not be grasped by the men involved. Maybe they were suppressed precisely because:

We love the criminal and take a burning interest in him, because

14

the Devil makes us forget the beam in our own eye when observing the mote in our brother's, and in that way outwits us [*Observer*, 24 May 1981].[2]

As women we are not blinded by that particular beam. Because of the enormity of Sutcliffe's acts, we should not hesitate in using the trial to point to the potentially horrific consequences of contemporary masculinity. Men deal with the requirements of their gender in diverse ways. Most do behave differently from Sutcliffe and the discourses exemplified here help them to feel far removed from the Ripper. But if similarities were recognised between the construction of Sutcliffe's sexuality and that of other men, it would be clearer to men that the reproduction of patriarchal discourses on masculinity not only promotes women's oppression, but is also against their own interests.

Because Sutcliffe admitted performing the killings, but entered a plea of guilty of manslaughter on the grounds of diminished responsibility, the trial took the relatively unusual form of turning on 'the state of the accused's mind at the time of the killings' (1 May 1981).[3] The way the question was represented to the jury by Sir Michael Havers QC (prosecuting) was as follows:

He had committed crimes which were beyond ordinary comprehension, but 'does it mean he must be mad – or just plain evil, plain bad?' [20 May 1981].

Therefore, 'we are really dealing here with motives, reasons, motivations. They are often very difficult to discern,' the judge told the jury before they were sent out to consider their verdict (21 May 1981). The jury's job – and consequently the job of the prosecution, defence, expert witnesses and reporters – was therefore to understand the reasons for, and causes of, Sutcliffe's action. Seventeen days later the jury, by a majority of ten to two, came to a verdict of guilty of the murder of thirteen women. (Sutcliffe had already pleaded guilty to the attempted murder of another seven.) It is because of this feature that the trial offers such powerful evidence of the patriarchal discourses on sexuality. They are to be found in Sutcliffe's own testimony, and other lay accounts; in the psychiatric evidence through which his so-called 'paranoid schizophrenia' is explored; through the arguments of prosecution and defence in explaining his actions as bad or mad. Then there is the influential way that the judge presented the issue to the jury. For example, he advised them that if they believed that Sutcliffe was deluded into believing that he had a divine mission to kill prostitutes and that at the time of each killing, his victim was a prostitute, then the correct verdict was probably manslaughter [21 May 1981].

These proceedings are only then relayed to us women readers after journalists – again exclusively men – have turned it into a newsworthy story.

Men's 'natural' sexuality

The lay, legal, psychiatric and journalistic discourses all shared an assumption about what is normal masculine sexuality. Mostly this remained implicit, although deducible from the lines of questioning used. However, one journalist, Piers Paul Read, made the assumption explicit, backing it up by 'scientific expertise':

As Anthony Storr says in his book *Human Aggression*, 'male sexuality, because of the primitive necessity of pursuit and penetration, does contain an important element of aggressiveness; an element which is both recognised and responded to by the female who yields and submits' [*Observer*, 24 May 1981].

To the extent that this assumption is never challenged, the patriarchal discourse is reproduced and strengthened by such an event as this trial. To the extent that explanations of Sutcliffe's actions can depend on people's acceptance of this 'truth', sexual violence, a most significant and deep-rooted form of men's oppression of women, goes unchallenged. One effect of the proceedings was to single out the Ripper as an abnormal phenomenon, explicable only by the difference between him and other men, thus reproducing the sexuality and relations of 'normal' men as unproblematic. It has been possible to achieve this with such consensus because of the scale of the murders. In one sense, any man who murders, or attempts to murder, a total of twenty women is different from the norm. The attempts to explain the aberration are therefore geared to accounting for that difference. If he was 'mad' this makes him quantitatively different from other men. If he was 'bad' it is more difficult to exonerate others: what made him different?[4] Able to provide no satisfactory explanation, the press split off his bad/mad side from the normal man offered to the public in such press comments as 'everyone who knew Sutcliffe thought he would have made an ideal father' (23 May 1981).

Mad?

There is one significant difference in the choice of 'mad' rather than 'bad' as an explanation of Sutcliffe's killings. Whereas 'bad' is a label which requires an understanding of the moral, that is, social, content of the acts, 'mad' is a label which is used as if it were a self-sufficient explanation: it is a form of diagnosis which avoids considering the content of the acts and thus avoids seeing the link between individual and society. Instead, psychiatry looks to biology for causes. Dr MacCulloch said in his report: 'I suspect there is a link [between the motorcycle crash and his madness] and that there is some organic impairment' (19 May 1981). However, it was Sutcliffe's representation of the 'divine mission' which psychiatrists relied on for an explanation. Mr Chadwin (for the defence) told the jury that 'he had to persuade them that Sutcliffe had, at the time of the killings, believed he had been receiving instructions' (20 May 1981). This would count as evidence that he was deluded, and be a major contributor to a diagnosis of 'paranoid schizophrenia'.[5] No one seemed to point out what to me was the obvious loophole in the psychiatric argument: the explanation that it was a delusion does not show *why* the voice told Sutcliffe to kill women. Whether it was God's voice, the Devil's, or the projected voice of Sutcliffe's own hatred makes no difference: the content derives from a generalised, taken-for-granted misogyny. The psychiatric discourse was one means whereby the legal process could avoid asking uncomfortable questions about male violence.[6] For example, when Dr MacCulloch was asked what he thought caused Sutcliffe to kill women he replied, 'I think it was the divine mission.' When pushed further, he explained: 'It is well known that in schizophrenia killings take place – and bizarre killings at that – and it is not possible to offer any logical explanation for the killings because of the nature of schizophrenia' (19 May 1981).

Bad?

The case for Sutcliffe being 'bad' rested, for the prosecution, on trying to prove that there was a 'sexual component' in Sutcliffe's attacks. This, and the 'divine mission', were contested as if they were mutually exclusive. Yet in the face of evidence of Sutcliffe's brutal attacks, only on women, a feminist analysis sees no incompatibility between a mission to kill women and this man's sexuality. None the less, the 'logic' of their argument powerfully illustrates the assumptions made about male sexuality. Dr Milne's position, that there was 'no underlying sexual component to his attacks', was challenged by Mr Ognall (prosecuting) in the following terms:

> Mr Ognall held up a seven-inch screwdriver which, he said, Sutcliffe had stabbed three times into the vagina of Josephine Whitaker. 'That indicates the most fiendish cruelty, deliberately done for sexual satisfaction.' [15 May 1981].

Despite the recognition of the act's 'most fiendish cruelty', a sexual component can only – to these men – mean 'sexual satisfaction'. Men's sexual desire is seen as an untainted urge, product of nature not society. So because 'there was no suggestion that he derived sexual pleasure from the killings', there was no sexual component. Sir Michael Havers thus draws distorted conclusions:

> Why had he stabbed one of his victims in the vagina? Why had he so often stabbed his victims' breasts? . . . Was he getting sexual gratification from these injuries? . . . If it was true that he felt repulsed by prostitutes and if he truly was seething with hatred for them, how was it that he had sex with one of his victims? . . . 'You talk about your mission. And then surprise, surprise, here's pretty little Helen Rytka and you have sex with her' [7 May 1981].

His reasoning goes that the woman's attractiveness (as sex-object) produces the man's sexual arousal and desire for gratification (as is so commonly argued in rape cases to absolve the man of responsibility). He cannot recognise the social meanings expressed through sexuality. But Sutcliffe's reply acknowledges those social meanings: 'To be honest, I pulled up her clothing to satisfy some sort of sexual revenge on her' (7 May 1981).

Sexual revenge

What was Sutcliffe revenging, and on whom? There are no isolated causes of feelings which are the product of patriarchal relations and which lead to violence against women – least of all a knock on the head or a divine voice. In fact, Sutcliffe's history in relation to sex and prostitutes seems fairly typical. He was given to boasting with his friends about sex with prostitutes, on one occasion telling a friend 'that two girls had followed him back to the car the previous night. He said he had one of them in the back and one over the bonnet' (8 May 1981). Men's acceptance of masculine sexual violence was shown in the testimony of another friend with whom Sutcliffe went on 'red-light jaunts'. This man told the court 'He said he'd followed a woman to a house somewhere. I think he said he'd hit her . . . He pulled a sock from his pocket and there was a small brick or stone in it' (8 May 1981).

He must have accepted this as fairly normal since, despite seeing the evidence, he did not pursue the matter. The patriarchal discourse sees as quite 'natural' a bit of aggression in men's sexuality (witness Storr's account cited above). To this extent Sutcliffe is normal. But what made him kill? Male sexual violence must be seen as a way of asserting 'masculinity' by exercising power over a woman. Sutcliffe's first murder came after a prostitute had accused him of being 'fucking useless' when he was slow to get an erection (7 May 1981), after which, he said, he felt a 'seething rage', and attacked and killed her. Clearly his masculinity was threatened by his impotence in the face of this woman's sexuality and her taunt. This is a matter which some of the men involved in the trial are quick to seize upon sympathetically:

> It is not hard to see how this cocktail of frustration, guilt and humiliation could lead to fury, and the fury to an urge not just for revenge but for the satisfaction in spirit if not in body of his sexual urge [*Observer*, 7 May 1981].

Sir Michael Havers, commenting in similar terms on the event, says of the prostitute's behaviour: 'Was this not a classic example of provocation?' (20 May 1981). By blaming the victim, Havers colludes in avoiding the threatening recognition that a man will kill when mocked about his sexual potency. Thus he avoids asking the question why – why did Sutcliffe kill women? – the answer to which would demand that he and other men faced the problem of masculinity. The ability to get an erection is the symbol of a man's masculinity, and it signifies his power. It is no coincidence that there is a common etymology for the words 'potency' and 'power'. When Sutcliffe had got his sexual revenge, he said he had a feeling of 'satisfaction and justification' (7 May 1981). But he went on to kill other women. Did they 'provoke' him?

Women blamed

Prostitutes, the main victims, were blamed for provocation. But it is on the generalised victim, woman, that the blame is laid. The search for a sexual component led straight to Sutcliffe's wife. If men's natural sexual urges were taken care of by the women whose duty it is to respond in a yielding manner, they would have no problems.[7] Hence Dr Milne could report, that he had been particularly careful to look for a sexual component in the killings. He was satisfied that neither Mr nor Mrs Sutcliffe was sexually deviant [7 May 1981].

Having accepted Sutcliffe's claim that he was not violent towards his wife, the psychiatrist appeared not to pursue questions concerning the quality of his relationship with this woman. Sonia Sutcliffe gets no such gentle treatment. After stating that she had been mentally ill, the report continues:

> She had shown no signs of a recurrence of her illness, but in interviews with Dr Milne 'she readily admits that she had been at times temperamental and difficult and freely admits that she has frequently teased and provoked her husband' [7 May 1981].

Note how the sentence construction 'but . . . she *admits* . . .' imputes blame. Often the conclusion which we are supposed to draw remains implicit, but Havers actually specified it:

> Or is [Sutcliffe's behaviour] because he was having a rough time after his marriage? Was his wife, also because of her own illness, behaving impossibly so that he dreaded going home? [20 May 1981].

A great fuss was made in the news of evidence from a prison officer (which the judge did not see fit to exclude as irrelevant) that 'Mrs Sutcliffe used to run the visits, she used to take the lead' on the basis of which he concluded she completely overwhelmed and dominated him in the situation (20 May 1981). Sutcliffe is presented as the henpecked husband who was driven to commit terrible acts because his wife dominated him.[8]

Peter Sutcliffe's behaviour to Sonia was worth consideration. He was obsessively jealous and on several occasions had fantasies that Sonia was a prostitute. But rather than blame Sutcliffe, the psychiatrist referred to it as delusion, thus incorporating it into the category of phenomena that have no explanation.

Women's sexuality

Sutcliffe's claim that 'God encouraged me to kill people called scum who cannot justify themselves to society' was eagerly seized upon by the press who failed to point out the inconsistency of the fact that for Sutcliffe only prostitutes fell into this category (and not, for example, the men who, like him, used and abused them). As prostitutes and feminists have pointed out,[9] the distinction between prostitutes and 'totally respectable' women victims clearly testified to a value that the lives of prostitutes were worthless, and that Sutcliffe's mission in wiping them out was somehow more justifiable. Thus Sir Michael Havers said of Sutcliffe's victims, 'some were prostitutes, but perhaps the saddest part of this case is that some were not' (*West Indian World*, 6 June 1981).

Whether Sutcliffe believed that all his victims were prostitutes became crucial to the verdict. Sir Michael Havers told him, 'Your story would have gone straight down the drain if you had to say to the doctors that six of them were not prostitutes' (13 May 1981). 'This can only be because the dominant discourse regards prostitutes as not 'innocent' (blaming the victim again), and indeed this is how Sutcliffe represents it:

> Sometimes after killing women who were not prostitutes he had worried that it might be the voice of the Devil. But he was able to tell that they were prostitutes by the way they walked. He knew they were not innocent [7 May 1981].

In fact there was no distinction between his feelings about his victims: 'I realised Josephine was not a prostitute but at the time I wasn't bothered. I just wanted to kill a woman;' and, 'I realised now I had an urge to kill any woman' (7 May 1981). Not 'scum of the earth', just 'any woman'.

Why was any woman in this category? The link is women's sexuality. 'By the way they walked' he could tell a woman was not innocent. Guilty of sexuality. In this society prostitutes symbolise sexuality. Images of women are split into the innocent and guilty: the virgin and the whore; Mary and Eve; the wife and the mistress.[10] Only the latter are meant to be 'guilty' of sexuality. The religious myth of the Virgin Mary represents the wife/mother as asexual, achieving what is impossible in reality by denying her sexuality while claiming her reproductivity. Sutcliffe had trouble maintaining his separation with respect to Sonia. He constantly imagined that she was having sexual relationships with other men and had fantasies that she was a prostitute. But from the 'voice', 'I had reassurance that she was a good girl and that the prostitutes were responsible for all the trouble' (12 May 1981).

Sutcliffe hated women for their sexuality, which he split off into prostitutes rather than acknowledge in his wife. Yet he was also obsessed by them. For it is against women's sexuality that men are motivated to measure their masculinity and because they must prove this at each encounter, their masculinity never rests assured.

Sutcliffe's desire for 'sexual revenge' was not satisfied by one murder.

The discourses representing women as sex-objects to be dominated pervade the culture: in sexist jokes; pornography depicting violence; and men's boasts. They not only address us women as sex-objects from the advertising hoardings, but often present the predatory man for the male public to identify with. The hoardings are beckoning men to live up to their masculinity by preying on women as sex-objects. It is through their sexuality that men are expected to prove themselves. As I stated above, woman-as-sex-object is not the only image which is reproduced. Men are torn between reverence, need and hatred of women and deal with these contradictions in diverse ways. But the threats represented by women as a result of these contradictions can contribute – as they did in Sutcliffe's case – to an extreme desire to punish women for their sexuality. That desire is legitimised by the patriarchal discourse which sees men's aggressive sexuality as natural. The lawyers, psychiatrists and journalists involved in the trial used and reproduced this discourse. But the 'voice' that Sutcliffe obeyed was the voice, not of God or delusion, but of the hoardings on the streets, of newspaper stands, of porn displays and of films. It is the voice which addresses every man in our society and to that extent, as the feminist slogan claims, 'all men are potential rapists'.

Notes

1. I have made no attempt to cover the reporting of the trial in all Britain's newspapers. The coverage in 'quality' newspapers such as the *Guardian* is a good deal less sensational, and often less blatantly sexist in its lines of reasoning. If the case I am making stands up from these reports, it would thus go for any reports – save feminist ones – of the trial.

2. The quotation is from Jung, but the *Observer* article ended with it. Maybe it was a covert recognition of the responsibility of men as a group for recognising the problem as one of contemporary masculinity and ceasing to blame the victim.

3. Unless otherwise stated, dates in brackets refer to articles in the *Guardian*.

4. After the trial, questions were asked why the Attorney-General, Sir Michael Havers, had been prepared to accept a manslaughter plea because 'it would spare the families of the victims' (5 June 1981). As the families had expressed a wish to see 'justice done', and felt that this would not have been so had Sutcliffe got away with a manslaughter verdict, Havers must have had other motives. I can only speculate, but from my arguments here, it seems likely that men would have felt much more comfortable if there was never any question as to Sutcliffe's insanity. Why else would four psychiatrists

unanimously find him mad on the basis of evidence that turned out, in the process of the trial and the eventual verdict, to be incomplete, partial and distorted?

5. The other symptoms cited by Dr Milne sound uncannily similar to normal masculinity:

> There were his preoccupations with prostitutes, his over-controlled behaviour, his illogical thinking, his lack of insight into the reasons for his actions, his feeling that his mind was being controlled, his distortions of thought and perception. [He goes on to mention Sutcliffe's jealousy concerning Sonia.] [20 May 1981.]

6. This discourse has a long history. In the case of Pierre Rivière, Foucault (1975) documents its use in 1835 in rather similar circumstances.

7. After the trial, Sutcliffe's father commented that it would never have happened if his son had married a different girl.

8. When Sutcliffe's upbringing was considered, blame was sought in his mother. When it became apparent that 'he was much fonder of his mother than he was of his father' (7 May 1981) the matter was dropped.

9. The fact that prostitutes and feminists demonstrated outside the court in order to make this point received almost no press coverage.

10. Read (*Observer*, 24 May 1981) refers to this dichotomy in images of women, but relates it specifically to Sutcliffe's Catholic background:

> There is undoubtedly a tendency among Catholics to be confused by this contradiction, and to solve it by dividing women into two – the pure and the wanton . . . loving one and desiring the other.

While this may be true of Catholic men, it functions here to mask the generality of the phenomenon in patriarchal discourses on sexuality.

References

Foucault, M. (ed.), '*I, Pierre Rivière, having slaughtered my mother, my sister and my brother* . . .', Harmondsworth: Penguin; 1975.

AL GARTHWAITE

All You Never Wanted to Know about Sex . . . But Were Forced to Learn

From discussion and consciousness-raising with revolutionary and other feminists in Leeds, with Women Against Violence Against Women, and women in the Patriarchy Study Group. First published in *Scarlet Women*, no. 13, Part 2

In December a sex shop opened on Chapeltown Road, Leeds. Shops line the road on both sides, it's near a crossroads, the local nursery and adventure playground. There's no window display of porn, but mags are listed on the white perspex in large red letters, together with 'Adult Books', 'Marital Aids' and a lit-up sign, 'Sex Shop'. Impossible to miss, in fact.

Why fight sex shops?

Because they have nothing to do with women's self-defined sexuality and everything to do with our degradation and humiliation in our own eyes and those of men. The porn they sell is not 'liberating', it reduces us to sex-objects, not our whole bodies even – many pictures just show our torsos, tits 'n' cunt. No heads to think with, legs to kick, feet to run away – just the bits men want to fondle and fuck (unless they're foot or mouth fetishists, of course . . .). Women in porn mags exist for them, eternally open and available, ready to be screwed, done over, and when they're finished, used to wipe their bums.

Most porn features violence towards women, usually by men. Some is openly sado-masochistic, that is, men getting off on hurting women, often pretty badly, the woman looking agonised but of course she must be 'pretending' and loving it. (We're really meant to believe that? That a ten-year-old girl undergoing anal rape would secretly enjoy the experience, and her tears were all part of the fun?) By being sold in 'family' newsagents, post offices and now

24

these unpleasantly sanitised and hygienic-looking sex shops in residential areas, what was previously regarded as sordid and nasty enters our everyday lives – *and our beds*. Sex shops help make our degradation *respectable*, especially by playing on the 'marital aids' angle. Few women can really believe that their marriage problems can be solved by nobbly Durex or the *Kama Sutra* – but the pressure to try is on them – it must be their fault, the marriage must be crumbling because they aren't sexual enough – sexual as defined by men, that is.

Faced by these pressures, women feel guilty if we don't feel sexual. It helps to push us into sex and/or relationships we wouldn't otherwise want or miss, and go along with a lot of 'sex games' that don't appeal at all, often sado-masochistic. Sex shops do a brisk trade in sex therapy manuals. Sex therapy is very much on the increase and promoted by the Marriage Guidance Council, agony columns in women's magazines and some women-only sex education courses. For instance, the December 1980 issue of *Cosmopolitan* carried an article on 'The Sexual Revolution', where Eileen's story was told. Eileen's marriage was on the rocks; married at twenty knowing practically nothing about her body, sex had never been enjoyable to her, and she would tell girlfriends that Tom was 'too rough in bed'. Their sex life dwindled and finally he moved out; panicked, she begged him to return. What could she do to persuade him? Improve sexually, he demanded. So she enrolled on the course.

> Now I know some of the basics about sex, like how my body works and how his works, I've come out of the Dark Ages. I now know how to tell Tom to be more gentle. I *never* tell him in bed; it's better done over dinner some night when we're alone. And he's encouraged to tell me some things in return, which has a renewing effect on our relationship. Sometimes I even initiate sex, which makes Tom feel good about himself. I'm just sorry I wasted so much time being stupid and stubborn.

Immediately after this, a psychiatrist is quoted:

> Right now, it's important to get women to take equal responsibility for their sex lives and to stop putting all the blame on their men.

I find this *horrific*. Yes, we must reclaim our bodies, learn about ourselves: but women's liberation does *not* consist of teaching women to be more effective sexual athletes to catch and keep a man, let alone discovering non-ego-bruising ways of hinting to him that he's *hurting* you; and learning orgasm, no doubt aided by masochistic fantasies we're told are 'value-free', will *never* our self-defined sexuality make.

Sex shops and the porn they purvey are promoted *by* men *for* men and for the financial gain of male-dominated concerns. While women remain financially and legally discriminated against, our protests curbed by the ever-present possibility of male violence, there will always be models for porn, but this is no more women's free *choice* than prostitution, wifehood, heterosexuality, or the badly paid boredom of the production line.

> *But sex shops are an outlet for male sexuality. Without them there'd be more rapes and sex crimes.*

A common reaction from women in local shops. They hate porn, but believe the liberal line – for which there's no statistical justification. Porn *encourages* men to see us as bits of meat and treat us accordingly – and the more socially acceptable it becomes, the less we dare complain for fear of coming over as petty or prudish. We've to laugh at flashers now, feel sorry for child molesters (even support their 'right' to maul our eight-year-olds for goodness' sake), our real anger, fear and disgust gets buried. Rape goes on, but is no longer defined as rape. Sex shops divide women into the 'prudish' (who object) and the 'liberated' (who don't). And who gains from our division?

What does it say about male sexuality if it needs this 'outlet', anyway? Pretty perverted.

Protest

A mixed community group called the first picket, from varied, and in some cases dubious, motives. Some who joined the picket, including a prominent local councillor, want the sex shop removed to the town centre. (So he can visit it without embarrassment?) But we don't want a Leeds Soho. Others are concerned for the image of, and life in, Chapeltown, already branded as a 'red-light' area: fair enough, but analysis can go deeper. Others, again, seem to be protesting because sex shops are big capitalist business with Mafia connections. The willingness of the firm's directors to give their names, and the public nature of the enterprise, are other examples of how acceptable it's become: organised degradation and exploitation of women has always paid, but been carried out furtively and illicitly: now, anyone can invest openly. However, the 'fight it because it's capitalist' analysis rather misses the point; we could equally be picketing Tesco's. The degradation of women is *central* to sex shops, not a by-product of it.

The first picket included placards with slogans some women disliked intensely, e.g. 'More sex, no sexploitation'. More sex for *whom*? on *whose terms*? Calls for more sex at present mean more male-defined sex; are likely to make women feel as pressured to leap about in bed as do porn mags and sex manuals. 'Any kind of sex is fun, but sexism is fatal.' *Any kind* of sex?? Rape? Bestiality? Necrophilia? Wife-swopping? Fun for whom? Always?

Even if it's consenting, is this *all* sex is? Sex is not a *thing*, it's an expression of a relationship between (usually) two people. As such it cannot but reflect the relationship they have outside the bedroom. In a society where power relations between the sexes are institutionalised, can this be broken down by individual couples in the bedroom, even if they want to? And usually, the man doesn't: no oppressing group gives up its power voluntarily, nor can it. Which raises the issue of how men can campaign against sex shops, porn, and violence against women, even if they are doing it from the purest pro-woman anti-sexist motives, with no taint of bandwagoning on the above issues, not to speak of political gain and/or feminist approval. Women want to organise autonomously, fight what oppresses us in our own way and on our own terms. We will not be co-opted by male lefties and told that if we live out of the area, for instance, our presence on the picket would be 'intervention'. *Women* 'intervening' in our own struggle??

I have to say here that these are my views and those of some, but not all, of the women I know. Personally, I cannot stand on a picket on such an issue with men I know to be anti-feminist, woman-hating; men who benefit from our oppression and degradation by porn – and all men do, like it or not. I don't want knights on white chargers fighting my battles and getting the credit. *Women* should close that sex shop, and be seen to do so. Men always get more credit and attention for taking up women's causes and women's roles than we do. Far from equalising matters, such actions increase their power. If men really want to help they can, but not publicly; let them carry out anonymous guerrilla actions on sex shops – take risks without credit. Support us financially and when we ask. Leeds Women Against Violence Against Women has asked four separate so-called anti-sexist men to ask for and buy under-the-counter sex-shop porn, so we'll know what's on sale and where to protest about what. (We've offered to pay, too.) Whinges of 'It's a heavy thing to do' have resulted and only one man has so far bought porn. Other men who have helped, usefully, in actions, have complained afterwards of being 'used' – despite endless concern and fuss from us about their safety.

A few more objections to sex-shop protest

(1) Protests increase trade. This can happen. But *not* protesting has yet to bankrupt a sex shop. And protesting raises women's consciousness, spreads our message.

(2) It's censorship. Porn incites sexual hatred of women by men – and makes *us* hate *our*selves *as* women, too. It is not censorship to object to and remove degrading, dehumanising distortions of what women are – any more than it is censorship to ban racist material.

(3) It's prudish. None of us wants to be identified with Mary Whitehouse, who identifies the causes of 'permissiveness' as working mothers, faithless wives, the breakdown of family life and religion, widespread homosexuality, etc., and concludes that women should return to our traditional roles – only thus can men be tamed and controlled. But lots of women have strong gut reactions against sex shops, and the Festival of Light is an obvious, public place to channel them into. Only by stating our feminism publicly can we provide an alternative. And a feminism that sees our liberation in being screwed by lots of men, or by one man in different positions, is not going to appeal to large numbers of women – nor bring about any sort of liberation. Anyway, I don't think Mrs Whitehouse likes lesbians.

Action

Women in Barnsley have *closed* a sex shop, after two months of picketing, and other less legal actions. 'Angry Women' in Leeds have so far set fire to three sex shops. Their press release, dated 2 April 1981, states that they

> are protesting and fighting back against images portraying women as sexual conveniences for men to abuse, hurt and degrade. Pornography in films, magazines and sex shops incites men to treat women as instruments solely for their use. It encourages rape, it increases men's power and control over women by humiliating and terrorising us. Porn is big money-making business based on the suffering of women.

> We will fight porn wherever it may be, whether in back streets or on main roads. Its very existence is an insult to all women, and as long as it is prevalent the streets will continue to be unsafe for women. We have resorted to illegal action as ten years of legal

activities and 100 years of feminist struggle have had no effect whatsoever on the pornography issue. We hope that these arson attacks are the start of a more active protest by women against all forms of pornography.

Women have been looking at porn, both 'soft' and 'hard-core', in women's liberation groups, sharing our feelings of disgust and anger, and raising the consciousness we need to fight it.

Notes

1. Swiney, Francis, *The Sons of Belial and Other Essays on the Social Evil*, p. 29.

2. Swiney, Francis, *The Bar of Isis*, p. 43.

3. Hamilton, Cicely, *Marriage as a Trade*, London: Chapman & Hall 1909, p. 36.

4. *Freewoman*, 30 November 1911, p. 31.

5. Pankhurst, Christabel, *Plain Facts about a Great Evil*, 1913, p. 98.

6. Hamilton, *op. cit.* p. 37.

7. *Ibid.*, p. 252.

8. *Ibid.*, p. 278.

9. *Freewoman*, 8 August 1912, p. 234.

10. *Ibid.*

11. *Ibid.*, 23 November 1911.

12. *Ibid.*, 15 February 1912, p. 252.

13. *Ibid.*, 7 March 1912.

KIRSTEN HEARN

Hands Off My Freedom

First published in *Merseyside Women's Paper*, Spring 1982

When I tell people that I have been sexually assaulted, they throw up their hands in horror, finding it disgusting that someone should take advantage of me.

They think it only happens to 'normal' women.

I am what society is pleased to call blind. I have a visual disability and use a white stick. Every day, wherever I am, people are touching me, taking my arm to guide me, pushing me about. Some people have used my situation and the body contact to assault me. This happens on the streets, on public transport and in public buildings.

When I was an undergraduate, I lived in a student hall of residence, at the back of our college. There were two routes to it – through a desolate street, badly lit, or through the main college building.

'Safe'

One night, I was returning from the student bar and chose to take the 'safe route'. The college porter let me in, locking the door after us, as was the practice, and he took my arm to lead me. We made polite conversation. After a while, he began to touch my breasts. I shook him off and tried to distract his attention back to our conversation.

Then he pounced on me, tried to kiss me and embrace me, running his hands over my body. I pushed him away and continued walking down the corridor, trying to pretend it hadn't happened. Then he pounced again. I became angry, broke away from him and ran down the corridor. As I got to the door at the other end, I slipped and fell. Struggling to get up, I remembered that the door was locked.

He made as though to help me up and tried to embrace me again. I pushed him away and began screaming. After a while he seemed

30

to think better of it and opened the door.

Another time I was in my local railway station, late at night. I had been led into the ladies' toilets, which led out into the waiting-room. When I emerged, I found a man standing in front of the door. I said that I wanted to get out. He grabbed me. I shook him off, but he grabbed me again, this time touching my breasts. I pushed him away, but he advanced, pinned me against the wall, and began running his hands over my body. I was struggling and started to scream. Then he pushed me more violently, so I hit him round the head and face, screaming again. No one came. He got angry and I kicked him and screamed even more. Then I was alone.

I have thought about these incidents and why they were happening to me. Both these men, alone with me late at night, under the guise of assisting me had the excuse to touch me sexually. Since society has told me that I must accept all assistance offered me with gratitude, I accepted the initial contact. I did not feel that I had the right to refuse, that I did not need their help. And, because I did not discourage them, they took advantage of me.

I have thought much about how to behave in these situations, when people try to manipulate me. It is their natural reaction to wish to control something they don't understand. They are afraid of me and feel guilty about my situation. But I am used to my situation and know what is best for me. I know that to be grabbed disorientates me, as they are pushing me in front of them and I don't have any control. I know that it is best that I take their arm, since then I am touching them and the control is in my hands, so that I can let go if I want to.

To many people we are seen as sexless objects. But we are contained in a female body, which our culture tells us is not our own, but an object of fantasy and eroticism. Men are brought up to believe that a woman's body is something for them to possess and control; that they can do what they like with it and society will acquiesce.

Culture

When a man comes into contact with a woman who is blind, his instincts are confused. She looks like a woman, but she can't see. When he takes her arm, he feels a woman's arm. Yet his culture tells him that she is sexless and something to be feared. So he becomes confused.

How can this be stopped? I say to all men: 'Get your hands off me! Ask me if I want any assistance. Don't push me about, but let me take your arm. I don't want your attention. If you are confused about the situation, then leave me alone.' Then I am in control.

This is only one facet of the whole issue of women and sexual harassment. It is an area which has been grossly ignored by the women's movement and by the labour movement, and I feel that it is time that this issue, and the struggle of people with disabilities in general, was actively supported by the women's movement and the labour movement.

After all, the struggle of people with disabilities concerns the same aims – the right to benefit from the advantages of this society, without discrimination or open hostility. *The liberation of people with disabilities is a political struggle!*

SANDRA McNEILL

Being Raped Is Not the Same as Being Mugged

First published in *FAST*, no. 7, Summer 1981

Rape is a sex crime. There have been some arguments for making it a crime of violence. First I shall summarise them. Then argue against them.

Arguments for rape as a crime of violence

(1) Rape and sex. Women do not experience rape as a pleasurable sexual experience. In fighting rape cases, we have been trying to get this across to the public, no easy task. 'You can't shoot a guy for trying to give you a good time,' said one of the jurors at Inez Garcia's first trial.

(2) What's rape listed with? Criminology texts frequently list rape next to victimless sex 'offences' like consensual homosexuality, giving the impression that rape is a trivial offence.

(3) Rape and power. Violence is one recognised way whereby any power group maintains its power over another group. Certain acts of violence then take on a special significance and maintain the subjection of the dominated group, e.g. lynching of blacks by whites in southern USA. By likening rape to that, something generally understood and recognised – as men do it to men – we can talk about rape as a form of control and a means men use to maintain their power over women.

(4) How it affects the trial/women's sexual history. If rape were defined as a crime of violence, there would be no justification for introducing women's sexual history.

Arguments against it and for keeping rape as a sex crime

(1) Rape and sex. First, rape, for men, is just one form of sexual intercourse. How many men 'make love' to unwilling wives as a

marital right? In fighting rape, we are fighting the notion that men have rights of access over our bodies, as long as he enjoys it, it's OK. Secondly, what does 'enjoy' mean for a woman? One woman who called a rape crisis centre had been gang-raped. By the fourth man she was detaching her mind so far from what was going on that she had an orgasm. That really freaked her – she felt betrayed by her own body. The fact that the victims 'come' is frequently cited as an excuse for incest. Surely to force a woman to come against her will is the ultimate act of rape?

(2) What's rape listed with? Does rape fit into a classification of bodily violence like these: maiming, blinding, rape, black-eye? If rape is listed as a crime of violence, what will it then be put next to? Mugging probably, to judge from comments made to me by media interviewers. They say, 'But men get attacked too – look at mugging.' Well, I've been raped and I've been mugged and it was not the same experience at all. Linking rape with crimes of violence which usually take place between men depoliticises rape. Rape is a mechanism by which men control women's movements *and behaviour*. Calling it a crime of violence serves to obscure this.

(3) Rape and power. Analogies such as lynching have limited use. Women, like other oppressed groups, are controlled by force and threat of force, economic dependence, and so on. What is unique to the control of women by men is sexual control – control by the exercise of male sexuality, which is seen as 'natural' or 'innate', e.g. if he is aroused he has got to stick it in. Splitting off rape from sexuality makes it appear that any exercise of male sexuality that is not rape is OK. Catherine MacKinnon, in *Sexual Harassment of Working Women*,[1] says that the approach to rape which says rape is violence, not sex, has made it harder to fight cases of sexual harassment at work. 'I mean, he hasn't raped her – which would be violence – and being forceful and aggressive verbally – making threats – is part of normal healthy male sexuality, isn't it?'

(4) How it affects the trial/women's sexual history. We have succeeded in the UK in restricting the introduction of the woman's sexual history – except, of course, where there was a previous sexual relationship with the rapist. If we can succeed in making rape in marriage a crime this will be another step towards removing the notion that saying yes once does not mean yes forever and whenever he wants it. So we can actually remove justification for introducing the woman's sexual history without making rape a crime of violence.

In Canada, women are going along the road towards making rape a crime of violence.

> The introduction of the past sexual history of the victim into the courtroom stems from the view that rape is just one form of sexual intercourse. It negates the fact that a distinguishing feature of rape is the use or threat of physical force and violence.[2]

In fact, many women 'give in' without marks to prove violence. In practice the man's size, age, fists, words, don't count as threats of force, only his having a weapon such as a gun or knife does. Rape is intercourse against our will whether violence is used or not.

I think that if a man uses violence in addition to the rape he should be charged additionally with this. To make rape a crime of violence would formalise the current *status quo* whereby women must prove *by the marks* that we resisted. Women who suffer 'only' rape would be in a worse position than now. If she has no physical marks, she would have to convince the jury and judge that she had suffered great psychological harm and damage. And how would you do that except by 'proving' you were some kind of 'unliberated prude', ultra-respectable, now thinking of yourself as damaged goods for life?[3] So women's sexual history would still come in – making rape a crime of violence does not mean it would be barred. And what would it do to a woman to have to 'prove' she was damaged psychologically?

(5) Other sex crimes. What about 'minor' sex crimes, like indecent assault? Currently, if a man molests us – touches us up, grasps our breasts, kisses us forcibly and says something like 'Let's fuck', we can bring a charge of indecent assault. If indecent assault were like ordinary assault, we would have to have the marks of physical assault to bring a case. If sex crimes involving additional violence get separated from those which don't, the way is more open for such crimes to be decriminalised. Already it has been suggested that 'flashing' be decriminalised. (She is not harmed, she must be a prude to be upset.) In fact, it is a hostile gesture and brings home the threat and fear of rape/murder to many women.

In conclusion, I think that to make rape a crime of violence would cause many problems and solve none.

Notes

1. MacKinnon, Catherine A., *Sexual Harassment of Working Women*, Yale University Press, 1979.

2. Lewis, Debra, Address to the National Conference of Rape Crisis Centres, Victoria BC, Canada. Quoted by Justice Minister Ron Barisford, in proposing changing rape to a crime of violence. See *Victimology*, vol. 4, no. 2, 1980.

3. Clark, Lorenne, and Lewis, Debra, *Rape: The Price of Coercive Sexuality*, Toronto, Canada: The Women's Press. In this book these Toronto rape crisis centre workers actually suggest that women are upset by rape because we view our bodies as a commodity for sale or rent.

LIZ KELLY

Who Needs Enemies with Friends Like Erin Pizzey?

First published in *Spare Rib*, no. 127, February 1983

I thought that reading this book[1] would make me angry
– I didn't know quite how bad and what a betrayal of women it was
going to be. I have been involved in Women's Aid for nine years
and have witnessed some of Erin Pizzey's attempts to keep power
and control over what she saw as 'her' movement. But all of that
seems insignificant compared with the potential damage this book
could do. It is sensationalist journalism at its worst and holds
women responsible for the violence men inflict on them.

Erin Pizzey has no scruples; she and Jeff Shapiro have totally
rewritten the early history of the refuge movement. She presents
herself as a martyr and the Women's Aid Federation as a
fragmented and naive movement. Apparently we refuse or are too
stupid to see that some women are 'addicted' to violence:

> Many of the genuinely caring people in charge of these refuges
> were so horrified by the violent attitudes of such women, that
> they quickly created selection procedures to protect other
> innocently battered wives from the chaos created by *violence-
> prone* [her emphasis] families. Others unable to make that
> distinction disintegrated into anarchy and had to close down. But
> some had social workers who proved able to cope with, say, four
> or five *violence-prone* families at a time and they did and still do
> excellent work.

The main point of the book is laid out in Chapter 6 where Pizzey
and Shapiro argue that some women are 'addicted' to violence.
Experience of, or witnessing violence in childhood (and it starts in
the womb) creates a chemical imbalance which, they suggest, is like
the high you get from drugs. Such individuals will seek out violence
in later life to get this 'high' – their pain and pleasure become fused.

Basically, it's an explanation of sado-masochism, although this is never said. They also say it explains at least twenty-five physical illnesses from autism to diabetes and 'charismatic' leaders like Hitler!

To cover themselves they say that there are two kinds of battered women – 'innocent victims' who love the man and hate the violence, and 'violence-prone' women who hate the man but love the violence. 'Innocent victims' come from happy families where they were loved and just picked the wrong man; 'violence-prone' women seek out men who are violent.

We are back to the old idea of 'good' versus 'bad' families. Violence has nothing to do with the structure of the family itself and the power men have in it. No explanation is given as to why experiencing violence in childhood leads *men* to be violent to women. The 'proof' for these ideas are fifteen disjointed case histories contained in the other five chapters. Some of this part of the book is pornographic in the voyeuristic and non-judgmental way horrific sexual violence is described. Many times they insist that for 'violence-prone' women death is the ultimate orgasm. The longer extracts from tapes (did they ask these women if they could tape these conversations and were they told they would be used in this way?) show Erin pushing her line in the most forceful way – not accepting women's answers and insisting that really they wanted a man to kill them.

No other research or refuge group has found anything to support these ideas. Instead, what we see are historical property rights that mean men expect sexual, emotional and domestic servicing and a submissive attitude from their wives. When any or all of these are not forthcoming men feel they have the right to 'punish' their wives and exert what they see as their rightful authority.

Men's behaviour is hardly referred to at all in this book – except where they fall into Erin's arms crying when they realise she loves them. Yet again it is women who are made to feel responsible for men's behaviour – one of the reasons many battered women find it so difficult to leave in the first place is because they blame themselves. This book reinforces that with a vengeance. Women, they say, are masochists who provoke men to violence. For the authors the only solution is to take the whole family into care for long periods of time. Just how or why this will 'cure' what they argue is a physical addiction to pain is mysteriously unexplained.

This book is *dangerous*. It has already been picked up by the media and gives an excuse for further denial of the needs of battered women – they like it, so why bother to help? It ignores totally the feminist analysis of violence against women, the political nature of personal relationships and power structures within the nuclear family. All of these are essential to an understanding of battering.

Don't buy this book – if you have to read it, borrow it.

Note

1. Pizzey, Erin, *Prone to Violence*, published 1982.

Letter to Sir Michael Havers, the Attorney-General, 13 April 1981

Subsequently issued as a press release

Dear Sir,

We are writing to you to express our deep concern about what we feel to be a gross miscarriage of justice. On 27 March, PC Peter Swindell was found not guilty of the manslaughter of Ms Pat Malone; yet he pleaded guilty to preventing the lawful burial of her body and was sentenced to five years. Swindell admitted that Ms Malone died in his house, that he dismembered her body during a two-week period, and that he subsequently disposed of it. He admitted taking part in sexual relations with Ms Malone – and other women – which involved the use of a rubber mask worn over the woman's face, severely restricting her breathing. It seems highly unlikely that PC Swindell was unaware that his bizarre sexual practices might lead to the death of the woman involved when he was reported to be obsessed with death. During his trial, both prosecution and defence agreed that Ms Malone 'probably' died from suffocation. Yet if PC Swindell did not kill her, the question of how she died remains unanswered.

That this question was never pursued by the prosecution, and that the defence had nothing to say on the subject, is in itself shocking. The implications of it remaining unanswered are even more so. From this verdict we can only conclude that a criminal can get away with murder if he mutilates the body of his victim, hides it for as long as possible, and if caught refuses to testify at his trial. In this way he cannot be questioned about what actually happened, making it virtually impossible for the court to establish with absolute certainty how death occurred.

Although in this case the verdict was handed down by a jury, it is the responsibility of the courts to ensure that everyone gets treated fairly, and in the same way. The effect of the prostitution laws is that every prostitute is regarded as a criminal even though she may be the victim of the crime. It is therefore crucial for the judge to be seen not to be biased, and for his summing-up and any directives he gives to the jury to counteract any bias there may be among members of the jury. From our experience we know that prevailing prejudice is against lesbians and prostitutes, and favours the police. We cannot help feeling that the police are given preferential treatment by the courts. In this case, the word and reputation of a police officer were obviously valued considerably more than the life of a lesbian prostitute. There can be no doubt in anyone's mind that were the situation reversed and a lesbian prostitute was accused of killing a policeman she would have been convicted, not of manslaughter, but of murder, and sentenced to life.

In addition, the prosecution counsel was at pains to tell the court that Ms Malone 'was in her private life a lesbian . . . who had been knocked about in the course of her life by people other than the defendant'. If the prosecution felt that Ms Malone was somehow asking to be killed because she was a lesbian and had been beaten up before, they played right into the hands of the defence whose only statement from a witness was to the same effect. It is scandalous that the prosecution made a better case of defending PC Swindell than of prosecuting him.

A verdict such as this is, in effect, a go-ahead to all men to rape and murder women, and to the police to abuse their power in any way they choose. It confirms our worst fears that if police powers are extended they will inevitably be used to attack the most vulnerable sections of the community – and the present laws on prostitution make prostitute women among the most vulnerable of all. It is already a well-known fact that very few complaints against the police ever lead to charges. When innocent people like Gail Kinchin and Blair Peach are killed by the police it is brushed aside as being in the course of police duty. Moreover the policemen who 'accidentally' shot Gail Kinchin, a pregnant woman, have now been recommended for a medal for bravery. When women's lives are held to be worth so little, men feel confident that they can get away with all kinds of violence, including murder. This attitude is reinforced by the media – the reporting of Pat Malone's case was typical of the sensational and trivial coverage given to stories concerning violence against women.

This case must not be allowed to set a precedent. We are therefore asking you to examine the facts of this case in order to ensure that in any future case the court will treat prostitute women without prejudice and will make sure that police officers are not above the law.   Yours faithfully, E.C.P.

JILL RADFORD

Retrospect on a Trial

First published in *New Society*, 9 September 1982

I wasn't too happy about moving to Winchester. I found it smug and narrow, and I was lonely. After a while I was amazed to discover that this conservative little town had a Women's Liberation group, which I immediately joined. It was there I met Mary Bristow who, over the next seven years, became not only a close and valued friend but, for me, the acceptable face of Winchester itself.

At first sight, I was rather in awe of Mary. She was magnificent-looking: dramatically tall – maybe six foot three in her bare feet – with all the conventional female virtues of beauty, grace and dignity. Added to that she possessed many virtues that the Winchester mentality would regard as manly – independence, vitality, an uncompromising regard for her own sensibilities, and an enormous measure of self-confidence.

As I got to know her better, I realised she was merely a woman who had achieved her own autonomy. She was almost blatantly happy; happy with herself, happy in her work, happy in her friends.

She had no sense of personal ambition. She had worked at the library since she came down from university and she had no burning desire to work anywhere else. She had her own home, she was well-known, well-liked, and Winchester fitted her exactly as a custom-made glove.

We shared many things. We were both mad about Jane Austen, we canvassed for the Labour Party together, and we joined CND and the Winchester Anti-Nazi League.

In my work as a criminologist, Mary was always enormously helpful. When Winchester Crown Court tried the notorious Asher case last year, and Gordon Asher received a suspended six months' sentence for killing his wife in a fit of petty jealousy, Mary was rocked by the aftermath of fear and dismay expressed by the ordinary women of Winchester. It was typical of Mary that she helped me write an article about the case and the significance, for women, of its outcome. Three months after we finished the work, Mary Bristow was herself killed by a proprietorial young man to whom she did not wish to belong.

How Mary was killed

On the night of 29 October 1981, Mary was clubbed with a meat tenderiser, smothered with a pillow, and strangled. On the morning of the following day, Peter Wood was charged with her murder and sent for trial at Winchester Crown Court.

I don't think I had ever spoken to Peter Wood. I registered him as a fitness-freak, and was vaguely aware that in the dim and distant past he had been Mary's lover. But in the years I knew her I found him a rather boring young man who hung around Mary and Mary's home. She was kind to him as she was kind to everybody, but he did grow in nuisance-value, even Mary had to admit that.

He had a habit of turning up on her doorstep with nowhere to go, no job and no money, and Mary would grit her teeth again and give him house-room. There usually was a lodger at Mary's, somebody with a temporary accommodation problem; she had the space, and she was not someone to slam a door in anybody's face.

She did lose patience with Peter Wood, though. One time she refused to let him in and he broke in. Another time she was so desperate she called the police to evict him, but they refused to be involved. Once, too, she hit on the idea of putting all his belongings out in the street, so he would have to go away.

But there was no shaking him off. He haunted her, and pestered her until some of us – but never Mary – came to the conclusion that he was dangerous. We knew, for instance, that a couple of weeks before she died, she had discovered that Wood had broken into her house, bored holes in her bedroom ceiling, and taken to spying on her from the loft. She had been livid, she told us, and made Wood understand that this truly was the last straw.

We knew, too, that ten days before her death, the ground floor of Mary's house had been gutted by fire; that Wood had been in the house at the time; and that the police had taken several statements from him in connection with it. We knew the incident had frightened Mary very much. I remember one of the last times I saw her; when she was doing her Friday-night stint at one of the local bars – she thought bar-maiding was great fun – she put her hands over all the ashtrays before emptying them to make quite, quite sure they couldn't start a fire.

Many of us took it for granted that we would be called upon to testify to the nature of Mary's relationship with Wood at the trial.

We assumed wrongly. It seemed to us, as the trial proceeded, that it was not Peter Wood on trial at all, but Mary Bristow, and that her defence was disallowed.

Wood's trial opened on 14 June 1982, and lasted for four days. It was heard by Judge Bristow – who was pleased to point out from the outset that he was not related to Mary – with Mr Simon Tuckey acting for the Crown, instructed by Mr Philip Melsh of the Director of Public Prosecution's office, and Mr Patrick Back defending. Wood pleaded not guilty to murder, but guilty of manslaughter on the grounds of diminished responsibility and provocation, according to the provisions of the Homicide Act 1957.

At first I have to grant that the proceedings almost resembled a murder trial. Wood admitted that he had habitually spied on Mary, and that on the night he killed her, he had watched her go out with a man friend and had got into her house to await her homecoming. Suggestions that he might have broken in through a top window using an otherwise unexplained ladder, were unpursued, as were so many details of the events. But it is clear that Wood watched Mary from the privacy of her own hall when she came home with her friend, kissed him goodnight, and came alone into her home.

Wood claimed that he then sneaked out of the back door, came round to the front door, knocked, and was admitted by Mary. The prosecution was content with Wood's claim that he and Mary then made love and his statement that he had admitted to her that he was in the house when she came home. He said she was 'livid' again and that he had selected this inappropriate moment to demand that Mary favour him with a monogamous relationship. When she refused, he decided to kill her.

According to his account, he then went to the kitchen to get a meat tenderiser, thereafter to the spare room for a pair of socks and a pillow. He put the tenderiser into the socks, went into Mary's bedroom and hit her over the head with the tenderiser. When she struggled, he throttled her and put the pillow over her face.

For myself and for all of Mary's friends this was grotesque news. For those of us who could believe she was dead at all, remained the hope that she died peacefully, that maybe he had killed her as she slept, and she never knew of his brutality. Nevertheless, it struck us as very odd that all parties to the case went to such pains to negate the facts of Wood's violence.

The judge deemed it unnecessary for the jury to be shown autopsy photographs of the extent of Mary's injuries. But we saw them. Sitting in the front row of the gallery, waiting in the corridor outside the courtroom, it was impossible not to see them, as the various gentlemen of the court passed them from hand to hand for their own edification. They seemed to want us to see.

Thereafter the killing was referred to in euphemisms – 'the incident', 'the events in question', and 'the tragedy of that night'.

Putting the victim on trial

The curious thing about the defence of manslaughter to a murder charge is that, since there is no injured party available as a chief prosecution witness, the prosecution's case is based primarily on the statements made by the defendant to the police. Similarly, the case for the defence relies on the one eye-witness, the accused. The case for Wood's defence was not different in tone from the prosecution's case.

Certainly there was little at issue between them. It seemed that the only way out of this deadlock was to put Mary Bristow on trial, at which they were ably aided and abetted by the British gutter press. 'Savage Killing of a Women's Lib Lover', the *Sun* headlined. 'Milady's Link with Free-Love Killer', said the *News of the World*. And the *Star* excelled itself with 'Kinky Secret Life of Beauty at Library', sub-titled 'Mary's sex games turned jealous lover into killer', and accompanied by a photograph of a naked woman captioned 'Victim Mary . . . enjoyed kinky sex games' – which, needless to say, was not a picture of Mary at all. There was nothing we could do about it. 'The dead,' our lawyer assured us, 'cannot be defamed.'

No doubt entirely secure in that knowledge, Wood's counsel proceeded with a relentless assassination of Mary's character, unchecked by any consideration of truth, logic or common decency. Mary's real qualities – her kindness, her concern for others, her strong feminist principles, her independence, her intelligence, her popularity, her political commitments – and even her age and her height, were used as sticks to beat her with.

Describing the relationship between Mary Bristow and Peter Wood, Patrick Back, defending, stated:

> There was between him and Mary Bristow what you may think of as a very strange relationship, in which a gifted and older woman took him in hand, and sought to fashion him into something she thought superior, but which his birth and background did not really design him to be. The six-year-old relationship was a Pygmalion or *My Fair Lady* situation in reverse. Mary had a brilliant intellect and an IQ of 182. She took the part of a female Professor Higgins, and he that of a male Eliza Doolittle. She was also middle-class, and as sometimes

happens with very clever people she was in a state of rebellion against the morality favoured by that class. She regarded marriage as, at any rate, something not for her. I suppose she thought of it as something that would restrict her freedom. She was a devotee of many causes. The Women's Liberation Movement, pro-abortion and CND demonstrations.

With such cant and insidious innuendo, Back hoped to take responsibility for Mary's death away from Peter Wood and cast it squarely upon Mary herself.

'Her rejection of him, perhaps in a rather nasty way,' he said, 'must have been like a stab in the body.' In other words, she was 'asking for it'.

Provocation, in law, means

some act or series of acts done by the deceased which would cause in any reasonable person, and did cause in the accused, a sudden and temporary loss of self-control, rendering him so subject to passion as to make him not for the moment master of his mind. The sufficiency of the provocation shall be left to the determination of the jury, which shall take into account everything both said and done according to the effect which, in their opinion, it would have on a *reasonable man* [Homicide Act 1957].

In this case, the alleged provocation was simply Mary's disinclination to enter into an exclusive sexual relationship with Peter Wood. And it was, according to Winchester Crown Court, enough. Thus, any reasonable man might be provoked into killing a woman if she has the temerity to refuse to marry him.

The second defence entered by Wood's defence counsel was that of diminished responsibility. In law, this means (according to the Homicide Act) that the defence must show that the accused was

suffering from such abnormality of mind (whether arising from a condition of arrested or retarded development of mind, or any inherent causes or induced by disease or injury) as might substantially impair his mental responsibility for his acts and omissions, in doing or being a party to the killing.

The Mental Health Act 1959 contributes a more comprehensive and enlightened definition of mental disorder:

Mental illness, arrested or incomplete development of mind,

psychotic disorder, and any other disorder or disability of the mind.

And the sixth (1979) edition of Smith and Keenan's *English Law* says:

A killing arising from drink or drugs is not covered, because the condition is self-induced. And jealousy, hate or rage are not covered because they are ordinary human frailties which the defendant is expected to control.

Psychiatrists appearing for the prosecution and defence were in almost total accord about Wood's state of mind before the murder. They had not, of course, actually met him at this stage, but they were happy to take his word as gospel. He was 'depressed', they agreed, because of his own admission that he had been 'drinking heavily' and was currently out of work.

These facts might have been easily ascertained at any time in the past five years from less expert witnesses: any Winchester bar person, for instance, or a member of the Department of Employment. However, the psychiatrists agreed that the cause of Peter Wood's stressful life was Mary Bristow's determination to live her own life in preference to one prescribed by Wood.

Both psychiatrists agreed, too, that when they met Wood after the murder he was not then, in their opinion, suffering from depression – because the cause of his stress (Mary) had been removed. This was enough to persuade the jury to accept a plea of diminished responsibility – implying again that, if a woman's life-style, independence and refusal to be ruled by a man is stressful to him, she is deemed to be responsible for any violent reaction on his part.

In his summing-up, the judge endorsed the view that Mary brought her death upon herself.

'Mary Bristow,' he said,

with an IQ of 182, was a rebel from her middle-class background. She was unorthodox in her relationships, so proving that the cleverest people aren't always very wise. Those who engage in sexual relationships should realise that sex is one of the deepest and most powerful human emotions, and if you're playing with sex you're playing with fire. And it might be, members of the jury, that the conventions which surround sex, which some people think are 'old hat', are there to prevent people if possible from burning themselves.

In drawing a distinction for the jury between murder and manslaughter, he explained,

> murder involves wickedness, manslaughter does not necessarily involve wickedness, as when out-of-their-depth and totally-unable-to-cope people do things which are totally foreign to their nature. There is a difference between a villain shooting a policeman, and a husband killing his wife or lover at a stage when they can no longer cope.

Effectively the jury were thus instructed that it is reasonable for a man to kill a woman he has slept with on a regular basis, if that woman behaves in a way which frustrates him. Such an idea not only denies women an equal status in law, it also denies them the status of persons. And the jury accepted it.

The implications of the manslaughter verdict are obvious. If women are more intelligent, stronger and more independent than the men they associate with, and if they refuse to be governed by those inadequate men, they are deemed in law to be responsible for their own deaths. Female strength and independence are construed as wilful acts of provocation which diminish men's responsibility for their violence. On this basis, Peter Wood will probably be free in 18 months' time.

*

I left Winchester after the trial. I doubt I shall ever live there again. The Women's Liberation group that had supported us all for seven years gradually disintegrated. It no longer exists. It is good to hear that a new women's group now meets.

Press Release from the Sex-shop Arsonists[1]

First published in *Leeds Women's Liberation Newsletter*, April 1981

Angry Women have so far set fire to three sex shops in Leeds. Although media coverage has been given to attacks on sex shops throughout the country, an important feminist point has been purposely ignored – that porn is violence towards women.

We are *not* against sex. We are *not* concerned about sex shops 'lowering the tone of the neighbourhood' or 'corrupting the young'. We are *not* against sex education literature for children and adults. We *are* protesting and fighting back against images portraying women as sexual conveniences for men to abuse, hurt and degrade. Pornography in films, magazines and sex shops incites men to treat women as instruments solely for their use. It encourages rape, it increases men's power and control over women by humiliating and terrorising us. Porn is big money-making business built on the suffering of women.

We will fight pornography wherever it may be, whether in back streets or on main roads. Its very existence is an insult to all women, and as long as it is prevalent the streets will continue to be unsafe for women.

We have resorted to illegal action as ten years of legal activities and 100 years of feminist struggle have had no effect whatsoever on the porn issue. We hope that these arson attacks are the start of a more active protest by women against all forms of pornography.

Note

1. Damaged by fire: Sex Shop, Chapeltown Rd, LS7, 11 February 1981; Fantasy, Woodhouse St, LS6, 14 February 1981; Cupid, Bridge End, LS2, 30 March 1981.

2 Forever Working

Introduction

What is women's work? Women continue to be in low-status jobs, often part-time, without associated benefits and with low wage rates. We continue to do the invisible, unpaid work in the home. The burden of domestic work gets heavier under the impact of continuing closure of essential social services, while choices open to women outside the home are increasingly narrowed.

Despite the Equal Pay Act, equal pay has *not* been won and women have had to initiate struggles to take more control of their work situation. Strikes have been launched for equal pay, better working conditions and against the cuts. Asian women, one of the most exploited groups in the British workforce, have gone on strike to force their employers to recognise their right to join trades unions.

Despite continuing prejudices from male trades unionists, women have now forced them to take up the issue of sexual harassment at work. Feminists have also drawn attention to new technology and its impact on women's present and future employment, the exploitation of women workers overseas, and the effects of this new technology on our health and lives. Others, accepting the inevitable, are investigating the possible advantages for us.

Over the past few years a very small number of women have been able to work in other ways, in small co-operatives and collectives. However, even in these alternative workplaces, women's position has not been safe – those women most vulnerable amongst us have suffered discrimination even here, as in the case of the Market Nursery.

We do need to continue to question the value of the work we do, and who benefits from our labour. Perhaps, though, the first step for feminists is to ensure that all the work that women do – a large part of it unpaid and unrecognised – is given the validation it deserves.

A Woman's Day

First published in *Merseyside Women's Paper*, Spring 1982; and reprinted in *Women's History, Women's Lives,* Second Chance to Learn – Harrison Jones School

The day begins about 7.45. I wash and dress the two kids (Scott five, Kelly 21 months), then I go down to make breakfast, which is usually porridge, toast and tea. I pour myself a cup of tea but don't sit down to drink it. I leave the two eating and run upstairs to get washed and dressed. I then start getting nappies and bibs and things together, to take up to my Mum's. Oh, I forgot, Scott's staying for packed lunch today, so I leg it back down the stairs. Kelly's got everything out of the fridge, there's food all over the floor, I must get a lock on that fridge door, she's doing it all the time lately. I pick everything up, sort it all out, she's been eating raw sausages, I hope she's not sick. I'm doing Scott's packed lunch, the doorbell rings, it's Scott's friend, I bring him in and get back to packing lunch. Scott and his mate are running like mad around the living-room and shouting. Kelly's in the fridge again, oh God, no, I'm getting a headache. If I take any more Anadin I'll be rattling. I keep thinking I'm going to be late.

I grab the two kids, put hats and coats on, Kelly's taken her shoes off, we can't find them anywhere, I'm looking all over the place, where are they, babe? She just smiles and says, 'Don't know.' Put her in the pram, tell Scott not to run down the street, I've only got to pick my bags up, and I can get on my way. My head's banging.

I take two Anadin with a drop of milk, there are Kelly's shoes at the bottom of the fridge, I get my bags, turn everything off, now it's time to run.

After putting Scott into school, I really do run with the pram, so I can have ten minutes with my Mum before catching the 9.30 bus. By the time I get there, I'm sweating, my head's still aching, I don't feel well at all, really. I mean I shouldn't be tired, I only got up out of bed about one and a half hours ago. I leave my Mum's a couple of minutes early today, I need cigs from the shop. When I get to the bus stop, oh no, there's nobody waiting, I've missed the bus, I'm just about to scream, very loudly, but there's the bus, I haven't missed it.

Now I sit back, light a cigarette and relax, I can think about myself today, well, half the day anyway. I'm on my way to my women's history class, so I'm feeling better already. No, I'm not going to sit drinking tea and talk a lot of chit-chat, I'm going to work, I'm going to learn things, things that matter and what's good about it is, it's really interesting. If I'd had a proper education when I was younger, there'd be no need to come here, so I suppose I'm glad in a way. I don't know what I'm grinning about though, I've got all kinds to do when I get back home.

LONDON LESBIAN OFFENSIVE GROUP
(LLOG)

By Parties not Connected with the Case

Paper presented at Lesbian Sex and Sexual Practice
Conference, April 1983

We are a group of lesbians who meet regularly to discuss
the causes and effects of anti-lesbianism – we find that we always
have plenty to talk about! The recent dismissals of two lesbian
nursery workers at the Market Nursery in Hackney, London,
crystallised several key points for us, especially as we have been
concentrating in particular on the anti-lesbian attitudes and
practices of people who have some understanding of sexism and
some commitment to oppose it.

We did not come to examine the dispute at Market Nursery with
an objective eye. From deeply rooted experience, we assumed right
from the beginning that if two lesbian childworkers were being
dismissed, and if 'extremist ideas' figured among the allegations
against them, heterosexist practices among those dismissing them
would be at the bottom of the dispute.

It may be true that lesbians have always been involved with the
nursery, but this in itself in no way proves that it isn't an anti-lesbian
workplace or that it has in any way incorporated a programme of
anti-heterosexism. To claim that anti-lesbianism has had no part to
play in the dispute, but has only been dragged in by those wishing to
make things difficult for the management committee, is asking us to
believe that Market Community Nursery is a paradise, a Lesbos-in-
Hackney, where contented parents come and go, delighted that
their children are being cared for and influenced by women with
strong lesbian identities. It is more than clear that this nursery is still
very much of this earth, and has not yet transcended it.

We know, too, that what has happened here among a group of
predominantly white heterosexual feminist and pro-feminist women
and men is the outcome in material form of the ideas they hold
about lesbians. The dispute has been shaped by alliances these men

and women make against us, and by the methods they have always used to maintain the oppressive dominance of heterosexually. They are by no means alone in their attitudes, which we have encountered over and over again.

For reasons which have a lot more to do with heterosexism than with individual temperament, most lesbians feel they have no choice but to behave as assimilated employees, going along with the general pace of things. Lesbians working within heterosexually-dominated feminist and socialist groups have often not raised the issue of their own suffering, insights, or even joys, of being lesbians, but have put their energy into a broad anti-sexist effort. Up until now, heterosexuals of both genders have assumed that (mainly because of their own 'tolerance') all was going reasonably well – and have not noticed the resounding political silence. They have been blissfully unaware of their own part in ensuring that silence. A major way they have brought it about is by the continuing marginalisation of lesbian politics as 'extreme'. Clothes, life-style and, above all, a manner which signals unavailability to men, are all ways in which we assert our identity. To some extent 'radical' heterosexuals have learned to accommodate these. But once we start to *articulate* the ideas and politics which lie behind these more visible aspects of our lives, they become alarmed and the very concept of turning away from men becomes the dreaded 'separatism': the dustbin into which all the 'bad' lesbians are dumped, while the 'good' ones remain those who will hotly deny any allegiance to such an outrageous idea.

Originally, separatist lesbians were those who tried to live every day in such a way that they had as little to do with men as possible which, after all, is neither a particularly mad idea, given the present state of the world, nor one without historic precedent. We note that men who try to live well away from women do not produce the same sense of outrage.

Whether or not the workers were separatists, hysterical rumour during the dispute, and subsequently in the media, insisted that they were, and they automatically became 'the kind of feminists who give feminism a bad name'. As the editorial in the *Daily Mirror* put it: 'That revolt [i.e. by women] has been natural and right. But like all revolutions, it has its excesses which cannot be defended.' The excesses referred to were apparently committed by Liz and Janet, and the editorial closes by calling them 'witches' (20 April 1983). By defining Liz and Janet as extremists, the Market Nursery management indicated that they found their ideas incompatible and indigestible.

On the whole, socialists who've been influenced by feminism no longer divide women up into categories of good and bad. However, they do not hesitate to propound that there are good – i.e. socialist – feminists, and bad – i.e. radical and revolutionary – feminists. And they share the steady conviction of those on the Right that lesbian separatism is completely and utterly the unacceptable face of women's liberation, even while proclaiming a general politics of the right of self-determination for other oppressed groups.

When we looked in detail at the ideas expressed by Janet and Liz that had caused the upsets, we found them to be exactly the kinds of ideas we might have expected to find being bounced around a radical nursery professing an anti-sexist policy. We know they have not been the first-ever nursery workers to oppose notions of a Father Christmas (or to substitute a Mother Christmas), and of course lesbians are not alone in finding such Christmas paraphernalia objectionable and silencing: Jewish and Asian workers and pupils, for example, lesbian or heterosexual, will have also had strong reservations. And to us it seems perfectly reasonable to question assumptions about being a bridesmaid, or for that matter a bride – this would be part of the education we *want* for our children (and something we would perhaps up till now have assumed most anti-sexists would want for theirs). And we also believe that a radical political education best begins at the earliest possible age to counteract the daily barrage of heterosexist and sexist (and otherwise oppressive) propaganda which bombards the under-fives.

We do not underestimate the difficulties management committees might have in persuading all parents and co-parents of the benefits of an anti-sexist approach in nursery work, but we do not expect them to require their workers to take an 'anything goes' approach just because the child is of tender years. In any case it is neither possible nor desirable for teachers and childworkers to reinforce every aspect of family- or media-promoted values that each child brings to them, as it is highly likely that among those values there will be racism, sexism and all other forms of oppression. On this occasion the management committee have not grasped that 'bridesmaids' are part of both sexism and heterosexism . . . it is to be hoped that others will before more such workers lose their jobs.

We are all in our group the parents or co-parents of children, girls and boys. We do not want to play tit-for-tat. But yet again (it happens so often) we do marvel at radical heterosexuals' pigheaded ignorance on the matter of who gets their family life reinforced in radical nurseries or elsewhere: after all, *our* children have theirs undermined every time an adult waxes lyrical in response to other children's recitals of bridesmaids' outfits and all the other forms of heterosexist culture they endlessly bring to the classroom and find there. *Ours* barely ever receive any kind of validation for lesbian family life – nor apparently did the Market Nursery management committee attach any importance to ensuring that this would be so for lesbian-parented children there, given they so readily became upset by remarks countering 'normal' family life. And once our children leave their radical nurseries (which most of them never attend) it's off to the years of school where they will bear the brunt of a daily and grinding prejudice; or oppression, as we prefer to name it.

Because they have yet to confront themselves with the fact that heterosexism is an oppression, many heterosexual radicals cannot see how lesbians can claim to be oppressed in a situation where they are 'allowed' to come and go relatively unharassed. The chairperson of the management committee expresses this short-circuit succinctly when writing his post-hearing dismissal letter to one of the workers: 'You claim to have been dismissed because you are a lesbian. Your *sexual orientation* [our emphasis] is your business and provided it does not diminish the standard of your childcare, is none of our concern.' We could not have found a more quintessential expression of heterosexism. Why is it, we continue to wonder, that heterosexuals claiming to be political radicals still insist that (a) lesbianism is simply a matter of sexual preference, and that (b) it has nothing to do with them?

Sexual orientation, under the virtually enforced dominance of heterosexuality, can hardly be a free choice, nor can it be lived out as if unconnected to the other. We're not just acting out a private sexual preference: we see the world differently because of heterosexism, and we want the world to be different yet again. We want to demand a say in how to bring those changes about, not just remain silent while the world rolls on, bridesmaids and all, with heterosexuals looking politely away as if we're 'none of their concern'. All this, of course, means heterosexuals must change, must *make* heterosexism their concern.

We know that classist assumptions also infected this dispute – assumptions which held that although 'non-sexism' (sic) was just about acceptable among working-class parents who used the nursery, anti-heterosexism (or an openly pro-lesbian policy) would not be countenanced by them. 'It's the alienation of the working-class parents I'm worried about,' said one middle-class socialist feminist supporter of the management committee. Instead of facing their difficulties in coming to terms with a politicised lesbianism, they projected them onto other people they felt were 'not ready'.

The two sacked workers were, like many of us who are politicised

around our own oppression, active in promoting workers' rights at
the nursery, something which caused, as it always does, a great deal
of upset among the management. This became centrally bound up
in the process which finally led to their dismissal. As lesbians, we
know the message very well: 'We *let* you come here. We're not
prejudiced, we *allowed* you to be lesbians . . . Why did you have to
go and spoil it all by being troublemakers?' Connected with these
sentiments is the management committee's shock and irritation that
other lesbians immediately rallied round to show solidarity, since
we easily recognised what was happening. Management responded
with accusations of lesbians 'bullying and intimidating' and called
them 'parties not connected with the case'. Throughout they have
insisted that 'it is an unpleasant allegation to make that you were
discriminated against on the basis of your lesbianism and we think
you appreciate very well that there is no truth in it', as if Liz and
Janet had deliberately cooked up a story to dupe the local lesbian
community who had responded sheep-like and rent-a-mob, with
uncritical support. We might say that for many of us the feeling is of
being only too intimately 'connected with the case', which we feel
we knew in detail before it ever happened, like a continuing bad
dream.

The 'case' is not the bad childcare of two lesbian workers: that
'case' fell apart during the hearing, and management were forced to
withdraw a number of allegations; the independent witness at the
hearing, who is also chairperson of Hackney Council's own
disciplinary committee, felt strongly that the final dismissal was not
in accord with the evidence presented. The real – but unheard –
case is the refusal of heterosexuals of both genders to recognise
heterosexism as a serious and universal oppression, coupled with
their current inability to study and analyse heterosexism's relationship to sexism (despite spending considerable time in socialist
re-evaluations of sexuality). They also continually turn away from
the self-evident fact that heterosexism's bastions are defended both
by and through an alliance of men and women, through heterosexuality in all its many manifestations.

The hapless Market Nursery management committee and its
supporters are very largely made up of those determined (seeming-
ly) to defend the heterosexual hegemony to the bitter end – even
though they have not yet consciously acknowledged themselves to
be a part of it. They have relied on concepts of their own 'tolerance'
and on the often necessarily compliant silence of lesbians, who
sometimes turn out to hold strong views countering those of
heterosexism. How can we take seriously their claim to be
'committed to an open and non-discriminatory point of view' when

they sack two lesbian childworkers in a climate where the very idea of lesbians working with children is simultaneously being ridiculed in the local and national press? For at the same time, the London Borough of Islington was being accused of 'employing gays to work with kids' (shock horror), and gay teachers at the NUT conference were being media-splurged as 'would-you-want-your-children-to-be-taught-by-these-people?'. And could this committee really not see what was likely to happen to Liz and Janet at the hands of the press? We quoted discreetly from the *Mirror* editorial earlier – there was worse. Yet we doubt that this committee can perceive they had any responsibility in these matters at all. In their view, we bring it upon ourselves, making such a fuss about our oppression when that wasn't anything to do with the way they treated us.

We find all these attitudes and practices common among the mass of those women and men on the Left who in Hackney, and virtually everywhere, have hardly got beyond half-hearted window-dressing with regard to their attitudes to lesbians. They are a part of a strong political tradition built up in the last twenty years where heterosexual anti-sexists have abused the energy and commitment lesbian feminists have consistently put into pro-women politics rather than into gay rights. While most of us will continue to identify ourselves as anti-sexist rather than pro-gay, we have come to see that heterosexual anti-sexists have flourished and benefitted from a lesbian contribution to feminist theory which has continued to exclude any attack on heterosexism.

What we have said may seem like a long journey around what happened to the two lesbians at a community nursery in Hackney! But to us it is all part of the same, long, sad story to which we would like to see a changed ending . . . not the same old tale of deeply held oppressive attitudes, long unchallenged, long validated throughout society, surfacing in the victimisation of two lesbian sisters. We are clear about who must change their ways. We would like them to begin, now.

Male Order

First published in *Scarlet Women*, 14 January 1982

The following is an extract from an interview with 'Angie', who works as a VDU operator for a mail-order company in the Midlands.

At the same time as you're working there are print-outs being made of each operator. There's a number of different print-outs they can get on you. One is your actual performance – how many times you sign on and off – and it goes right down to seconds. Then there's another print-out that comes on a weekly basis which tells the management how many letters you've logged out, so they can check the scores you've handed in. They know how much of the time you're actually working and how much work you do. They can measure it right down.

Up until the beginning of May they were quite lax on the score, there was no pressure to get the score. But in May they introduced this figure of sixty, that was the number of queries a clerk was expected to deal with each day. They really clamped down. Every day we have a score taken. You start from the day before, because at four o'clock your final score is taken. What you do from four until a quarter to five is taken at eight-thirty, and they'll take another score at eleven and another at two, and then you hand in your score sheet at four. I have my own system. By eleven I'll try and get twenty done, and then by two I like to have done about forty. And then I know I'm going to get sixty. But if I'm nowhere near by that time there's not much point in me doing sixty.

Some people are scared of not making their scores, some people say they don't give a damn. I think underneath we're all scared. I am. I have to really push myself sometimes. You know, mentally you have to push yourself. That's why there's all the friction. You get a lot of friction amongst the girls. Bitching and back-biting over really stupid little things. I think if the job was different you wouldn't have that. I'm sure of it. The difference in atmosphere between where we work now and where we worked before, doing the job manually – there's just no comparison.

Now, obviously, if there's down-time on the line, they take that into consideration. That means there's a fault on the line that comes to the terminals. It means you can't enter anything into the terminals. It's a fault in the system. Sometimes it might only last a few minutes, sometimes it could last hours. It usually goes in days – you might go for three or four days and nothing goes wrong and then the day after it's off a few times, but not for very long. That's worse, people don't like it going down for a few minutes. It's just frustrating because you've still got to get your work done. If it goes down for longer – half an hour or an hour – it's a bigger break. But then they start dishing work out. If they know it's going to be off for a few hours, then they give you other things to do. The relief people feel when they book you off – when you know the line's down, it's just unbelievable. You might not be at your desk when it happens, but you can hear it. The whole place just goes 'phew!'. Everybody starts talking and messing about.

Recently, since they've imposed all these conditions, people have become a lot more aware of the system, the set-up, the regime. People say it's just like a military camp. It's just so dictatorial, it's terrible. The absenteeism has really gone up. A year, eighteen months ago, nobody, just nobody would say, 'I was away yesterday because I didn't want to come in.' You'd make a story up and you'd lie because you just don't have time off work saying you're ill when you're not ill. That was the attitude. But now people just don't care. At one time even friends wouldn't admit to each other they were just fed up. But now . . . If they asked for voluntary redundancies they'd get loads, people hate it so much.

LIZ ELSIE

Typists on Strike

First published in *Merseyside Women's Paper*, Autumn 1981

Out of 510 typists, secretaries and machine-operators working for Liverpool City Council, 450 are in the union NALGO. On 28 May 1981 they voted overwhelmingly to start a work to rule. The city council retaliated by immediately suspending twenty-three women, and NALGO, in turn, began selective strike action. Then, in a secret ballot, the women voted overwhelmingly to come out on full strike on £20 a week strike pay as of 6 July. Their strike brought the work of the city council to a stand-still and the council leader, Liberal councillor Trevor Jones, had to set up an emergency committee to keep things running.

Liz Elsie went to interview the six members of the strike committee. Just before this interview, all the strikers had been sent letters asking them to return to work and implying that if they didn't do so, they would be sacked.

The strike was over pay and regrading and showed what a farce the Equal Pay Act is while women are confined to the lowest-paid jobs.

Liz: Can you tell me what the dispute is about?

Helen: The typists', secretaries' and machine-operators' scale has this year been completely deleted. They've now introduced new scales which apply also to the lower-paid clerical officers and technical staff, but all Liverpool City Council has done is assimilate us to these new scales at the same salaries as the old ones.

May: We're one of the worst-paid in the country. In Gwynedd Council, their starting salary is higher than women's who've been in Liverpool City Council for twenty-five years.

Liz: Does the strike involve any other demands?

May: Yes, equal opportunities. Normally when clerks and technicians, predominantly men, come into the service, they have about three O-levels, but come September, they're immediately sent off on part-time courses in administration to gain qualifications to enhance their careers, so they can go shooting up the scale to £8500 p.a. We come in already qualified in shorthand and typing, and there we stay. In fact, our director of Personnel and Management services very proudly told me that he started off as a clerk, and I said, 'You're proving my point.'

Liz: What effect has your strike had?

Margaret: None of the students are getting their grants because we've stopped the cheques. No houses are being let or sold. Stocks in schools have gone right down. We've affected the wages a lot and the council have lost over £100,000 because of people being paid sickness benefit as well as their average wages. We've stopped all the council meetings. Rates demands or rebates aren't being sent out. We've affected the courts as well.

Rose J.: Nobody realised how essential we were, we're in everything, you see.

Liz: Have you noticed any changes in the attitude of the strikers?

May: They're more politically aware now than they've ever been.

Helen: Councillor Pyne has said that the 400 women are terrified of the six women who sit round this table.

May: They look it!

Helen: Every mass-meeting we go to, we walk round with our whips, don't we?

May: They bring out the old reds-under-the-beds of course, which has been going since the year dot. If you take action about anything, you're bound to be getting your orders from the Supreme Soviet.

Liz: What about attitudes of family and friends?

Rose J.: We couldn't have stuck it out if we hadn't had support. I mean, we work so hard, some nights it's 10 o'clock when we get home and we've been on the go since 6 o'clock that morning.

Helen: And if you do have a husband, he does need to be understanding and sympathetic because otherwise we'd have been in the divorce courts by now.

Liz: How do you feel about the reactions of the council and the media?

Rose D.: When the picket women are on the steps, you get men in top positions saying, 'Oh, you'll be here in the winter, hope you've got your boots.' They wouldn't say that to a man, but they're passing remarks daily.

Helen: But when Trevor Jones came past last week and asked were they all OK and would they still be there in the snow, one woman turned round and said, 'Well, we'll be here but where will you be next May at the elections?', and he just clammed up. And we've tried to get across to him that when he talks about the ratepayers, he's actually talking to them – his idea of a ratepayer is a male.

May: Councillor Pyne said we were destroying their image of the wives, sweethearts and sisters of the citizens of Liverpool, as if all the 'citizens' were male.

Helen: When we walked out of the council meeting last week, it went out on the 4 o'clock news that we were 'angry typists' and by 7 o'clock we were 'hooligans'. We're also very angry that on Friday they were saying that thirty of the women had returned to work and that the strike was crumbling. What they didn't say was that twenty of them went back within the first two weeks of the action. I think it's amazing just how many haven't gone back to work after the threatening letters we've received.

Liz: What do you think you've learnt most from being on strike?

Helen: I think the women themselves have realised that, when they do go back, they will never, ever be used the way they have been, and that is a very big point. Because we've had women at meetings saying, 'Well I'm employed to type at 35 w.p.m. and when I go back to work, that's what I'll do, even if I type now at 65 w.p.m.'

May: There'll be no more making of tea and coffee to the same extent either and no more taking over while the bosses are off, quietly doing their work for them in the background to make sure the public isn't damaged. In future, it's too bad, they'll have to stand and fall on their own merits. I think what a lot of people don't realise is that we don't just sit there with a pair of hands and a disconnected brain at a machine.

Barbara: Yes, in fact I spend half my life re-writing what others have written.

Helen: All day, we correct the grammar, the spelling mistakes. It was totally amazing when the industrial action started. One of the points of the work to rule was 'type as is' and the way the letters went out was absolutely appalling.

May: One of the things that the councillors have said is that other city typists had been prepared to accept new technology. But in this city, we've got typists who've never been acquainted with the *old* technology! They're still working on manual machines. Many years ago, someone at the university did a PhD thesis on energy used in various kinds of work and they said that a typist, in an 8-hour day, uses as much energy as a coal-heaver. Now since then the mines have become mechanised, so those of us on manual machines are the only coal-heavers left in the business!

Margaret: The next time we go on strike, we'll be organised from day one. I mean this. We've learnt by our mistakes, and it's cost us.

Postscript
The strike was lost, and they had to return to work without any of their demands being met.

CAROL OSGERBY

How Our Brothers on the Left Support Us

First published in *Hull Women's Newsletter*, November 1981

I do not describe myself as a socialist feminist, and feel very cynical about the precarious nature of reformist political 'victories'. But it is impossible to ignore the need for a defensive action to protect women's interests against massive attacks from this government, and essential to attempt to achieve some improvement in women's position. Over the last couple of years I have therefore become actively involved in my union, the Civil and Public Services Association, and joined the Broad Left Group. On the weekend of 7/8 November, I went to CPSA Broad Left Conference in Leeds.

If this introduction makes you think I have a need to justify myself, you're right: some of the things I get involved in make me think I must be crazy.

Despite the fact that 70 per cent of the membership of CPSA is female, about 80 per cent of the people at the conference were male. I got a strong impression that many Broad Left members do not attempt to recruit women, whom they see as very conservative.

The first day's business was pretty boring, almost all motions being passed without opposition. After the elections had been completed, disinterest in the business was quite blatant from a lot of people, and it was difficult even to hear the debate above the general talk – the usual booze and sex, and slagging off Militant members. Sexist jokes were excused on the grounds that female NEC members were fair game so long as they were right-wing.

There was a crèche, though it was practically impossible to find it. Some women had to stand in the doorway at lunchtime, because their children weren't allowed in the bar (and there wasn't anywhere else to sit). The fact that the conference took place in the Trades and Labour Club reveals a lot about entrenched attitudes to women in the labour movement.

On the second day was the debate on women's rights issues,

which were dealt with as a block. The motions concerning the national abortion campaign were unopposed, as were motions vaguely supporting greater involvement of women in the union, and advocating more crèche facilities, and union meetings in worktime. In so far as the motions concentrated on freeing women to work for socialist issues, they were uncontroversial. Speakers offered women sympathy and concessions, but made it clear that feminist demands were not to be tolerated.

The two motions which caused most controversy, and which were both lost, were the only two motions which suggested any practical means of achieving improvements, as opposed to the pious platitudes in the successful motions.

First, there was a motion calling for total support for the Civil Service Women's Rights Group, which takes up feminist issues through all the civil service unions. This failed because the group's business meetings are for women only, thus denying men control of the group. The counter-arguments were that women-only meetings were divisive, that they encouraged undesirable feminist debate (!), and that the suggestion that women were unable to join in debate on equal terms with men was 'patronising'. By failing to support the CSWRG, the male Left in CPSA made plain their opposition to any autonomous, self-directed action by women.

The other crucial motion which failed called for positive discrimination – giving priority to women on union schools, allocating conference time to women's issues, appointing a women's officer. Speakers said that there was no need for special efforts to encourage women to participate, merit being the only criterion for success, which led to the inescapable conclusion that they felt that, in a union with 70 per cent female membership and less than 50 per cent female involvement, men are simply worth more. The argument that women should not be advanced at the expense of men means in effect: 'We'll promise not to oppress you, sister, so long as you let us keep our power.'

I listened to no more of the debate after the section on women's issues. I was extremely angry – and more angry with myself than anyone else, both for being so surprised at the resistance to feminist ideas expressed in debate, and at my own failure to join in the debate. (I felt too angry to be coherent.)

Of course, my impressions of what happened at this conference will seem naive to many women. I know that the tactics of the male Left in subverting feminist arguments and paying lip-service to the need to fight for liberation, whilst supporting patriarchal institutions, have been described before. But there's nothing like seeing it at first hand.

Men are the enemy, and this is no less true of men in the Left with whom we may share political views. In spite of the occasional man who is sympathetic to feminism, men are the upholders of patriarchy. I feel angry and frustrated that feminists in trades unions have a double fight, in having to use the framework of the hierarchical, male-dominated union to fight male domination in society.

SARAH and FUGEN

Homework: So What's Changed?

First published in *Outwrite*, no. 8, November 1982

I am a homeworker and experienced machinist. As a housewife I know it is the only job that I can do at this time because I have a three-year-old boy to look after and my home. I think something must be done about it so that the homeworkers get a better wage.

Homework is, simply, paid work done at home. Many homeworkers are machinists, sewing clothes in their homes for factory-owners, who will then sell the finished goods to, for example, chain-stores and mail-order firms. Others make Christmas crackers or children's toys.

They are usually paid far less than workers doing the same job in factories – often as little as 40p an hour.

Nearly all homeworkers are women, mainly black and immigrant workers and women with disabilities. For nearly all workers, homeworking is not a positive choice but the only way they can earn money and look after their children and do the housework.

I have to decide how much I must make for next week. It's up to me. I have to earn that money. What payments I have to make.

The money Ayshe earns from machining clothes in her home every day is a vital part of her family's income. She, like all workers in the clothing industry, is paid according to how many garments she finishes a week (i.e. piecework rate).

If she stops work for whatever reason – even for a day – she and her children are affected in some way by her drop in earnings.

Like most of Britain's 400,000 homeworkers, Ayshe is regarded by her employer as self-employed. In fact, the employment status of homeworkers is complicated and Ayshe, like many other immigrant women, says she is unclear about her own position.

Should it be her or her employer's responsibility to pay her income tax and national insurance contribution, for example? She's never had any clear guidance about this so she has simply been forced to accept her employer's assertion that he is certainly not responsible for her in any way: she is not down in his books as an 'employee'.

Most homeworkers are in a similar position. By calling Ayshe self-employed, Ayshe's employer doesn't have to give her a contract (which he would have to do if she were an employee). Therefore, he doesn't have to give her continuous employment, a consistent rate of pay, sickness benefit, maternity pay, redundancy pay or holiday pay. The safety of the machine she uses, like her light and heating costs, is her problem, not his. Also, if she was an employee with a contract of employment she'd be covered by a wages council. This would mean that she could contact the wages inspectorate who would investigate the levels of pay where she works and make sure the workers were getting paid the legal minimum rate.

> I can never bargain with my employer. This is the working home. If you're not satisfied with the work you have to find another job. If I know another job I can look for it but I cannot make any bargain with him. I'm stuck with him no matter whether he's good or bad. So many people have been stuck with them [their employers] so many years and they cannot make any bargains with them about the prices or the work.

In some industries and areas, employers have to register any homeworkers with their local authorities and the health and safety inspectorate. Registered homeworkers tend to earn slightly more than other homeworkers (although their pay is still extremely low), but they make up only a small fraction of the homeworkers in this country.

It is not just a handful of bad employers who are responsible for the low rates of pay and appalling conditions. Homeworking has always been a part of British industry. Big and small firms alike employ homeworkers because they need a dispensable workforce at as low a cost to themselves as possible.

By using homeworkers, employers save on their running costs and national insurance contributions and thus maximise profits on workers' labour.

> I cannot sleep in the night-time for my back. I cannot lie on my back . . . I been to the hospital for an X-ray, it's my muscles being bent all day they told me. They said I have to stop working for a while, but I can't afford to stop. I have to work.

The speaker is a Turkish-Cypriot woman who has been a home machinist for fifteen years, ever since she left school at the age of sixteen. She is not surprised that she has almost constant backache, she knows many people whose health has been much more seriously affected by long hours at the machine.

For her it is far more worrying that fifteen years of boring, unrewarding, isolated work have badly affected her nerves and her relationships with those closest to her.

Stress is a major cause of ill-health amongst homeworkers. As the vast majority are women, they often have domestic responsibilities as well as their full-time job. Indeed, it is typically because of the need to stay at home and look after young children and/or elderly or disabled relatives that women start homeworking in the first place.

Long hours at home, often in badly lit, badly heated accommodation with all the domestic responsibilities associated with looking after a home, children, a husband and/or relatives, cause severe depression amongst many homeworkers. But of course their depression, like their wages and working conditions, remains hidden.

Homeworking is an isolated and isolating job and so it is very difficult for homeworkers to get together to change their situation.

For all of them, the small wages they earn are vital to their families' income. Alone they are dispensable and for most any confrontation over pay and conditions would mean losing their jobs.

The labour movement could and should be moving to halt the exploitation of women like Ayshe. But there are difficulties. Women, and particularly immigrant women, who already have painful experiences of British public male-dominated institutions (like the Home Office), are naturally reluctant to come forward and talk about their working conditions. The ambiguity of their employment status – the fact that income tax and national insurance contributions are often not paid at all, either by the employer or by the women themselves – makes them fear the repercussions of identifying themselves.

Nor do they necessarily see any connection between themselves and British trades-unions. How might the unions help, they ask, and would they, concerned as they are with the pay and conditions of male white workers?

Some progress is being made, though it is pitifully slow. The TUC has a 'Statement on Homeworking' which is meant to 'provoke active consideration at all levels of the movement'. Again, at this 'concerned' level, the General and Municipal Workers' Union has since 1977 been committed to integrating homeworkers into their trades-union organisation, negotiating on their behalf when this is possible and putting pressure on employers to furnish complete and comprehensive lists of the homeworkers they employ. What has been achieved is another matter.

Perhaps of far greater significance for homeworkers (because it might actually *affect* them) is the decision by some boroughs to appoint a homeworking officer to liaise between homeworkers, employers and officials and to represent homeworkers' interests. This at least suggests local boroughs are recognising that a problem exists and that homeworkers should be given a voice.

If the situation of homeworkers is to improve, two things have to change. First, homeworking has to be a choice. Women must be free to work outside the home if they want to. Adequate childcare facilities and day centres for the elderly and disabled would free many women from the absolute necessity of staying at home.

Secondly, homeworkers must be given the same rights and protection that other workers are entitled to. Homeworkers need to understand their position, to know whom to go to for help and information about their employment status, pay and working conditions.

Ultimately, of course, the situation confronting homeworkers has to be understood in the context of a political and economic system which defines women's – and particularly immigrant women's – work as less 'important' than men's work. This *all* women can fight to change.

JAN PARKER

A Right to an Income

First published in *Spare Rib*, 117, April 1982

If you're a housewife or a married woman, to take just two possible 'categories', do you call yourself a wageless woman? The very name of some groups that have been set up recently – Wageless Women – is telling. It *is* important for the Left to focus on fights against redundancies. It's also easier to stand on a picket line and talk about a woman's fight to have that job, than to tackle all the other issues that affect as many women who don't even have the 'luxury' of a job to start with. 'Wageless' sums up the situation of thousands of women and calls for a completely different 'ball-game' than the 'right to work' and unemployment campaigns.

After working out a Charter for Wageless Women at a Conference of the National Unemployed Movement, Wageless Women groups have begun to be set up. Jan Parker talked to Fran, Monika and Sarah, three women involved in Wageless Women, about a complementary but different demand to 'the right to work' – the demand for a woman's independent right to an income.

S: After the NUM conference in Newcastle, women met and discussed the Wageless Women's Charter. It's very difficult, but the one thing we all thought was important was to campaign for a woman's independent right to claim benefit. That's the central thing; it entails a completely different benefit system, but it's our main reason for existing.

F: I'm a woman who signs on and what I most want to do is contact other women in a similar position. It means knocking on estate doors and getting very little response for a long time; it's hard work, but it's about building up our strength as women. I also think a lot more women can identify with the call for an independent income than the right to work. The majority of women involved with WW are unwaged, but it's also open to part-time workers because many women are part-time for the same reasons we're unwaged.

S: After the announcement about child benefit changing to a monthly payment, we had women running after us down the street in Sheffield to sign the petition on it. Many of them were saying it was often their only income to keep the family on, especially if their husbands didn't give them any money that week. And it's going to be paid in arrears as well!

Most of the benefits are bad news for women. Sickness and maternity benefits are dependent on NHI contributions, in other words, a history of paid employment. Supplementary benefit is a safety-net benefit for anyone whose income falls below subsistence level, but a married or cohabiting woman cannot claim as it's assumed her husband will support her. If he has no income he can claim for her, but she still has no income in her own right, and if she does earn money herself, it's assessed as *his* income. One of the most discriminatory provisions is the housewife's non-contributory invalidity benefit for married women. To get a non-contributory invalidity pension, a man simply has to show he's incapable of paid employment from a doctor's certificate. A woman has to fill in a three-page form that's full of questions about shopping, cooking, cleaning, making the beds. There's categories for able, almost able, unable; it's so demeaning. If she can do them she *doesn't* get the benefit and she gets . . . nothing.

M: Many of us aren't in a position to go and get a job, for example if you've got dependent relatives at home or small children and no access to nursery facilities. On top of this, a recommendation of the recent Rainer Report will prevent women from getting benefit unless they can prove they have childcare arrangements already worked out for when they might be offered a job.

Our benefits are low or non-existent. If we choose to live with a man we don't get any money. Then there's the problem at benefit offices. We get hassled by officers who come round to check if you're cohabiting and if we've got kids we often get asked questions about our sexual behaviour. We have to justify everything all the time.

S: Anyone who doesn't have a job should get a benefit without any kind of means test.

M: And we're not asking for a wage to do housework, for 'fulfilling our role' either. We don't recognise housework as a woman's job anyway. Wageless men have the right to an independent income and it's not tied to whether they do housework. What we're asking for is very basic – our own money – that every woman gets her own Giro or book through the door. We've decided, after a lot of talking, not to concentrate on a figure; it's a bit dangerous when prices change so much.

F: There's a lot of talking going on at the moment about how to approach our demand: as a guaranteed minimum income; whether you should have to register for work or if there should be a contributory system. It's difficult to get clear proposals and still be something that we can identify with easily as a campaign. But wageless women have always been ignored. That it's a 'difficult issue' doesn't mean it's OK to make excuses for doing nothing. Our demand is also a challenge to low-paying employers. A lot of married women take the shit jobs because they don't get benefits, so they end up with the low-paid work. It's extraordinary what you can earn up to and actually be worse off. It really is a poverty trap. As you start earning a little you begin to lose rent and rates rebates, free prescriptions, milk tokens, and so on.

S: The trouble is, a lot of women still think that having their own independent benefit would be scrounging off the state.

F: That's a rampant attitude. Men are accused of that too, but they don't come up against it as much as women because of the ethos that if there was a job, he'd be doing it. People don't think of women in those terms.

S: Unless you start talking about keeping or creating shitty jobs for the sake of everyone having a job, you're also inevitably talking about women having a choice and about *improving* social services like nurseries and old people's homes.

It means society changing in a lot of major ways and it also means thinking of being on benefit in terms of everyone's life being productive, whatever we're involved in. Whether we're being paid by an employer or not, our lives are still productive.

URSULA HUWS

Domestic Technology – Liberation or Enslavery?

First published in *Scarlet Women*, no. 14, January 1982

Any investigation of the effects of new technology in the home has to start with the incontrovertible fact that *the technology which has so far been introduced has failed to liberate women from the role of houseworker and from the reality of many hours of unpaid household labour*. Despite much liberal theorising about the 'symmetrical family' and changes in the boundaries between 'men's' and 'women's' work in many homes, housework is still seen as the woman's responsibility, and such research as has been done on hours of labour in the home suggests that, if anything, the amount of time spent by the average woman on housework is actually going up – from around 60 hours a week in the 1920s to over 70 in the 1970s, and this during a half-century when there has been an unprecedented increase in the number and variety of 'labour-saving' appliances, household chemicals, convenience foods, and so on. What can be the explanation for this phenomenon?

It appears that several different factors make a contribution to this state of affairs.

The first of these is *ideological*. Barbara Ehrenreich and Deirdre English have shown in much of their work the power of ideological forces in bringing about the 'manufacture of housework', as they call it. The education system, advertising, the advice of 'experts' in medicine and psychiatry have all combined to persuade women whose grandmothers made do with an annual spring-clean that every corner of their homes must be disinfected weekly, or even daily, that clothes should be washed after each wearing, and that children will suffer extreme deprivation if not given undivided continual attention. So well have they done their job that none of us is immune from the crippling guilt which comes from believing we have neglected a child, or put someone's health at risk by allowing germs to breed in our filthy kitchens.

A second factor is a direct consequence of the *privatisation of domestic life*. Each housewife, isolated in her own home, duplicates the work of every other housewife, and requires her own individual washing-machine, fridge, cooker, Hoover and all the other items which make up a well-equipped home from lemon squeezers to chip-pans, many of which are probably out of use 95 per cent of the time. There is thus no economy of scale, which is often the main saving which automation brings. Getting out the food-mixer, assembling the bits, dismantling it, washing it up and putting it away again takes as much time whether one is cooking for two or twenty, and the same applies to hundreds of other operations which all women carry out separately.

The third factor, less obvious but perhaps even more pervasive in its effects, results from *applications of technology and science elsewhere in the economy*. As areas of paid work are automated and 'rationalised' to maximise profits and efficiency and minimise labour costs, so more and more unpaid 'consumption work' (as it has been labelled by Batya Weinbaum and Amy Bridges) is foisted on to consumers – in other words on to women as housewives. Thus, since the beginning of this century, a whole new range of self-service tasks has been added to the traditional responsibilities of the housewife. If someone is ill, it is no longer the doctor's paid time which is spent travelling to and from the home, but the patient's unpaid time, travelling to and from the clinic and, once there, waiting. The housewife is now expected to transport herself to the nearest supermarket, find the goods she wants, take them down from the shelves, transport them to the checkout, wait, and transport them home – nearly all tasks which used to be somebody's paid job. The increased size of supermarkets has meant that distances to travel are much further, which in its turn has led to increased reliance on home storage of food, e.g. in freezers (so the retailing industry is even managing to transfer much of its storage costs on to the consumer).

Many other examples could be quoted of this trend towards what Jonathan Gershuny has called a 'self-service economy'. What male economists like Gershuny fail to point out is that in a society in which unpaid work is equated with women's work, such self-service tasks will inevitably fall preponderantly on women, thus reaffirming the low value placed on women's labour in the wider economy, in a self-confirming circle, and perpetuating women's oppression in the home.

The roots of the fourth factor which contributes to extra housework lie in *women's role as carer*. She is expected to take responsibility for the health and safety of the entire family in and around the home, more particularly that of children and aged or handicapped dependants. As paid workers have discovered, new technology leads to new hazards, and, as a result of the scientific and technological developments of the past century or so, the home and its immediate environment are now a death-trap for anyone who is not able-bodied, quick-witted and literate. Perhaps the three most important 'advances' of the twentieth century – the internal combustion engine, the many-branched growth of the chemical industry, and electricity – are also the three greatest killers, as anyone who has had to keep a toddler safe will appreciate. Outdoors, the danger from traffic is a constant nightmare; indoors, poisonous chemicals are used for everything from cleaning the lavatory to keeping mummy tranquillised, while sockets and trailing leads make every room potentially lethal. Safety advertisements on TV and in clinics emphasise, with guilt-provoking details, that it is mothers who are responsible when children are mutilated and killed, and it is actually a legal offence to leave a child alone. Childcare has thus become a tense, fraught, 24-hour responsibility, and again science and technology have added to housework with one hand, while seeming to lighten it with the other.

In any discussion of the disadvantages of the new technology or science there is a danger of appearing to glorify some pre-technological, past golden age. That danger exists too in the discussion of housework. It is important to remember that it's always been hard and that technology has brought about advances for women in terms of reduced physical effort, more choice, freedom from some types of diseases, etc. But we must always remember that it's contradictory. Just as contraceptive technology *has* given some freedom of choice to women about whether or not to have children, although it hasn't brought our liberation from male domination of our bodies, and has created new health risks, so domestic technology has brought some advantages, while in no way bringing about our liberation from housework.

In some ways, the effects of technology in the home parallel very closely the effects of technology in the factory, as analysed by Harry Braverman and his many followers. The workers' skills and knowledge are appropriated, and incorporated in the design of the machines. Just as skilled craftspeople, such as lathe-cutters, suddenly find themselves needing only to know which button to press on the computer-controlled machine, so the housewife can now discard all her expert knowledge about, for instance, different methods of washing different types of fabrics, and need simply select the right program on her automatic washing-machine. Similarly, cooking may become a simple matter of following the instructions on the packet – the only skill required is literacy.

Dependence on the 'expert' is also increased. We no longer understand what things are made of and how they work. In the workplace, this leads to a polarisation between the few high-status jobs at the top and the mass of unskilled workers at the bottom. In the home, it leads to an increased helplessness and dependence on the part of the housewife. She does not know why the label on the aerosols says 'Caution, do not use near pets or foodstuffs; keep away from children', and so has no alternative but slavishly to follow the directions, abandoning any possibility of creative improvisation with the materials to hand. She also spends ever-increasing amounts of frustrating time waiting for the 'expert' repair man, gas-fitter, etc.

The effects of all this are very contradictory. On the one hand, the fact that household tasks have become easier and less specialised means that anyone can do them. This opens up possibilities of men taking a larger share in housework and potentially liberating women. On the other hand, it also gives men a greater confidence to criticise when work does not come up to the standards the advertisers claim for their products. The mysteries once handed down from one woman to another are now common property, and do not command any respect. For older women in particular, this can lead simply to a feeling of dispensability and interchangeability with other women which results not in greater liberation but in increased economic insecurity. This closely parallels the experience of older, skilled industrial workers who feel themselves devalued and made redundant when their jobs become easier as a result of new technology.

There is another sense in which these developments adversely affect women economically. A fully operating home these days requires a much bigger capital investment than it did in the past, and while most women earn little more than half men's wages, that can mean that a woman who decides to leave her man and set up on her own is plummeted into quite extreme deprivation, going as she does from the standard of living of a 1½-income family to that of a ½-income one. As society is increasingly reorganised on the basis that every 'normal' household is equipped with a telephone, fridge, TV, etc., surviving without these things becomes increasingly intolerable.

What are the implications of all this for socialist feminists? In our personal lives, many of us find liveable solutions – we live collectively with other women or cheaply on our own, push men into doing their share of housework or find sufficiently well-paying jobs to buy our way out of the worst problems (though we often pay a price for this in perpetual exhaustion, or enforced childlessness). When it comes to formulating demands to benefit all women, things become more problematic.

Clearly, it is not enough to take on new technology just in the workplace. We must recognise that it affects every other area of our lives too, and find ways to resist its worst effects. Community organisation might provide part of the answer. Perhaps we should start demanding more home visits from doctors, DHSS officials, midwives, etc.? Or delivery services from supermarkets? We should definitely continue with campaigns for daycare facilities for children, the aged and the handicapped, and for safer streets and play-areas and better-designed housing.

We must also, I believe, clarify what we mean by the socialisation of domestic labour. It is possible to imagine a society in which just about all the things now done by women in the home are automated or carried out as paid services without capitalism having been dislodged or women achieving liberation. We must start defining what sort of services we want and insist that they are brought in under our control.

References

Ehrenreich, Barbara, and English, Deirdre, *For Her Own Good*, Pluto Press, 1979.

Gershuny, J., *After Industrial Society: The Emerging Self-Service Economy*, Macmillan, 1978.

Oakley, Ann, *Housewife*, Penguin, 1974.

Weinbaum, Batya, and Bridges, Amy, 'The Other Side of the Pay Cheque', *Monthly Review*, July/August 1976.

3 Racism

Introduction

Is racism on the increase in this country? Will recent legislation, particularly the Nationality Act and the proposed Police Bill, strengthen already held racist attitudes? Black people are amongst the most vulnerable to unemployment, redundancies and the erosion of the welfare state. The threat of deportations, checks on Irish people and their homes, more police surveillance and harassment of black people in inner cities, demands for proof of nationality when dealing with government agencies and virginity tests all show the racist policies and practices of the police and the government.

This has been met with resistance and some successes. Virginity tests ceased after massive opposition by Asian women. Several deportations and attempts to divide families have been resisted: Halimat Babamba for instance won her fight against deportation with the support of the first women-only anti-deportation campaign group in Leeds. However, in this particular area, where the new immigration rules make black women's situation increasingly precarious, there is a constant need for vigilance and action.

As this book shows, things have become increasingly difficult for all women in this country during the past few years, and particularly so for black women, both in personal day-to-day experiences and in conflict with the institutions that govern our lives. It has become necessary for us to form specific interest groups based on our shared identity and personal history, to feel safe and able to define and state our priorities. 'General topic' women's groups are not able to do this, are no longer sufficient, and in fact need to be challenged.

For reasons of space and the difficulties of prioritising one campaign over another, we have decided not to include articles about fights against racism and imperialism in other countries, nor about women's involvement here in supportive anti-imperialist struggles. The recent formation of several women's anti-racist and anti-imperialist groups has drawn attention within the women's liberation movement to the specific oppression of women in other countries, especially in the Third World. *Outwrite Women's*

Newspaper was established in March 1982 to give a voice to these struggles, and to reflect feminist struggles internationally.

This section overlaps with *Challenges*, in which there are articles about feminists failing to question our own racism or to tackle the racism around us. While it is important that women in this country involve themselves in solidarity groups, surely it is no less important that we look at continuing British colonialism and its obvious repercussions as expressed in the dissatisfaction of, and demands made by, black people here today.

During 1982 Israel invaded the Lebanon in a major international political act, the reverberations of which are still being felt world-wide, including within the British women's liberation movement. Women here formed the Women for Palestine group and were quick to react, criticising the state of Israel for its imperialistic act. Many Jewish, and non-Jewish, feminists felt that those recriminations contained deeply ingrained anti-semitic sentiments, and the debate quickly became volatile and polarised. However, the complexity of these issues *needs* to be tackled: anti-semitism *has* to be recognised and fought against; but, in this instance, current Israeli imperialist practice deserves the same response.

It is important that feminists work together through such major, and destructive, world events, listening to each other's demands and experiences, and stay steadfast in working together against racism and imperialism.

The women's liberation movement *is* slowly changing and groups already active on these issues have contributed a political awareness that can no longer be ignored.

Eenie, Meenie, Miney, Mo

First published in *Shocking Pink*, 1

I was asked to write something about racism in schools –
I thought this would be quite hard to do as racism is not just 'racism
in schools'. It's not that simple. The best place I decided to begin
was junior school.

At junior school, racism was not prominent to me. This was
probably because I was so young and not aware of being black and
what it meant. Racism mainly occurred in the form of school
literature – things like little black children called 'Sambo', and
images that took the form of black people called 'Gollywog'. Things
for me at that age were pretty clouded because I enjoyed school,
and at the age of eight, black and white children were less struck by
colour differences. While writing this, something I remember of
junior school feels quite painful now and, as I remember it, did
then. It was when a teacher had to pick a team and started chanting
'Eenie, meenie, miney, mo, catch a nigger by his toe, if he screams
then let him go, eenie, meenie, miney, mo.' I looked at him in
disgust and vowed never to speak to him again, and I didn't much
either.

Well anyway, of course you begin to age, and you can't get your
enlarged bodies into Wendy houses any more. So the educational
system decides to move you to a larger Wendy house in the form of
domestic science rooms. But unknown to us happy tomboyish girls,
your whole world which revolved around playing football, marbles
and penny-up-the-wall with the boys, stops! You can't be a pilot any
more, because you're 'black' and a 'woman'. The labelling process
begins. You're streamed into O-levels or CSEs and you're not
allowed to do woodwork *and* metalwork, or cookery *and* needle-
work. The steady build-up of the educational system reinforcing the
status quo and the role in society 'they' want you to perform.

It's a fact that while black girls visit the career officers to decide
what subjects to pursue, we are persuaded (shoved) into domestic

83

science and social science CSEs (is this a conspiracy of adult society to have more black tea ladies and low-paid typists) and are encouraged to continue with athletics, winning on 'behalf' of the schools. (Where does the winner's cup go?)

Then the girls go home after five years (well, at weekends as well) and parents ask, 'Why didn't you do this, why didn't you do that – you had the same opportunities as the rest?' bla, bla, bla, 'You'll have to go to college then!'

Parents sometimes fail to realise that at school we're being continually patronised about our attitudes, the way we speak and our lack of progress. (Yes! young women, we're to blame for the position we've got ourselves into. It sounds like pre- and post-Conservative Manifesto material.)

Teachers often, if not always, fail themselves to see the educational system, even society, in its true light. For instance: (1) *Our attitude* – Don't we come from different cultures? Attitudes are different. Have teachers or the educational structures ever stopped to look at our culture and realise that we're fed up with 400 years of domination and oppression from the 'ruling-class' values and culture? Why should we become uniform in attitude? Well, I mean, they put us in uniform dress – but that's not enough, they also want us to have uniform attitudes. (2) *Our language* – Yes! it would be nice to speak and write the Queen's English, wouldn't it? Just because a teacher fails to understand what we are saying, that makes us ignorant, rude, etc. But when we are being thrown into domestic science, it's hard to speak Queen's English to cakes and pies – even typewriters don't respond well. Or when in class you're asked to read, and you read with your West Indian, African or Asian accent, reading rubbish about the 'whites civilising the blacks', rather than 'white capitalists infesting the colonies to rob them of their wealth and exploit cheap labour'.

If we react against this demoralisation, we're put in disruptive units. There are classrooms which do not facilitate pupils with any education and are labelled ESN (educationally sub-normal). Also we're left in there for very long periods.

Who the hell wants more education in the form of college? And anyway, we leave with no 'real' qualifications, negative self-images, and like me with identity complexes. I went to a secondary school which was all girls, only about 3 per cent of which were black. Some of my friends were brainwashed into thinking that everything is equal for the 'good black student'. So after leaving school qualified, all they got from employers was 'You're very highly qualified' (for a black woman, they mean). Then the final stab-in-the-back cliché, 'Have you any experience?'

Then, if you do get a job, it's probably second-best. If you were like me, a 'bad student', then the next step was the dole office since there are so many black women on the dole queue of all ages.

That's just as bad, as we have to be trodden on, chewed up and spat out before we get our £16.35 a week. This ultimately numbs your ambitions, self-expectations and self-recognition.

This society has a knack (conspiracy) to provide useless diversions. It's a lot easier to go and play with the space-invaders than to read 'real' books about black women. We are not so much dropped as kicked into societal traps. Lots of black girls get pregnant, not so much because of a lack of knowledge about contraception, I think, but because of a lack of trust of necessary agencies. Or it might provide their 'independence' from parents, as they can get their own flats. What about bills, however? 2 a.m. feeds? Continual shit to clean. And obligation? Black men as well as black women get picked up on the police rules called 'SUS', where the innocent are guilty and the guilty doubly guilty.

We fight at school for equal education and non-sexist education. We fight at work against discrimination of sex, wages and race. We fight in the dole offices for our share of nothing. I'm fed up of us black women propping up our black men, to help them prop up this society, while continually getting kicked in the face. My patience is running out and so is this society's time.

SHAILA,
with support from the Third World/Black Feminist
Group and the Black Lesbian Group

Angry Opinion

First published in *London Women's Liberation Newsletter*,
no. 244

Dr Rani B., a feminist doctor, works on a radical
medical/health programme, which is part of a development project
called 'Chetana Vikas' (consciousness-development) which operates in several villages in a large rural district in Maharasthra state,
India. So far, a large number of women resident in this area (mostly
poor peasant women) have been given dangerous intravenous
contraceptives. Dr Rani B., in her efforts to encourage and provide
safe contraception for the women, requested me to send her twenty
cervical caps initially, in order to see how these would be received
by the women. I requested financial donations for these caps, which
I got, and enough money was collected to enable me to send these
caps to her last month. My thanks to all the women who
contributed.

Unfortunately, the matter does not end there, as it should have.

Two black sisters reported to me that they were present on two
occasions when 'opposition' was voiced by two white feminists who
disagreed with my having sent the caps. This 'opposition' stated that
my decision to comply with Rani B.'s request was reactionary as I
had thereby supported the institution of heterosexuality. One of
them further suggested that the true 'feminist' solution would be
that 'we' (by which I take it she meant 'they') should instead be
going out to India to 'convert these women to lesbianism'.

In true missionary tradition, but this time it's white lesbian
feminists!

These two (and more?) women obviously have no idea or
understanding of the reality of women's lives beyond their own.
Their comments display sheer ignorance, arrogance, inconsidera-
tion and racism. This has made several black/Third World sisters
and myself very angry.

I am not prepared to enter into any discussion with these white
women about my so-called 'support of the institution of heterosex-

uality'. This is not the issue. As far as I am concerned, both the right to a self-defined sexuality and the right to control our own bodies are fundamental feminist principles, and universally acceptable. And these are just that, i.e. a woman's right to a *self*-defined sexuality as opposed to a *white*-defined sexuality. Do not export and impose your white-identified understanding of feminism, or what constitutes women's liberation, or your experience and understanding of female sexuality on black and Third World women. It is inadequate: it is inappropriate.

We, as black/Third World women, do not need your opinions, your approval or disapproval of our Third World/black feminism, politics and actions, especially from uninformed ignorant white feminists. *We* can judge for ourselves what is best for us. You cannot. We will define feminism for ourselves, a feminism that will be based on our experience as Third World/black women, lesbian and heterosexual.

For too long, western white feminists have organised WLM, and developed a theory and practice of feminism to suit their needs, in their countries to suit particular political climates, and further, wrongly imposed this limited ideology and practice on women in Third World countries, i.e. most of the world.

Surely a white supremacist feminism that dares to believe that it addresses the needs of all women, and proceeds to present itself as the norm, is just another expression of yet another kind of white imperialism? This must be combatted, not just by black women who have constantly had to challenge this power base, but by white women in the WLM in this country who are committed to revolutionary change *throughout* the world for *all women*.

We regard the crass political analysis supplied by the white women on the caps as just one more indication of the ignorance and white-identified/defined nature of feminism in this country at present. We reject this, and demand that we, as Third World/black feminists, be left alone to define and develop our feminism as we see fit, a feminism that will be internationalist and voice the experience and perspective of many women, who have so far been ignored, ridiculed and silenced.

In anger with the white women who inspired this response. In sisterhood with those who supported.

A Revolutionary Anger

First published in *Spare Rib*, no. 110, September 1981

As the most recent wave of uprisings of black people has died, and the establishment media has no more 'sensationalist' events to report, the consequences for black people in this country are increasingly frightening: excessive police surveillance, raids on black people's homes, an increase in hostility towards us daily, the introduction of almost militaristic control of our movements . . . While the country was stupidly gasping over the Great White Wedding, young black women and men were, and still are, being picked up, convicted, fined exorbitant sums, imprisoned – the charge being that we dare to exist. The white media remains silent.

A lot of political work lies ahead of us – I feel deep respect for black men and women already involved in various ways, such as those working especially now in defence committees. I feel positive that the fight back against the racism of the state is gaining momentum, and that a kind of revolutionary anger is being expressed when we say we will no longer tolerate this.

But I feel I also need to single out some of the reactions I have had as a woman. There has been the paralysing fear which prevents me from participating actively in a show of solidarity and strength as expressed through street conflict. I feel powerless, afraid.

But I do not believe that not being on the street battlelines equals non-participation. Women *are* an integral part of this struggle – some of us are mothers, daughters, wives of those convicted, injured, imprisoned, and some have taken to the streets too. However, I do feel that we have been on a different receiving end of the uprisings and their consequences, and may therefore have different responses. Black women have nursed those injured, we have been directed to control our children (if we fail, *we* are charged), and many women have found themselves suddenly having to cope on our own with our families and in our partially destroyed homes.

It seems clear to me that the form that the uprisings are taking, of violence at a street level against police presence and attacks, and as a protest against the racism we face, is a form that allows men to participate more easily. Many of us are powerless to fight on those terms and with that kind of strength. The anger, tension, fear is in all of us; we are all victims as *black people* . . . but as women we also face the sexual abuse that accompanies the racist violence we encounter.

Can women realistically participate on equal terms with the men? We have been mostly silent. We have not been given a chance to speak of how unemployment affects us differently, worse, than it does men – for many women unpaid 'employment' in the home *continues* while the faint chance of possible outside employment vanishes altogether. Our relationship with bad housing conditions is more immediate – the world of women is more contained in those homes.

For me, I cannot follow a male-defined pattern of fighting back – I have to find different ways of directing my anger positively.

I need to know that I can trust that black men will fight with women's interests in mind as well as their own. Obviously I feel solidarity with *all* black people. We need to unite to protect ourselves and each other.

But my allegiances are divided . . . and my identification with black women is total.

Despite what we share, I feel that as black women we exist in a different reality from men too – our perspectives are different, and we must realise that *our* chances to gain independence in a white patriarchal society are even more remote.

There is a war going on and we are being attacked, degraded, humiliated, killed. I feel the time has to come when an increasing number of black women will organise to fight our oppression, demand freedom from the forces and power that control our lives, and lead a struggle on our own terms.

ROS

Race Riots: What Was I Doing There? What About My Own Racism?

First published in *Manchester Women's Liberation Newsletter*, no. 30, July/August 1981

I write about the Toxteth 'riots' hesitantly because, although I was there, at the time I wasn't sure whether it was a race issue only, or more. I wasn't sure I should be there at all if it was a black fight against white supremacist harassment and authority. There were, however, a lot of white people taking part. I am hesitant because I'm afraid of being racist, stupid, unaware and insensitive about those race issues, as seen from my view, a white woman's view.

There is nothing more annoying to feminists than a man trying hard to be 'right-on'. I don't want to seem like that to the black people and their fight: if I do seem like that at the end of this, I'll have to accept it and go on from there. That said I know, unless we white women start facing our own racism, especially within the feminist movement, and start talking amongst ourselves, we shall continue to be ignorantly racist. And there is no excuse for that. I don't *feel* racist, but I expect I have lots of attitudes which are so ingrained that they would anger and hurt black people. As a feminist I feel I have to dig these attitudes out, and sort them out. At the moment I tend to keep quiet if I am in doubt, and so I make little progress.

Being at Toxteth brought up so many feelings. First of all, I'm not sure it should be called a riot. That might be a derogatory term imposed on the fight by white patriarchal authority. 'Protest' seems too mild a word. What do black people call it? Is it a riot? If black people themselves choose to call it a riot, it seems to me to have a strong meaning of disgust and rage about years and years of white racism, imperialism and terrorism. Perhaps only a 'riot' can show the extent of that rage. Then I think: am I using the wrong/right

90

words? Am I assuming an awful lot of things, and being patronising in writing about this at all?

Toxteth began basically, and a long time ago, because of police racism. Other factors are housing and job discrimination against black people. White people joined in the riot. They are discriminated against because of their position of poverty too (in Toxteth), but they are not discriminated against because of their colour.

So, were there two fights going on alongside each other? I think so, even if there was mutual support.

If, on the other hand, it was one joint fight, did black people want white people there? This seems to be the same sort of question feminists ask about whether we want men fighting actively with us. Surely, there can't be many feminists who don't feel we should act separately at times, if not most or all of the time? And one black woman said: 'Whites get out, this is a race issue.'

Can we white people really give black people support by joining in as at Toxteth? I'm not sure we ever can. Whatever we do as white people, we are privileged over black people because it's a white-run society. And yet, I stayed out all night. Partly I have to admit I was overawed by the drama of the fight and the burning buildings, and a sense that this was an historical event. Does that make me a voyeuristic, parasitic white? Another part of me wanted to be there to try to understand it all. Is this patronising? As a privileged white in a safe financial position, I have rarely felt moved to active anger against the state, and yet I hate the way the state functions, etc. I want to be angry and yet somewhere deep down I expect I control it to protect my privileges (I was brought up middle-class), which in turn keeps black people firmly in the place allotted them by whites, women, men and the capitalist patriarchy. I stayed at the riot also because I saw abhorrent mainstays and protectors of white capitalism attacked: the police, a judges' club, a bank, a local rich man's business. Also I have friends living in Upper Parliament Street, and those streets nearby.

Is our best anti-racist stand to attack any racist acts and comments by white people, and to keep out of the black 'riots'? I am confused. I'd like to talk with other women. White feminists, we must sort out our own racism. We can't escape it and we shouldn't avoid it.

PROTASIA TORKINGTON

Black Women and the NHS

First published in *Merseyside Women's Paper*, Spring 1982

Black women in the National Health Service

Although this article focuses on the position of black women in the Liverpool area, the problems discussed apply equally to black women in other parts of the country.

Black women have had a double role in relation to the National Health Service: as employees and as consumers.

Employment

First, black women have contact with the National Health Service as workers. Many of them have been recruited from their own countries to come and staff the service, especially those parts which are shunned by the indigenous white women. Their concentration, in consequence, has been in psychiatric, sub-normal and geriatric hospitals. Such institutions do not only rank low in status within the organisation but also have a heavy, dirty workload, poor working conditions and low rewards in terms of job satisfaction and career structure.

Whilst some black women have reached the position of ward sister, very few have found their way up the central power ladder to top management. A large number of black women came to Britain and joined nursing in the 1950s and 1960s. One would expect a number of them to have reached senior positions by the 1970s. After the reorganisation of the National Health Service in 1974 there was and still is a dearth of black women in strategic positions in the health regions, areas and districts. In Liverpool there is not a single black woman who holds the position of divisional nursing officer and very few are nursing officers.

In some parts of the country black women have been and are still mainly employed as state-enrolled nurses and auxiliary nurses. But in Liverpool even this area is being blocked and a large number of black women are falling into the never-to-be employed category. In some hospitals auxiliary work has become the domain of part-time white women who have been pushed into this area by the recession in other sectors of industry. But the Liverpool Area Health Authority is not unique in its failure to provide equal opportunity in employment. In Liverpool black people have the highest rate of unemployment and this has no doubt aggravated the situation, and then in the boom periods not many private or public employers had black people among their staff.

Recently pressure has been exerted by various black organisations and at present many employers including local councillors are expressing intentions to adopt equal opportunity policies. This sounds good in theory, but we are as yet to see the practical application of those intentions.

Black women as consumers of the NHS

As consumers black women face real problems for which they are blamed. The Black Report of 1980 stated that there are marked inequalities in health between social classes in Britain. Working-class people on the whole suffer more health hazards, have poor health generally and experience a higher mortality rate than their middle-class counterparts. In the deprived inner-city areas black and white people live cheek by jowl and share similar health needs. But for black people there is an added dimension of racism in the wider social, political, and economic structure which makes black people, situated at the base of the structure, so much more the victims of all major illnesses from infant mortality to post-natal depression than the white working class. The racist assumptions which lead to blaming the victim are well illustrated in the case of rickets.

Rickets – blaming the victim

The strategy of blaming the victim has been illustrated in the government's response to rickets. Rickets is an old deficiency disease which crippled many working-class white children before the first world war. The response then was to encourage parents to give vitamin-D supplements to their children during the time of the war. But the government knew, as it does now, that this was not the most reliable way of eradicating the disease, since it is known that few people keep up treatment for any length of time and this is particularly true if the condition treated is not an acute one and is not likely to lead to immediate death, if treatment is discontinued.

In view of this it was decided that the safest way of dealing with the problem was to fortify certain foods with vitamin D.

Rickets has now re-emerged and made its appearance first among the Asian communities. The government response this time has been quite different from the one adopted during the war. The emphasis of the rickets campaign launched in 1981 is on educating Asian mothers on the kinds of food with vitamin D on which to feed their children. The use of vitamin-D supplements which was found inadequate during the war is now being pushed forward as a solution to the rickets problem. The emphasis is on educating black women and the implication is that rickets is caused by the ignorance of black women. But as the Brent Community Health Council argued:

> White mothers are no better informed than Asian ones about the need for vitamin D in the diet. Yet all the publicity about the inadequacy of Asian diets creates the impression that Asian mothers do not know how to feed their children properly.

But how inadequate is the Asian diet? The diet is vegetarian, low in fat and sugar and high in pulses and fibre. By DHSS standards this is a healthy diet since in its booklet *Eating for Health* (DHSS, 1978) the recommendations are for the British public to eat less meat, highly refined products, dairy products and fatty foods and to increase the consumption of less refined starchy foods, pulses and lentils. What the DHSS recommends for white British is very much closer to the present Asian diet and viewed from this point the Asian diet is far superior to the British one. And yet the emphasis of the rickets campaign is on educating Asian mothers about British foods which contain vitamin D.

Does the amount of vitamin D in these foods warrant the adoption of a British diet with all its food-based western diseases? The highest contributor of vitamin D is margarine which has been fortified with vitamin D since 1940. Asian communities do not eat a lot of margarine but they do eat butter. If butter was fortified in the same way as margarine, rickets among the Asian community would be under control.

Fortification of food

But the government has consistently refused to consider the question of fortifying foods that would benefit the Asian community. The fortification of chappati flour was rejected on the grounds that it would lead to toxicity for those who do not need extra vitamin D among the Asian community. This was not considered a problem when fortification of margarine was undertaken. Besides, an individual would have to take a fairly high dose of vitamin D before getting toxic. Milk was rejected on the same grounds with the additional problem of food adulteration to which the British public might object. But the British public is constantly consuming adulterated food. You only need to look at the foods sold to realise how many are advertised as vitamin-enriched, and the government does not intervene with such food adulteration.

The role of sunlight

It has been argued that because Asian women wear all-embracing saris and tend to stay indoors, they do not benefit from sunlight which is another source of vitamin D. So in the campaign Asian women are advised to change their culture. The emphasis is on exposing their arms and legs and going out for walks in order to get some sunlight. This argument is not supported by facts. First, there is not enough sunlight in Britain for the amount of vitamin D that the body needs. Secondly, a study has shown that Asian and white adolescents have the same level of exposure to sunlight and yet Asian adolescents still suffer from rickets. The skin pigmentation cannot account for this because some Asians have a lighter skin than people from the Caribbean. If skin pigmentation is the barrier to the absorption of sunlight then Caribbeans and Africans should have more problems with vitamin-D deficiency. All the publicity about the Asian diet and their culture has done little more than blame the victims who suffer because of the DHSS refusal to fortify foods consumed by the Asian community.

Patrick Jenkin – witch-hunt

Black women in Liverpool, and elsewhere in England, are going to face more problems when Patrick Jenkin's proposal to check a patient's eligibility for treatment is in full force. Given the existing racist attitude which sees all black people as 'immigrants', such proposals will encourage the harassment of black people. When black women do not attend ante-natal and post-natal clinics for fear of the witch-hunt, they will be blamed for neglecting their health and endangering the lives of their babies.

Conclusion and recommendation

The problems that black women face stem from British racism. In employment they are exploited to meet the needs of the National Health Service. In times of unemployment they are squeezed out of the market to make room for white workers. Their ill-health is blamed on their culture, giving the impression that it is inferior and that black mothers are ignorant.

There are no easy solutions to any of these problems. But it is obvious that any solution will not be initiated by those who hold power in the NHS. Real changes will only come when black workers and consumers combine their efforts and make their demands known to the National Health Service. In Brent such an initiative has been taken by the Black Health Workers' and Patients' Group, an organisation which is active in

> supporting black workers in their struggles, pushing for better treatment of black patients, and monitoring racism and racist policies on health [Black Workers' and Patients' Group: *Black Health Bulletin*, no. 1, November 1981].

The formation of such a group in Liverpool would be a start in the right direction.

Stop This Racism: Sheffield Conference on 'Women, Immigration and Nationality Laws'

First published in *Outwrite*, no. 10, January 1983

On Saturday, 11 December 1982 a conference on 'Women, Immigration and Nationality Laws' took place in Sheffield. It was organised by the Women Against Racism Group with the aim of sharing information about the new (proposed) Nationality Act and the racist checks taking place in the National Health Service. What was most obvious was the way in which the laws are biased against black people, and against black women especially.

The Nationality Act comes into operation this month (January 1983). It is very complicated and anyone needing details should seek advice.

Some of the overall effects of the Act will be:

– To narrow down the definition of British citizen so as to take away many rights from former Commonwealth citizens, in particular the right of abode in this country.

– To make women who are not full citizens totally dependent on their husband's status. If their husband is deported, then so can they be, and their children. However, this does not apply the other way round. Also, women who are not full citizens do not have the right to bring in their husbands to join them here. Men, however, can bring in their wives. This implies that women should always follow their husbands, not vice versa.

– To make a whole section of the population stateless. A black person born in this country who has a mother (or father, if the mother was married to him) who is not a British citizen, will not be given British citizenship. Thus, children born in this country who have known no other home will not be given the automatic right to live here.

These laws, whilst they may in reality only apply to a few people, will in practice be used to police and harass the black community.

The status of any black person will be in doubt, and the effect will be that all black people will be forced to carry passports and other identification at all times. An apartheid state is being set up under our noses, with noticeably little protest from white people.

This increasing harassment of black people is being put into practice in many ways. The new race checks in the National Health Service, which were introduced in October 1982, are an obvious example. To get free treatment people will have to prove that they have been 'ordinary citizens' in Britain for one year and/or that they are 'loyal to the British State'. If they do not qualify they can get free treatment only as an out-patient, for contagious diseases and for psychiatric treatment under sectioning. Maternity care will no longer be free and this will, of course, particularly affect women. Although only a small number of people will actually qualify under these provisions for payment for health care, everybody who is suspected of not being a resident in Britain for one year will be forced to go through a series of questions on admission to hospital. This will obviously be used most against black people, who again will be forced to justify their right to be here.

In addition, the concept of 'free health care for all' embodied in the NHS has disappeared. What sections of the population will be forced to pay for treatment next?

All these laws discriminate against black people, and in particular black women, who are seen as appendages of men. The wealth of Britain has been built on the backs of the people of the former Empire, and still thrives on cheap black labour both here and in the Third World. These laws need to be actively opposed by large numbers of people. Black people have as much right to live in this country as any other people, and to live free from harassment, the threat of deportation, and the increasing racism of the State.

SHEILA SAUNDERS

'That's Funny. You Don't Look Anti-Semitic'

First published in *Leeds Women's Liberation Newsletter*, March 1982

Sheila Saunders . . . you have even taken my name and forced me to anglicise it. My real name is Sara Yetta Bat Dvorah.

The title of this chapter is taken from an article written by an American Jew about his experience of anti-semitism on the Left. When I read this article I thought, thankfully this does not happen in the women's movement here, and I sank back into my assimilated radical lesbian feminist pose. Now, some years later, I feel like that man who wrote of the American straight Left – me identifying with a man after all these years; me with my fantasies about cyanide in the chicken soup and the 'Solidarity with Sophie Portnoy' campaign – why am I backed into this corner with this man? Because we are both Jews and the stick that beats us equally is anti-semitism – anti-Jewishness.

I was born just after the second world war, a time of devastation for all Jews. We approached the future with a mixture of grief, guilt and relief that we were the ones who had survived. We were the children of the new, improved world – after all, I was told that Britain had won the war. Britain had saved world Jewry from extermination and we were lucky to be British and safe. I was part of the new generation, the smell of rotting corpses would not reach our noses – the ultimate nose job – the plastic surgery of assimilation was successfully performed. It is not surprising therefore that with this background I have managed to exist inside the women's movement here in Britain thinking that their fight is my fight and my fight is their fight. I believe that the personal is political and that the political is personal, after all I have been in the movement since 1969, it is my movement . . . or is it their movement?

In the early days we spent a great deal of time discussing our own personal struggles. We believed very strongly that our own struggle was the main struggle and that solidarity with other sisters was the life's blood of the movement – I still believe that – but do they? I have been told recently that being Jewish is most unfortunate but that there are cures for it, one does not have to remain Jewish. After all, it is not visible, and therefore not as bad as being black, for instance. Being Jewish means being religious and therefore it is to support an exceedingly patriarchal religion. The sisters did not hear me say that I was Jewish, they only heard me say that I support religion. In fact the sisters did not hear me say anything very much because they launched the anti-semitic attack on my non-Jewish sister for wearing the same Jewish identification symbols around her neck as I do.

Perhaps I should state here and now that I am not religious, nor have I ever worn religious symbols, however the same arguments would apply even if I were a religious Jew. Anti-semites do not care whether or not a Jew is religious, only whether she or he is a Jew. At the risk of over-simplifying Jewish religious ritual I feel that I must point out that Jews do not worship anything other than their god – or goddess for some Jewish feminists – there is no symbolic worship equivalent to the Christian symbol of a dead Jew on a cross. The symbols that my sister and I wear around our necks are derived from women's superstition and tribal identification. These symbols are recognisable identification to all gentiles. In the past Jews have been forced to wear such identification on yellow armbands. My not-so-kosher sister was told that as a lesbian she must fight as a lesbian and wear her own oppression around her neck. Needless to say, some of us do not need to wear any identification for society to conclude that we are lesbians – they know. Three years ago this sister walked into work wearing a Jewish symbol around her neck for the first time, two days later a man at work called her 'a Jewish bitch': she did not deny it. She has since then faced a lot of anti-semitism because of those chains around her neck. I live in a house with two other women, neither of whom is Jewish. When the knock comes on the door how will they know which one of us to take if we are all wearing the same identification?

A sister told me that they would not take my children away from me because I am Jewish but only because I am a lesbian. Well, let me tell you, sister, as women we all risk losing our children whenever and wherever the patriarchy decides. As Jewish women we risk losing our children not just to one man but to whole armies. Our children have been burned by anti-semites, gassed by them, experimented on and tortured. Our children are psychologically tortured every time they set foot inside English schools. I was tortured as a Jew long before I had ever heard the word lesbian.

I was a happy six-year-old child who skipped into school one day only to be told at lunchtime that no one must sit near me as I had killed Jesus. 'Who is he?' I thought to myself. Then I remembered what my mother had told me about him and how I was to respect other people's beliefs even if I personally did not believe them. So I respected their belief about my hand in Jesus's murder and as I sat alone at the school dinner-table I had an asthma attack – a sure way of getting home early. Once I was safely home I opened the wardrobe door in my mother's bedroom, stood in front of the long mirror and just stared at my reflection in disbelief. I looked just the same as I had looked when I left for school that morning. I hadn't grown horns or turned green, so what was so different about me? Well, sisters, I'll tell you what was and still is so different about me. I am Jewish, that's what's different. Then as now I cannot and would not deny or change this one fact about myself. I stood in front of that mirror and repeated over and over to myself, I'm Jewish, I'm Jewish, I'm Jewish. I told my mother, she told the school, the school told the kids, the kids told me – I was to blame. From then on I understood that this was my struggle.

I never told anyone again, not until now that is. This time the girls at school are not so blatant, their feelings have changed but mine are the same. The girls at school no longer blame me for the death of Christ because now they blame me for being a Jew in an anti-semitic society and for expecting my sisters to support me. They confuse religion with culture, they confuse culture with men. Jewish women have a culture too, sisters. Jews are not all men, many of us are women, many are still children, many are murdered by anti-semites in the name of some just cause or other.

Let me tell you, sisters, that if you think that it is hard being a lesbian you should try being a Jew. If it is possible to make political statements about lesbianism, why then is it not possible to make political statements about Jews? My not-so-kosher sister and I have been out-lesbians since 1970, we were wearing lesbian feminist symbols when many of our sisters were still wearing wedding rings, or fighting for their liberation inside male organisations. We do not reproach our sisters for this. We have grown up in the movement, we have also grown with the movement. We believe that every sister must struggle from within herself in order to struggle in solidarity with other sisters. Our struggle is everywhere, it is black, it is white, it is Jewish, it is Muslim. There is no country which does not hate women. There is no country or state in the entire world that I can live in peacefully with my children as a Jew, as a lesbian, as a woman.

DIANE HUDSON

'That's Funny. You Don't Look Jewish'

First published in *Leeds Women's Liberation Newsletter*, March 1982

The title of this chapter is taken from the remarks usually made to me by people when they see the symbols I wear around my neck. These remarks are prompted by what I now call 'unconscious anti-semitism', and are made by people who would be horrified to be called anti-semitic.

I was born in 1946 and brought up on the notion that Britain had saved the world from being overrun by Nazis. I don't remember anyone mentioning Jews at all. I do remember first learning about concentration camps, but not about who was in them. As I grew older I found out – from books – what had happened to some people called Jews, and wondered why no one had mentioned this horror in my circle of relatives. When I asked questions no one wanted to discuss the subject. When I got older still I learned about English concentration camps where Jewish refugees fleeing from Germany were interned with Nazis. I learned how Jews trying to get to Palestine after the war had their craft sunk by English gunboats, and how the Jews getting to shore were gunned down by English soldiers. I stopped believing Britain had fought the war 'to save world Jewry from extinction'.

Who were these people who provoked such hatred in every country in the world? I'd never, knowingly, met one. I'd read about them – Shylock and Fagin – I knew of their personalities – Jewish meant money-grabbing. I knew what they looked like, from cartoon pictures and book illustrations – long, hooked noses, shifty eyes, rubbing their hands together, talking in a strange way.

'Funny, you don't look Jewish,' people would say when I objected to anti-semitic remarks. And in those days I said, 'I'm not, but I don't feel people should be treated that way.' 'Oh, I agree,' would be the reply. 'It was horrible the things that happened to them, but still . . .'

It was my anger with the 'three dots' conversations that prompted me to wear symbols that identified me as a Jew – and the world changed overnight! I had come out as a lesbian in 1970. Before that time I had struggled alongside lesbian sisters to fight our oppression, even though at that time I wasn't sure if lesbian oppression was part of *my* oppression. But some of these sisters found something blocking the extension of solidarity towards my taking on board an oppression that wasn't mine. Yet those same sisters and I would march against SPUC, hoping that as lesbians we'd never need the freedom for abortions we were fighting for. These same sisters would work with Women's Aid, yet some of them, and I, have never been beaten in our homes by men who were our husbands and lovers.

In my personal/political struggle as a non-Jew showing solidarity with my Jewish sisters, I have discovered that I attract two kinds of anti-semitism. For sisters who know I am not Jewish, I become a 'funnel' for anti-Jewish remarks which are said to 'nearly-kosher-me' and not to my 'totally-kosher' Jewish sister. That, I call 'unconscious anti-semitism'. For people who assume that I am a Jew, I attract hatred of an intensity I have never encountered before. When I was beaten on the streets by men who hated me for being a lesbian, I knew I had innumerable sisters around me. When I am abused for being a Jew, I feel isolated. My family accuse me of putting them in danger by associating with Jews; they are convinced there will be a knock on the door one day, and they will be taken for collaborating with Jews.

I am told it is my choice to take on board this struggle – by white women who struggle against racism, and who seem surprised when I point out that they have a choice about anti-racism because they are not black.

During the war, when Denmark was invaded, the Nazis demanded that all Jews in Denmark should wear the Star of David on their arms. The day after that proclamation, King Olaf told the Danes they should *all* wear the Star of David, and appeared in public wearing one. Most of the population followed suit. That was their choice, to show solidarity with the oppressed against an oppressor.

All women's experiences are different. Phyllis Chesler, an American-Jewish feminist, was verbally attacked by Israeli feminists for wearing the Star of David around her neck, 'a symbol of patriarchal oppression'. Her reply was that to live outside Israel in the midst of anti-semitism prompted the choices that one made. Her statement, to wear the Star of David, was based on her experience of fighting anti-semitism, inside and outside the WLM, and so she made her choice.

Sisters, I've made my choice, based on my experience. Give me the freedom to make my statement.

4 No Nukes

Introduction

US Cruise missiles have been installed in this country, despite one of the largest public protests that we have experienced. Women's involvement in the protest has been major. Women from different political backgrounds have come together to voice their opposition to this government's policies to instal nuclear bases here.

Despite the usual anti-lesbian and anti-women media coverage, which has attempted to trivialise their efforts, the Greenham women have been instrumental in bringing together various women's peace action and anti-nuclear groups nationally. Massive demonstrations have been staged, notably embracing the base on 12 December 1982, and the International Women's Day for Disarmament, 24 May 1983. Many local actions and other peace camps have supplemented national efforts.

These have predominantly taken the form of non-violent action, which seems to have confused police reaction at times. Women have staged 'die-ins' on major roads in many cities to disrupt traffic, Greenham gates have been blockaded by women lying in front of them, women have forced entry into the base itself to then *dance* on the tops of the silos. As this section will show, many questions have been raised about women's participation in the anti-nuclear struggle:

- Should feminists not be focusing on issues that affect us exclusively as *women*, rather than wider issues such as the anti-nuclear movement?
- Why do black women choose to put energies into other campaigns?
- What happens to other feminist concerns, nationally and internationally, if we invest too much energy in anti-nuclear campaigns?
- Does the insistence on women's concern with peace and nurturing reinforce stereotypical notions of women's passivity?

Other criticisms have been voiced. The assumption that the fight for disarmament is *the* crucial survival issue ignores women in Third World countries fighting for daily survival. Non-violent action is an easy option for those already in a position of relative privilege –

women fighting in national liberation struggles may have no alternative but to take up arms. Despite these contradictions, thousands of women not previously politically active have bravely come together to focus world attention on women's opposition to the nuclear threat.

KRIS

. . . Ain't We Wimmin Too?

First published in *Lysistrata*, no. 2, Winter 1983

I am a womun of colour who has been working for some time within the wimmin's peace movement. I've written this article not only to clear my head of things I feel need to be said, but also to bring out into the open what is a relevant part of my life and work within the movement. I ask anyone who reads it to consider what I'm saying to be relevant to her life as well.

When I used to think of the peace movement what came into my mind was: CND marches (once a year if they feel like it); vague reports in newspapers about the effects of nuclear war; politicians talking about disarmament; videos about what happened at Hiroshima and Nagasaki; all things that reinforce the belief that nuclear weapons will only be used if 'they really have to', that nuclear war *is* going to happen, we're all going to be blown to pieces, and there's nothing we can do to stop it.

Recently wimmin have begun to realise our potential for taking things into our own hands, and changing what we don't like. For so long wimmin have only been seen as halfway equal to men. Now, through the wimmin's peace movement I can see things are changing fast! Now that cruise missiles are due to be brought into this country, wimmin have taken the initiative in the peace movement, through Greenham Common and other wimmin's peace camps. They've started up because wimmin have wanted to be together. Things are changing for wimmin in society – but slowly. Within the peace movement I can see things changing much faster because wimmin are doing it themselves.

Through my involvement in the wimmin's peace movement I have seen things the way they should be, or the way I'd like them to be. But there are still things wrong. I'd like to think that the wimmin's peace movement has now shed its image of being white and middle-class, but I can't see this happening through the media coverage we're getting. The problem is that the desired image seems to be one of 'ordinary', dedicated and sincere wimmin with descriptions like 'housewives', 'grandmothers', 'mothers' in all the papers. This is only one type of 'ordinary' womun that is being shown.

The wimmin's peace movement should be welcoming to *all* wimmin. I'd seen things about Greenham before and never had I seen one black womun's face. When I was at Greenham on 12 December I saw only three other black wimmin amongst the thousands that passed me. I'd been up to the camp before and seen no other black wimmin there and I thought, hang on a second, what is going on? 12 December should have been a time when *all* wimmin came together, when I should have been able to feel that there were more wimmin like myself doing things. The mentality behind cruise missiles and nuclear weapons, everything I don't believe in, is part of the same system. All the male stuff that is being put on us. And at a time when all wimmin should have been able to come together to make their protest felt, for me to only have seen a few of my black sisters present was, I feel, very sad.

I saw the video *Critical Mass* which spoke to me as if I was married with X amount of kids, which is total shit because I'm not – I'm a lesbian and I've got no kids. It also assumed you'd had an academic education and could relate to all the facts and figures it gave. But the video changed my life. What it accused me of was exactly what I'd been doing – letting other people do the work. I also hadn't thought of the peace movement as being one in which wimmin can play the most crucial part.

At the same time as changing the attitudes 'out there' we should be looking at ourselves. Obviously the conditioning we've had can't be wiped out simply by being part of the wimmin's peace movement. What about the words we use? Our lack of interest in understanding wimmin with different cultures and backgrounds to us? Our assumption that our racism will be pointed out to us? We've got to start thinking about how our own attitudes are stopping other wimmin from joining us.

If we expect to get an interview on television, for example, we must make sure that we haven't just got the same wimmin doing it all the time. As many different wimmin as possible must be seen so that wimmin who watch television can relate to those wimmin individually. The danger is that if only a few wimmin can relate to the wimmin's peace movement then, of course, it's only going to grow one way. We need millions of wimmin and I don't think we are going to succeed in our most immediate aim – stopping Cruise missiles – unless our numbers increase.

I feel that because I am a womun of colour I should be looking at how we can get more black wimmin into the movement, how we can get more wimmin of all nationalities, more young wimmin . . .

What we're doing is so important that it can't just be down to me because I'm black to think about it. It must be down to *all* wimmin to think about what they can do. It is our problem as a movement. Personally, I'd like to see a video made, and this is only a small part of what we can actually do, a video that could be shown on television. Television reaches millions of wimmin. It would be a video that *all* wimmin could relate to because it would cover a wide range of viewpoints given by all kinds of wimmin. The video I'd like to make would not only go to wimmin's centres because a large proportion of working-class wimmin wouldn't go there. It would be shown in community centres and other places that would be accessible to them. We have to make sure that it isn't the kind of video that speaks in words of over 600 syllables! It'd have both black and white wimmin in it, and young wimmin would have their say.

I think our most immediate aim should be to get more wimmin into the movement – now! Time is running out. Every womun is a part of it. Every person in the world should be working towards getting rid of attitudes which I, for one, find abhorrent. Things like racism, like sexism, attitudes based on power; the kind of thinking that says this doesn't affect me directly so why should I worry about it? It all goes towards making this world a much harder, unhappier place to live in. And that's what I really want – a world in which everyone can be happy, everyone can live as they need to, no one has to starve, no one has to even worry. A world where we're in tune with nature, because we're a part of it. A world where we haven't got the threat of violence and death hanging over our heads. The kind of world where, if I wanted to, I could feel happy to bring life into. A world where I'd want my life to continue. I'd like to live to see that. I think we all would.

L.B.

Letter to *Lysistrata*, 1

First published Winter 1982

Dear sisters,

I saw *The War Game* when I was fifteen. Banned by the BBC, but showing at a few cinemas up and down the country, I'm sure I would never have known about it if my boyfriend hadn't taken me to see it. When we came out of the cinema he said he still thought Britain needed a nuclear deterrent. I said I thought that was the craziest thing I'd ever heard (I'd never really liked him anyway!).

By the time I was a bit older and had slightly more confidence in my convictions, CND was all but dead. My feelings lingered on, occasionally nourished over the years by extra information from the media.

It wasn't until three weeks ago that I saw Helen Caldicott's video, *Critical Mass*, at Brighton Women's Centre. I came out halfway through to have a cigarette, and tried hard to suppress my desire to pierce a dagger through the tightly stuffed uniform of a high-ranking member of the male military establishment. Almost any one of them would have done.

Then I went back to see the rest of the film but it was almost finished so I saw it round a second time. Then I cried a lot. I stood in the little yard at the back of the Women's Centre with its solitary tree and looked at the sky. A light rain was falling and there were occasional blue flashes heralding an electric storm. And a picture in my head of a bald-headed Hiroshima victim which it was all too easy to see duplicated all over the Northern hemisphere sometime within the next few years.

If we don't take them by force, play them at their own game, fall into the old male traps and act as if we're no better than our enemies, then we've got to get them some other way. But it's got to be good. It's got to be force without violence. And it's got to be something that *all* women can do irrespective of commitments which for many women it would be unrealistic to abandon, e.g. children, families, jobs, etc.

110

And it must also be something that holds them to ransom, something that they have to sit up and take notice of and preferably something which they cannot restrain us from doing within the bounds of their existing legislation. I want to get beyond patriarchal law.

But where does men's control of women end? What is it that makes us indispensable to men, which so far men are still a short distance away from being able to perform without us? The continuation of the species. Yes, that very thing that they are also hell-bent on destroying by means of a perverted technology.

Just as workers can withdraw their productive labour power and go on strike, so all women can withdraw their *re*-productive labour (!) power until our demand for a peaceful world is met. We are entitled to argue that unless certain environmental conditions are resumed, it simply isn't worth our while going to all that trouble.

What's the point anyway of bringing a child into the world if it's only got a 50–50 chance of reaching its third birthday? Those are the current odds being quoted by the joint chiefs of staff (USA); the lunatic, power-crazed, nihilistic male button-pushers who, as Helen Caldicott rightly says, have the arrested emotional and intellectual development of a thirteen-year-old delinquent boy.

I would like to suggest that we seriously attempt to get as many heterosexual women as possible from all over the country interested in the idea of a token stoppage, i.e. withdrawing from sexual relations with men. (Eighty per cent of abortions are the result of contraceptive failure so it's no good kidding ourselves that sex with men and pregnancy are separate events nowadays; they never were and they never will be.) No one can stop us if we so choose and all women can, in theory at least, participate without any loss of time spent on other commitments. Indeed, it would actually provide most of us with slightly more time than we're used to!

The women of Ancient Greece are said to have gone on a birth strike to prevent their men from starting a war and they were apparently successful.

The strike could take many forms:

(1) All out for a month nationwide with the threat of further strikes if our demand to remove cruise from British bases isn't met.

(2) Regional and for longer periods than a month.

Objections to this proposal include:

(1) Lesbians don't have anything to do and participate by default, so to speak!

(2) More seriously, heterosexual women may object that they couldn't keep it up or don't want to. Well, maybe if you've got a reputation amongst the women at your workplace or amongst

friends for having a bit of an insatiable sexual appetite perhaps you could get them to sponsor your period of abstinence! Funds to Greenham – 20p per week or something.

The advantages of this idea are:

(1) The action is above the law whilst in no way conflicting with action that isn't.

(2) It cuts across the social, racial and class barriers between women.

(3) All women, whatever they do, whatever life-style they lead, can participate without altering their life circumstances.

(4) It brings our protest down to basics; the futility of women's creative nurturing powers under present conditions of male destructive powers.

SALLY DAVISON

Women for Peace

First published in *Link*, no. 36, Spring 1982

The Pioneers

Women have played a strikingly important part in the peace movement throughout this century. The Women's International League for Peace and Freedom (WILPF) was set up in 1915, and campaigned through the war, and against the harsh terms of the Peace Treaty of Versailles. They played an important international role in the days of the League of Nations, and national sections, and although cut off from each other in the second world war, were involved in resistance to the Nazis. After the war they were heavily involved with work on behalf of refugees; in protesting at the development of the cold war system and working in the United Nations.

Looking at the history of WILPF there are recurring themes. Women acted as mediators, breaking through national and ideological barriers; they focused attention on the suffering of war victims; and they protested at the lack of representation of women amongst those taking decisions on war and peace. Many of the original members of WILPF were involved in the suffrage movement. Although WILPF and other older women's peace campaigns are set in a different cultural mould from women's groups today, the central issues they addressed are still the most pressing for the women's peace movement.

Women have tended to be quicker than men to see through the jingoism to the human suffering of war, and they are largely excluded from higher levels of government. In particular, women generals, diplomats and ministers of war are thin on the ground. Because of this there has always been a strong motivation for women to come together to express their opposition to war through their own forms of organisation. This forms a strong basis for co-operative efforts in the peace movement.

The new generation

So when the peace movement began to grow in the late 1970s, it was not surprising that women almost immediately became very involved in the campaigns. At this time, however, the older women's peace groups were weak, and were almost exclusively involved in the international peace scene – making representations to the UN continuing the traditional role built up in the 1920s and 1930s. Many feminists saw the older groups as being too concerned with stressing the role of women as mothers. Groups like WILPF and Women for World Disarmament really wanted to get involved with younger women, but there was a wide cultural gap between the newcomers and the pioneers.

In fact, the whole peace movement at that time had a bad cultural image, but this began to change with the new urgency of the threat of nuclear war. The transformation of CND, from being regarded as a bunch of cranks who couldn't forget Aldermaston, into being the most popular mass movement in Britain, had important implications for the women's peace movement. The story of that transformation needs a book, but for present purposes I'll just mention briefly those issues that affect the involvement of women. (At least) two significant events occurred between CND's first flourishing and its revival – the growth of the Women's Liberation Movement, and (obviously related) the development on the Left of a more open approach to politics. The strategy of the Broad Democratic Alliance, largely contributed by the Communist Party, was an important factor in this development.

All this influenced the politics of CND in its second phase of growth. It has been very conscious of the need for political campaigns to be open and accessible, and has paid more than lip-service to the ideas of the Women's Movement, in its attempt to be non-hierarchical. There is also an intimate connection between one strand of feminism and the non-violent movement, an important trend within CND.

So women's special concern for peace, combined with a political movement more than usually accessible to women, has led to a fruitful interchange of ideas between women from the WLM and women in CND. Women within CND have met together to challenge some of its practices that are oppressive to both women and men, and though things have not always gone smoothly, there is a continuing dialogue.

During 1979 and 1980 women from the peace movement and the WLM started coming together to consider the specific contribution that women could make to the peace movement. The older women's groups were largely outside this discussion, though they were pleased that younger women were involving themselves in the peace movement. There were arguments as to whether women should organise specifically as women, how to react to women who identified primarily as mothers, whether the mixed campaigns were worth linking up with. The discussions took place against a background of increasing activity by women, nationally and internationally.

WONT

At this time there was a Women and Non-Violence group that was investigating the relationship between male power and militarism, and several feminists against nuclear energy groups, looking at patriarchy and technology. These women formed the basis for a network of Women Opposed to the Nuclear Threat (WONT) groups that sprang up round the country, autonomous groups that were concerned to develop a specifically feminist analysis of the arms race, and to intervene politically as feminist groups.

In Manchester, Doreen Henshaw started the Manchester Women's Peace Movement, because she felt that the CND group was intimidating, and she wanted to form a group for 'ordinary people' such as herself. In Hornsey, a sub-group of the local CND set up 'Families against the Bomb', to emphasise their concern for the future of their children. Two Quaker women, both pensioners, donated a substantial part of their life savings to send a group of mothers to the Soviet Union and to the USA, to talk to mothers there. This formed the basis of a 'Mothers for Peace' group. The older peace groups were revitalising, and women in CND were expressing their desire to work together as women.

In Europe, especially Northern Europe, there were flourishing women's peace groups. In the Netherlands in 1979 there was a torch-lit procession by 10,000 women at The Hague, to coincide with the NATO decision to deploy Cruise missiles. In 1980, in Scandinavia, there was a women's petition against nuclear weapons that collected over a million signatures in a few days.

All these activities were carried out by women specifically as women's campaigns, but many women involved were not overtly feminists. This has been one of the major points of discussion in the women's peace movement, but has been usually resolved by an agreement to tolerate each other's different approaches, and by being non-exclusive in terminology (e.g. referring to parents rather than to mothers, and by not excluding women who are not parents by organising events for mothers).

Turning outwards

Against this background a number of women from all the areas of
the women's peace movement decided to form an association called
the Women's Peace Alliance (WPA), which would allow autonomy
to the groups already in existence, both nationally and locally, but
would act as a coordinating group for the exchange of information.
This structure is not a new one for the women's movement – it
reflects the very different forms of activity that women involve
themselves in, and the respect that women give to each other's
projects. But the Alliance also wants to be visible, in a way that the
WLM sometimes isn't. So there are plans for affiliations, and for
setting up a national office. The Alliance is still in its early stages,
but it has done a very good job on informing different women in the
peace movement about women's activities. It now needs to turn
outwards.

The WPA was able to respond effectively as a network when the
women's peace camps were set up. These were probably the most
significant women's peace activities since the regrowth of the peace
movement. They are organised in a non-hierarchical way, and are
an immediate, emotional form of protest activity.

The camp at Greenham Common was set up following a march by
women with their children from Cardiff to Greenham, calling in at
several military installations along the way. The march was
organised partly as a British response to the Scandinavian women's
march from Copenhagen to Paris last summer (1981), itself an
extremely important new event for women. When the women (who
call themselves Women for Life on Earth) arrived at Greenham,
they were very disappointed at the media response. They felt that
their activity was important and should be reported. So they
chained themselves to the railings at the base, to make their point
more forcibly. They were allowed to stay, and decided to take
advantage of the establishment's fit of repressive tolerance by
making a permanent camp outside the base.

Since that time, the camp has received very widespread support
and publicity, as a very human form of protest. It points out sharply
the contradiction between people going about their daily lives,
producing and reproducing, whilst just down the road a massive
apparatus of destruction is being created. Local people have
responded enthusiastically with hospitality. Even base personnel
have engaged in dialogue with the women. Just after Christmas
1981 another camp was set up at Molesworth, by women in the
Fellowship of Reconciliation, a Christian group committed to the
ideas of non-violence. Another camp is due to go into action very

soon. This kind of activity, starting from a fairly spontaneous act, but gradually spreading across the country at grass-roots level, is in strong contrast to a centralised distant national campaign. Although there are men at some camps, they are women-initiated and -led, and the whole atmosphere there is informed (sometimes unconsciously) by a feminist approach.

The women's peace movement is still growing, and will continue to make a significant contribution to the fight against nuclear weapons.

SARAH BUCKLE

Women's Peace Action

First published in *Lysistrata*, no. 1, Winter 1982

On 6 August 1982 women in Brighton mourned the women, men and children who died at Hiroshima in 1945 when the first atomic bomb was dropped, by staging a die-in. In a die-in those taking part lie down in the road as if they are dead. One idea of this is to confront people with the horror of the nuclear threat by giving them some picture of the sort of chaos that would be caused by a nuclear bomb, although of course it's not realistic.

For me, this action is effective because stopping the traffic achieves two things. First, it disrupts people, nearly all of whom object, which allows the opportunity to reply: 'Look, if you object to this tiny amount of disruption, why aren't you objecting to the threat of nuclear war? – you won't just be disrupted, you'll very likely be dead. And if you're not, you'll wish you were.' Second, it attracts attention and shocks people – it's easy to ignore people handing out leaflets, but if there're several 'dead' women in the road, and queues of traffic with horns blaring, people are more likely to want to know what's going on.

In the morning at 8.30, fifteen women lay down in the London Road. Other women handed out leaflets and talked to passers-by and motorists. After about ten minutes a passing policeman cautioned some of the women and they got up. Several male motorists asked the policeman whether they could remove us, and he authorised them to do so, saying that they should first ask us to move. One made a half-hearted attempt to do so, but the others just grabbed women and dragged us from the road. My impression was that the men were very glad of the chance to vent some of the anger and frustration they felt towards us for daring to disturb their routine by being as rough as possible – women were dragged by one leg, pushed and shoved, had arms twisted and heads banged on the pavement. In this situation it was very hard not to react violently, but for me it reaffirmed the importance of non-violent action – if we had fought back, the situation would have degenerated into a free-for-all, and the point of what we were doing would have been lost. I felt our strength derived from our non-violence. My impression of people's reactions to us was mainly of hostility and impatience, but the leafleters said that although some people refused to take a leaflet or stop and talk, others were interested and encouraging, and one woman said how brave we were.

At 1.30 we did another die-in by Barclays Bank in North St. This time we attracted a huge crowd, whose reactions were very mixed – amusement, curiosity, some hostility and some approval. Some people were really supportive of what we were doing, but I heard someone right by my head say, 'Bloody youngsters, they weren't even alive then, they don't know what they're talking about.'

It's strange, this idea some people seem to have, that if you haven't experienced something, you haven't got the right to object to it. The trouble with nuclear war is that once we *have* experienced it, it'll be too late. Why can't we learn from the victims of Hiroshima? After about ten minutes the police arrived and two of us were arrested. We were charged with wilful obstruction of the highway, and our case was adjourned until 6 September.

When our case came up in court we pleaded guilty. We acknowledged that technically we had committed the offence with which we were charged, but pointed out that the laws of this country allow us no right to cause even minor inconvenience, except at the discretion of the police. This is in spite of what we are told, that in this country we have the greatest democratic rights in the world, of freedom of speech and political power. People have been trying to exercise these rights, using conventional channels to campaign against the existence, and therefore likely use, of nuclear weapons for over twenty years, and yet the situation is becoming far worse. We also expressed our horror at the reality of nuclear war – millions dead and dying in agony, no shelter, no medical care, food and water contaminated – there will be nothing left to live for. We want to go on living, and so we feel that we must use whatever *peaceful* means we can to prevent a nuclear war.

We were pleased to have one woman magistrate, in an otherwise male-defined and dominated set-up, and felt that she at least listened to what we had to say. We were both given a conditional discharge for twelve months.

I feel it is really crucial for more people to get involved in anti-nuclear campaigns. I know that we all only have so much energy, and we can't put it everywhere, but I feel that if we don't fight this fight, we won't be around to fight any others.

Sometimes when I face up to the threat of nuclear war I feel so much fear it incapacitates me – which is why I ignored it for many years. But ignoring it isn't going to save us.

I feel we must acknowledge our responsibility – to ourselves, to each other and to the earth – and take action to make the world nuclear-free, if we want to go on living.

SOPHIE LAWS

An Open Letter to Women in WONT and the Women's Peace Alliance

First published in *Catcall*, 13, December 1981; also published in *Breaching the Peace – how dare you presume I went to Greenham*, Onlywomen Press, 1983

The Women's Peace Alliance is a national coalition of women who want to work together to halt the arms race. Their priority is nuclear disarmament in Britain. The Alliance aims to involve all women in working for peace and to form a network to share information and link up activities.

WONT (Women Oppose the Nuclear Threat) is a network of feminist anti-nuclear weapons/power groups in Britain.

Dear sisters,

I want to ask you some questions about the politics of what you are doing. Nothing I have read of yours has made me feel I really understand why feminists are going into these campaigns. My concern has been mostly set off by reading *Nuclear Re/Sisters* by Feminists against Nuclear Power[1] and more recently by reading the Women's Peace Alliance's statement of aims.[2]

It is very difficult to ask questions about campaigns against nuclear power/for peace – they tend to take on an almost holy status, and you feel you are just being perverse – or there's always the suspicion that you haven't understood the risks. I want to make it clear that I believe that it is highly likely that nuclear power in one form or another will produce either total destruction or slow poisoning for us all in the near future. The issue I want to discuss is what can be done about it – and especially whether for women to involve themselves in existing campaigns, or to replicate these campaigns in women's groups, is a useful thing to do.

So, some questions:

– Is nuclear power a feminist issue?

– What is a 'feminist issue'?

– Men created nuclear power. Is a group of women opposing it then inherently feminist?

– Nuclear power is the highest, maddest expression of patriarchal reasoning. Is it wise for us to start at the top?

– When we are denied rights over our own bodies, how can we fight for everyone's survival?

– What is the strategy you propose? Is it a distinct, feminist approach, or are you adding your voices 'as women' (whatever that means) to E.P. Thompson and Co.'s movement?

– Is the new Women's Peace Alliance really what it appears to be, an alliance based on keeping quiet about women's oppression? It seems to me that an organisation with no stated commitment to women's liberation has no place in feminist publications such as *WIRES*.

– Do the women in WONT see feminism and the fight against nuclear power as quite separate issues, as those who wrote *Nuclear Re/Sisters* seem to? Or do they think women have a different relationship to nuclear power than men? If not, why are they working in women's groups? The only reason given for this in the *Re/Sisters* pamphlet is that it is more comfortable not to have to confront men all the time.

So what are the problems with the CND-type strategy? What does it mean for feminists to use reformist methods – marches, petitions, etc.? It implies that we (the people? women?) have the power to change it – now. It implies considerable faith in parliamentary democracy.

What you end up with, I am afraid, given our present government, is essentially support for a Labour Party committed to unilateral disarmament by a party conference. Does that remind you of anything? Wasn't it the 1964 Labour government that was elected with a disarmament programme?

They lie.

Surely you know they lie?

Has anything changed since the last mass-scale CND campaign? From the developments in the arms race since then I can see grounds for panic, perhaps, but no new grounds for hope. What is new is a world recession producing yet more insane (democratically elected) governments in many western countries.

Is nuclear power to be seen as the ultimate expression of patriarchy? Then what's the sense in women trying to put a stop to it without destroying patriarchy? Men have not often been seen to give up power voluntarily. What makes you think they'll give up the greatest power they have harnessed? Someone has to find a power base from which to challenge it.

Ending male domination begins with women developing a sense of our identity as women, with focusing on what we have in common as women. A primary empowering step is to see that we are not deficient men, we are different from them and oppressed by them. An important political act is to stop taking on guilt for the crimes of men – it is they who made this world as it is. We have to start from where we are, recognise what power we have and what we do not have and will have to fight to achieve.

It seems to me we should be trying to unpick the power structure from the bottom. How do women in WONT[3] and the WPA see us gaining the power to make real changes? As an alliance based on femaleness saying nothing about female oppression? An alliance with nice men in the hope that 'enough people' can sway the power élite towards sanity?

I hope that the women I am writing to will not see my questions as negativity – I want to see these issues debated. My fear is of large numbers of women abandoning women's liberation struggles in favour of what is seen as a 'larger cause'. It runs deep in all of us to put aside our 'special concerns' for the human race. My anxiety is particularly intense because my own involvement in similar campaigns in years past has led me to an interpretation of the world which makes me think that the fight for the 'larger cause' as it is currently being fought will only lead to frustration.

The parallel that haunts me is with what happened to the first wave of feminism in this country when the first world war began. I want to be reassured that this is not an appropriate parallel.

Notes

1. *Nuclear Re/Sisters*, by Feminists against Nuclear Power, c/o Sisterwrite Bookshop, 190 Upper Street, London N1.

2. In *WIRES*, no. 118, September 1981.

3. This article was written before actions leading up to the establishment of different peace camps nationwide, including the one at Greenham Common, and while WONT was still a small organisation.

LESLEY WEST, Leeds WONT Group

Reply to An Open Letter to Women in WONT and the Women's Peace Alliance

First published in *Catcall*, no. 14, August 1982

It seems to me that you are asking questions that can be applied to various different feminist activities and thus your questions are basically about feminism itself, although they are specifically directed at feminism and nuclear power/war. To me, feminism is about caring, sharing, co-operation, equality and life. In addition, it is about change, as you can't achieve those things externally without internalising those values first. However, feminism has other facets for other women, and that's fine by me. I see diversity as a strength, for patriarchy needs undermining at all levels and in all ways in order to get the madness to stop, and I know that personally I cannot fight for every issue, so I'm happy to see it being done by women whom I support for doing it. Why waste energy trying to get everyone to think the same way as you and that there's only one approach to the problems? For surely that reeks of patriarchal thinking which is: 'I'm right, so you do what I say, otherwise I feel threatened.'

If we could allow the differences to exist, and support women doing what they feel is right in their fight against patriarchal madness (instead of seeing diversity as a weakness), we would save so much time and energy. I can't fight for every issue that is of importance, like abortion rights, power over our own bodies, an end to the degradation of all women, etc., because I don't have all that energy, so it is great for me to know other women are doing that. For myself, I found I was so scared for my life that I had to fight for it, and not to fight to improve the quality of my life when I didn't believe I would live long anyway. So naturally, I work with women in a leaderless, co-operative, caring, sharing and life-loving group to end the threat of nuclear war and to bring about a peaceful feminist (as defined before) world.

The way in which we work together is all-important, for the means are as vital as the end. How can you work for a feminist community in a violent or hierarchical manner? Now, how, you ask, are we fighting the threat of nuclear war? Well, again, in every aspect that we possibly can – which does include supporting other peace groups to a degree – but the answer lies in this. You say nuclear power is the greatest energy harnessed by man. Well, I think the greatest energy exploited by man is women's 'power'. So, it is only by reclaiming that energy in every way, which includes working together as women supportively, that we can hope to redress the balance of nature which is wobbling precariously on the brink of disaster in the patriarchal system. So let's support our sisters and not excommunicate them.

I hope I have answered some of your questions; and this brings me to the last point that was made: 'large numbers of women abandoning women's liberation struggles in favour of what is seen as a "larger cause".' How sad. Isn't feminism a large cause? Feminism is not fixed with a set number of women in it – it is growing, varied, and so attracting more and more women to it. I'm sorry you see women fighting the system at its most crazy expression, that of destroying the earth for egotistical con-games, as weakening feminism. I see it as strengthening, as attracting more non-feminists, and as necessary as it is natural to fight for your life in the way in which you want to live it. If you feel other issues are being weakened, then surely you must see them as being dead (i.e. fixed, unchanging), for otherwise they would attract women in their own right, with a perfectly natural turnover. If they don't, then perhaps there's something inherently wrong with the way in which they are set up, who knows?

'. . . don't shut your sister out, trust her choices, her intuition of her own way to grow . . .'

JOSEPHINE

Letter to *Lysistrata*, 2

First published Winter 1983

As is often the case with grandmothers, I spent my Christmas holidays with my son, his wife and my baby grand-daughter. They live at High Wycombe. The conversation turned to the proposed missile site to be built there and to the American base already there.

My son and his wife are not nuclear disarmers, even though as a small boy, in the 1960s, he marched to and from Aldermaston. It is the proximity of the base, coupled with their role as parents, that led them to think of the awful implications involved in policies of nuclear armaments. They are impressed by the Greenham Common actions and wanted to visit the new peace camp at Dawes Hill.

So, reluctantly on my part (I wanted to sink into Christmas sloth), we walked up to the camp to say some words of support.

That day there were four people present – two men and two women. They had a tent (for how much longer?), a fire, and the usual trappings of camp life but without chairs – their main shortage at that time. The banners were flying, the blackboards were in evidence so that all knew who they were and why they were there. The camp is beside a busy road and it was very heartening to hear the approving hoots and see the arms waving in salute by passing motorists. Whilst we were there a man delivered *everyone* a pair of warm wellies! The protesters told us how they had been inundated by Christmas gifts.

However, our mood of optimism about the camp soon vanished when we walked around the perimeter fence and thought of the real issues. A handful of brave protesters is not enough. A government embarrassed by Greenham may see Dawes Hill as a soft option. We must make sure they see our energy and our commitment at *all* the peace camps – even the 'mixed' ones. I think *that* is our first priority – and it's not just because my beautiful, naughty and clever grand-daughter lives only two or three miles away, though that is part of it. I'd like some *great*-grand-daughters too.

5
Up Against the State

Introduction

Britain's first woman prime minister has been in power for five years, and during that time we have seen a dramatic decline in the quality of life for women. In spite of the fact that the Conservative Manifesto for the 1983 General Election made feeble gestures towards equal opportunities, the effects of their policies have had serious consequences for women in paid employment and for women in the home. These particularly affect the poorest sections of the population, including single mothers and the black community. The infamous return to Victorian values, in which the woman is the sustainer and symbol of virtue in the private sphere – based in its day on a vision of middle-class prosperity supported by numerous servants – is particularly meaningless now, when only one in ten households 'conforms to the family ideal of male breadwinner, full-time housewife and dependent children'.[1] Cuts in welfare provisions for the elderly and the young mean that the responsibility for caring for them is thrown back on the home. The real value of child, unemployment and sickness benefits drops year by year, and cuts in housing expenditure by local councils mean fewer and fewer housing options. Bad living conditions add to the burden of women in the home, while there are fewer permanent alternatives for women who want to leave violent men.

All these things affect women in paid employment too. Jobs in the public sector, where so many women work, are put at risk as cuts are implemented and as areas are privatised. It is too simple to say that Thatcher's policies are forcing women back into the home. Indeed, until now women have not been losing jobs more rapidly than men, but as the service sector begins to suffer under the monetaristic policies of Thatcher, women are more likely to be made redundant. What Thatcherism has done is to increase massively women's workload, and with general unemployment levels rising, the choices we can make about whether or not to go into paid employment – or to leave it – are much more restricted.

The Thatcherites' belief in the free play of market forces at whatever the cost has been justified by an ideology of the family in which the self-sacrificing little woman as usual plays the supporting role. Of course, the state and the government are not synonymous. Anti-woman legislation existed long before this government came to power, and patriarchal assumptions are expressed, for example, in the attitudes of judges in lesbian custody cases. However, under this government, new repressive legislation has been enacted. The racist and sexist Nationality Act has recently been strengthened, and used extensively against black women. Campaigns have been launched to stop black families from being divided, and to press for women's right to stay in this country, independent of men. The Police Bill, under debate at the time of writing, proposes to increase state surveillance and police powers. By the time you read this, we will be well into 1984. No doubt the government will continue to evoke the spectre of totalitarianism to justify dismantling the welfare state and local government. The rhetoric of individualism and free choice will continue to have a special irony for women, whose responsibilities are ever increasing and choices narrowing.

Note

1. Segal, Lynne, 'The heat in the kitchen', in *The Politics of Thatcherism*, Lawrence & Wishart, 1983.

FRANKIE RICKFORD

The Hidden Victims: women and public transport

First published in *Marxism Today*, May 1982

When the Law Lords ruled the Greater London Council's public transport subsidy illegal they stimulated a major debate on urban transport policy which, despite the government's reluctance to participate, is unlikely to die while London fares remain the highest of any capital city in the world.

The economic and environmental arguments for attracting people out of cars with a cheap and reliable public transport system have been widely accepted. The London Chamber of Commerce and leader writers on the *Financial Times* have been among the many and varied voices to call for higher rates of subsidy to reduce traffic congestion, pollution, noise, road damage, accidents, fuel consumption and the waste of valuable land for car parks.

Much less attention has been paid to the fate of those Londoners unable to opt to travel by car when the fares doubled, whose experience will only be officially recorded by their absence from the tubes and buses. They are that growing chunk of the population with very low fixed incomes – the young, the unemployed, low-paid and part-time workers and single parents. Their only alternative to forking out 40 pence or more for a mile's journey is to stay at home, as thousands will be forced to do.

Yet it is precisely these groups who are the biggest users of public transport all over the country, entirely dependent upon it as they are for their everyday business and much less frequent pleasure.

Young women

According to the Department of Transport's most recently published National Travel Survey (1975–6) the most frequent bus travellers are young women aged between 16 and 20 years. They make more than twice as many journeys to and from work as any other group in the population – an overall average of 2.63 a week.

129

They also make greatest use of public transport for social, entertainment and holiday purposes – not because they go out more than their male peers but because men of the same age are more than three times as likely to have the use of a car. Young women are also the lowest-earning group, so high fares may not only prevent them from going to films, discos, evening classes or to visit friends but may also force them to refuse available jobs because they cannot afford to travel to work or give up jobs they already have.

The same problem confronts older 'unskilled' women whose husband and childcare responsibilities debar them from full-time jobs. I've personally met three women in London who said they had to leave jobs when the fares doubled, and I doubt if they are the only ones. If you are paid £1.50 or so an hour for 20 hours a week work and have to find £2 a day for fares as well as the other expenses incurred by going out to work, such as clothes, union dues and gifts for workmates, the job gets very expensive.

Nurses, office cleaners and catering workers on late-night and early-morning shifts also face the problem of poor or non-existent bus services at the times they need them. As a result of the fares increase and the anticipated drop in passenger traffic, London Transport has reduced all bus services especially during 'uneconomic' off-peak periods. All services now start half an hour later and finish half an hour earlier, and the entire night bus service may be withdrawn.

For women, waiting in the dark for a bus that does not arrive, or trying to cadge lifts, hitch-hike or walk is not only inconvenient, but dangerous. Assaults by men on nurses have now become so frequent that the Royal College of Nursing has taken up the question in an official campaign.

Early this year a young woman was accused of 'contributory negligence' by an Ipswich judge sentencing a man who had admitted to raping her after picking her up as a hitch-hiker. After a second woman hitch-hiker was raped in the same area two weeks after the trial finished it emerged that the last bus left the nearest town, Bury St Edmunds, at 5.30 in the afternoon. How many thousands of women must there be in rural areas trapped at home every single evening of their lives by such hopelessly inadequate public transport services coupled with the threat of male violence?

Not surprisingly there is a direct link between car availability and household income. (The London Borough of Bromley, whose council initiated the legal action against the GLC fares policy, incidentally, has the highest number of cars per household in Greater London – three times the rate of Tower Hamlets.) But from the sex-based information available on people's travelling habits it is clear that where there is a car in the family, the man keeps the keys. About 60 per cent of employed men in the DoT survey drove to work, compared to 36 per cent of women. One in four women and one in ten men bussed.

Non-job travel

But if the media, MPs and even the GLC leadership have neglected the problems of these carless commuters, they have completely ignored the importance of non-job-related travel. Only 29 per cent of the 62,000 bus trips in the national survey sample were made by people going to or coming from their jobs.

No passenger statistics can directly express the need of different groups in the population to travel. What appears to be an essential journey when you can afford the fare may have to be jettisoned if you cannot, and while for one person 'social' travel may mean going to a party, for another it means regular visits to a sick and aged relative who would otherwise be in an institution. Bus fares vary wildly from city to city – in Bristol, for example, you are well advised to carry a credit card for what in Sheffield would be a 7p trip – and London Transport is certain to find some sharp changes in the results of its monitoring programme after 21 March 1983.

London Transport's current monitor indicates that 57 per cent of bus passengers and 60 per cent of tube passengers are women, and according to the national survey women use buses about 35 per cent more frequently than men. Women's need to travel locally is greater because they carry the main burden of domestic and parental work. As well as shopping to feed and clothe a family, women have to visit family planning clincs, ante- and post-natal clinics, take their children to school, doctors and dentists, 'keep an eye on' elderly relatives and are generally held responsible for sustaining family relationships.

The importance of public transport in carrying out these tasks is increasing week by week as small local hospitals and schools close, shopping facilities become more centralised, GPs leave their street-corner surgeries for bigger health centres and families are dispersed by housing transfers. London Transport chairman Sir Peter Masefield's suggestion that hiking or walking would be a healthier alternative to expensive buses may be true for the childless in areas where the atmosphere still contains more air than exhaust fumes. But a two- or three-mile trek with a couple of miserable under-fives and a stone or so of shopping in the Borough of Hackney or Lewisham is not going to improve anyone's constitution.

For people dependent on supplementary benefit, public transport fare levels can make the difference between a tolerable and an intolerable existence. Two-thirds of supplementary benefit claimants are single parents, predominantly women, occupying some of the worst housing in our inner cities. High fares mean only absolutely essential journeys can be made, with the result that the parent and children can be literally trapped within buggy-pushing distance of home for days on end.

An added problem for many lone parents is their vulnerability, because of poverty and stress, to having their children taken into local authority care. In such circumstances, a court considering an application from the parent to take the child home will take account of the number of visits made to the residential home or foster parents – visits which usually require a bus or underground journey. London Transport's introduction of adult fares for children after 9.00 p.m. is a further blow to the freedom of the capital's 150,000 one-parent families.

Pensioners enjoy travel concessions in most parts of the country so are not directly affected by fares increases. But as the second largest group of bus-users they have to put up with the service, however bad. A free pass is little comfort when you've been waiting at a bus stop for three-quarters of an hour on a winter's night for a bus that is full up when it eventually arrives.

Isolated and demoralised

I have concentrated here on the impact on some groups of working-class women's lives of local public transport policies. Other groups, including schoolchildren, students, and unemployed men and women have also been severely punished by the Law Lords' ruling and the government's refusal to legislate for subsidised fares in London. And it is worth pointing out that black people are over-represented in all low-income groups.

The people worst hit by an attack on public transport are those most isolated and demoralised by exhaustion and poverty. To then immobilise them by pricing travel beyond their means removes them further from society, confirming their sense of powerlessness.

TESS GILL

The Family Wage Debate

First published in *Link*, no. 35, Winter 1981/82

The family wage debate is concerned with the effect of
women's wages and conditions of framing wage demands in terms of
the need for the male worker to earn enough to support himself and
a family. The model presupposes a male wage-earner, with a
dependent wife and two children. With 60 per cent of married
women at work, this is clearly not a typical case.

In fact, only 5 per cent of workers (40 per cent of whom are
female) at any one time fit the model, according to the *General
Households Survey*, 1978. There are nearly 1 million one-parent
families, most of whom are women. The fact that the number of
families below the poverty line would probably treble if married
women stopped work indicates that most employed women support
dependants, either as the sole breadwinner or jointly with a male
wage-earner.

Another crucial factor is the continuing low level of women's
earnings. There are 9 million working women and 12½ million
working men. Yet 60 per cent of all these women's hourly earnings
worked out at less than the poverty wage (£76 per week) compared
to only 18.5 per cent of the men. This stark fact underpins women's
generally oppressed position in society. It makes female economic
independence very difficult when most women never earn enough
to support a household or even themselves in average comfort.

The idea that the individual male breadwinner has to earn enough
to keep a wife and children is historically fairly recent. It developed
in the nineteenth century, when the shift from household to factory
production meant that the unit of production was no longer the
family but an individual – who was almost invariably male! Since
then, demands for a minimum wage, supplemented by dependants'
allowances, have been strenuously opposed, even within the labour
movement. Eleanor Rathbone's campaign for family allowances
between the wars is a case in point. Hilary Land attributed this
opposition to the fear that family allowances/child benefits could be

used against the interests of organised labour. However, a powerful and committed labour movement could prevent this.

Wages and the state

The family wage question opens up a number of areas for discussion. Perhaps the most important is the role of the state. What degree of family support should be sought from wages and what proportion from the state? Opponents of the family wage suggest that wage bargaining should only aim to obtain sufficient to support the individual, and the needs of the dependants should be met through the social security system. They say that trade unions should reorientate themselves to this end, and that they have as much ability to obtain it from the state as from the employer.

The other approach which equally accepts the need to end wage-bargaining strategies centred on the male breadwinner is that the family needs to be redefined. Why should socialists accept an individualistic approach to wage bargaining that looks on earnings in terms of self-support only and relies on a welfare state under declining monopoly capitalism as the best provider for dependants? Why not redefine the family in line with reality and feminist objectives, so that one bargains for the wage-earner (male or female) to earn enough to support themselves and their dependants, whether they are aged parents, children or partners at home with childcare responsibilities. It would, of course, be false to counterpose this argument entirely to the previous one, so that one is either for or against state support. One can argue for higher child benefits while recognising that they will not entirely provide for children and still look to wages to provide some support for dependants.

A further important question is the distribution of wages within the family. If a man earns enough to support a family, the family does not necessarily receive the surplus. Child benefit is good for women, as it goes straight into their purse. Increases in child benefit as against child tax allowance (in the past) or the married man's tax allowance (in the future) are often opposed for depleting the male wage packet.

Low pay

Redefining the family is not made easier by a sexist social security system which debars cohabiting women from any entitlement and frames all calculations according to the male breadwinner and dependants. This is where the argument as to how wage claims for the low paid should be framed becomes important. At present wage negotiators for the low-paid workers often include a demand that all wages exceed the low-paid threshold. This can be defined as the gross pay equivalent to a social security entitlement for a married man and two children.

Against this, it can be argued that low-pay bargaining should not attach itself to social security standards which are unacceptably low but should only be tagged to a proportion of earnings.

Moreover, this method does not help when one is bargaining for the majority of the low paid, i.e. women, as the employer is able to point out that the calculations do not apply to them. It is contradictory to argue both for equal pay for women and for a family wage for men, which perpetuates the idea of married women's economic dependence.

Ideological effects

It is difficult to assess the actual effects of the family wage argument on wage levels. Family wage arguments are not always utilised and usually only apply to the basic wage. It may well be that at the negotiating table the family wage element in the wage demand has little or no effect. On the other hand, it provides an insidious long-term ingredient of general ideology about women wage-earners being temporary, marginal, working only for pin money, and neither deserving nor needing equal earnings. It is this ideological content which tips the balance against any tendency to dismiss the whole discussion as irrelevant. Whichever way we move, we cannot be seen to continue to bargain for the male breadwinner.

JULIE GASK

Behind Closed Doors: disabled women and the DHSS

First published in *Manchester Women's Paper*, February 1982

Last year (1981) being the International Year of the Disabled, the Equal Opportunities Commission (EOC) carried out a survey to gauge the opinions of disabled married women, and of married women caring for the disabled, on the discriminatory social security benefits relating to them. These benefits are based on the out-of-date assumption that when a woman marries, she becomes a dependant of her husband.

The EOC placed adverts in *Woman*, *Woman's Own*, *Woman's Realm* and *Woman's Weekly*, and on 6 January 1982 published their report, *Behind Closed Doors*, on the strength of over 9500 replies received over a two-month period:

> I was examined by two civil service doctors and my own GP and told both verbally and have it in writing that I was unfit for clerical duties. Eventually I applied for HNCIP and was turned down for this pension – how ridiculous that I am not fit for clerical duties, but fit for heavy housework.

HNCIP (Housewives' Non-Contributory Invalidity Pension) is not automatically available to a married woman incapable of paid work. Her traditional role, as the name of the pension implies, is that of housewife; therefore, she has to undergo a test to prove that she is also incapable of housework (normal household duties)! Disabled married men, however, receive an invalidity pension regardless of their ability to do housework. As if this wasn't bad enough, it seems that in order to qualify for HNCIP, a woman must be completely bed-ridden or thereabouts.

> It appears to me that they expect you to be both incapable of shuffling around and completely mentally retarded. Unfortunately, I am only crippled with rheumatoid arthritis.

136

Of course, she can always take her case to an appeal tribunal, but often she cannot do this unless someone goes on her behalf, as she cannot manage the journey. Also if, like most of us, she is unaccustomed to tribunals, she will not know how to put her case.

This woman was fortunate in having a solicitor:

> She had originally been told that because she could walk as far as the shops (but couldn't carry anything), and because she could cook vegetables – if she was sitting down and they were already prepared for her – she was not entitled to HNCIP. Her case was heard by the tribunal, who were astounded that she had been refused, and the pension was granted immediately and back-dated.

This ridiculous and humiliating household duties test has got to go – and as soon as possible. But until it does, women who have been refused HNCIP and wish to appeal can obtain help with their appeal from their local Citizens' Advice Bureau.

> Help should be according to need, not to the wearing of a wedding ring.

A married woman who stays at home to care for a disabled relative or friend does not have to suffer any tests or tribunals – she isn't entitled to any benefit at all. If, however, her husband did the same thing, he would be entitled to Invalid Care Allowance. This discriminatory arrangement saves the government a lot of money:

> Of course, I could put my daughter into hospital and lead a normal life. This would cost the government a lot more than if they gave me an allowance for caring for her.

Until very recently, the facts about these two discriminatory benefits (and there are others) have been all but invisible. Hopefully, this report will trigger some positive action amongst the people who are in a position to do anything about it.

SARA HARDY

Trial of a Lesbian Mother

First published in *Spare Rib*, no. 107, June 1981

Dear women,

Enclosed is a poem about lesbian custody. It was written out of anger and terror over the turmoil that a sudden custody case thrust us into – 'us' being Sue, myself and Sue's child Sally. This sudden court case changed our lives, our life-style, we had to tone down everything for fear of welfare officers finding anything to use against us. This meant stripping the house of any lesbian or feminist identification, it meant that the two other women in the house had to leave, it meant a frightened, demanding child, it meant a tense, steel-eyed mother, it meant that 'justice' can put the boot in at any time, especially when you least expect it.

Lesbian mothers are never safe as long as their husbands are alive. Lesbian mothers never actually win custody for keeps. That's the way the law works. I wrote this poem out of anger and desperation because I knew there was nothing I could do – it was all so big and uncontrollable.

Now the case is off; Sue's ex-husband withdrew from the case – maybe because it was proving too expensive, maybe because he realised what he might be doing to Sally – he's seen her on average twice a year for the last nine years, he could have won, but maybe his pride wouldn't risk it.

So, maybe you'd print the poem? There are a lot of lesbian mothers freaking out over custody around the country, they need support, they need recognition. Women with children have a tough enough time without having to fight for the right to keep hold of them as well.

Yours in womanhood,
Sara Hardy

The trial of a lesbian mother

Careful   Careful   Careful

Watch what I say
Watch what I do
Must not betray
A Custody Clue

Careful   Careful   Careful

Yes we sometimes sleep together
No the child has no disorder
Yes we are at ease together
No there's nothing under cover
Yes she is my only lover
No the child did not discover
Yes we thought it right to tell her
No we didn't tell the father
No we wouldn't tell that fucker!

Careful   Careful   Careful

Yes I've heard of feminism
No I'm not familiar with them
No there's rarely any friction
No it's never scared the children
No we do not share a bedroom
Yes she knows, we're clear and open
No no signs of alienation
No we are no women's 'faction'
Yes we are prepared for Action!

Careful   Careful   Careful

I am going to be compliant
Smile so sweetly undefiant
Subjugate my hate and passion
Denounce my Self to gain compassion
Kiss the patriarch that bleeds me
Piss on him for *I will be free*!

Careful   Careful   Careful

Lesbian Mothers: 'Moral danger'
Warp the child, contaminate it
Hail the Judge our overseer
See the father pale and pining

Hardly knows his frightened daughter
Prick too proud to pass this battle
Property – his right to fight for
Prejudice his moral armour
Patriarch the social norm

Welfare visits notwithstanding
All the tell tales tucked away now
Posters books and badges long gone
Even dresses on display
Nothing Left to compromise one
Nothing but the Awful fact
Lesbian mother Lesbian lover
Unnatural parent Moral trap

'Save the child Oh save the children!
Contamination must be stopped
We see the child is loved and cared for
Acknowledge good reports and such
But your problem is distressing
And the Child we must Protect
Trust the law "she" will protect you
Trust the law for we know best'

See the Judge his seat of power
Arse splayed wide his wig askew
Finger on the scale of justice
Great Protector of the few
Moral danger is his Playboy
Keep the courtroom clean and straight
He never touched that public schoolboy
Never bought it, never raped

See the child now so bewildered
Questions all designed to trap
'Do you sometimes hate your mother?
Does Daddy buy you this and that?'
See the mother drawn and tight now
Compromised and blown apart
See her fight until the end now
See her win?
                    See her lost?

JILL RADFORD

Marriage Licence or Licence to Kill? Womanslaughter in the criminal law

First published in *Feminist Review*, no. 11, June 1982

With particular gratitude to Mary Bristow who helped me write the article, and was ironically herself the victim of male violence, dying in tragic circumstances three months after this article was completed.

This article emerges out of the fear and anger experienced by us as women on hearing the outcome of a case tried at Winchester Crown Court in June 1981. In this case Gordon Asher was found guilty of the manslaughter of his wife and received a six months' jail sentence suspended for two years. This sentence allowed him to walk free out of the court, allegedly to his engagement party. For this man, wifeslaughter was more economic than divorce.

Our immediate reaction was to write in outrage to all national and local media. It was only, and perhaps ironically, the *Sun* newspaper which chose to print our protest, and as a result of that coverage, the *Southampton Echo* printed a few lines.

Coverage in the national press was a new experience for us. We were not surprised to receive phone calls and letters – supportive, hostile, some recording experiences of being battered by husbands and some asking for our help and support. We were surprised at the amount of emotional energy required to handle these calls. We insist that in no way do we regret our decision to publicise our feelings on this issue and the local and national support from women we received was encouraging, though at the same time tragic.

This was our initial reaction. On reflection we feel that this horrific case of male violence and the legal response raises many important issues for women. In order to develop these issues, unfortunately, it seems necessary to relive the frightening incident.

141

The details of the case as covered by the media are as follows: Asher was alleged to have murdered his wife, Jane, in the bathroom of a house where a party was being held, during a quarrel about other men she had been with. He denied intending to kill her and claimed that he held her by the throat and suddenly she collapsed on the floor. He then drove six miles to a roadworks site and buried her. Mr Paul Chadd (prosecuting!) said Asher was clearly a model husband, and devoted to his children. Jane Asher, however, was portrayed in court as a 'flirt', a 'two-timer' and someone who 'made up to other men'. The last straw seems to have been the fact that she disappeared for half an hour at the fatal party and then started dancing with another man.

He was found guilty of manslaughter and was given a six months' suspended sentence.

Central questions of concern to us are: the extent of criminal violence against women in 'domestic' situations; how the legal system responds to this (i.e. how typical was the Winchester case?); what protection does the criminal law offer to women if married or in a relationship with men?

The law in theory

Theoretically, with the exception of rape, itself an issue of much contention, a husband can be prosecuted for all other 'offences against the person' on his wife – murder, manslaughter, attempted murder, wounding or other act endangering life and the various forms of assault. Susan Maidment, an academic lawyer at the University of Kent, writes reassuringly: 'There is no doubt that the criminal law contains adequate provision for dealing with violence between any two persons, including husband and wife' (1978: iii). However, even in terms of its formal provision, the legal system treated 'wife assault' as something different from other forms of violent crime by excluding it from the scheme initiated in 1964, through which victims of criminal assault can claim compensation from the Criminal Injuries Compensation Board:

> Where the victim who suffers injuries and the offender who inflicted them were living together as members of the same family, no compensation will be payable. For the purpose of this paragraph where a man and a woman were living together as man and wife they will be treated as if they were married to one another [1964].

The popular explanation for the exclusion of 'wife assault' is

...ces currently recorded as homicide by relation of victim to ...ipal suspect

		Number	%
...e, cohabitant or former spouse,			
...abitant		137	24
...or former lover		24	4
..., son, daughter		93	16
...family		12	2
		119	21
...ssociate		31	5
	Sub-total	416	73%

...ot acquainted with suspect

			less than
...fficer (victim)		1	½%
...f terrorism		1	½
...ranger		119	21
...ct		41	7
	Total	578	100%

...fences between spouses recorded by the police

	Total	Victim Wife	Victim Husband	% of total in which women are victims of men
...anslaughter,				
...d murder,				
...murder	200	163	37	81.5%
...acts				
...ng life, and				
...sault	5721	5263	379	91.5%
Total	5921	5426	416	91.6%

...e Office, 1979.

...he facts presented above, that we as a civilised society
...it crime, and that the highest proportion of violent
... in a 'domestic' context where men as husbands are
...gly the aggressor – how can the suspended sentence
...sher be explained? Is this a typical sentence?

perversely the large number of claims that could be brought. As will subsequently be discussed, criminal violence in a domestic context constitutes a very high proportion of serious crimes of violence. Another argument cited for its exclusion is that 'public interest' is not concerned about criminal violence which occurs in the privacy of the home. On the contrary, we would suggest that it is a matter of central public interest as defined by the male legal system in that it goes towards preserving male dominance. While men can legally rape their wives, it is difficult to imagine male judges awarding compensation to wives for injuries received at the hands of their husbands.

Adrienne Rich notes in a different context that the 'law of a male sex-right to women' is used to justify prostitution and to defend 'sexual slavery' within the family on the basis of family privacy and cultural uniqueness. The male perspective as reflected in 'objective' legal wisdom renders sexual abuse and terrorism of women by men invisible, natural and inevitable, thus hardly eligible for compensation. To quote from Adrienne Rich in legal thinking, 'women are expendable so long as the sexual and emotional needs of the male are satisfied' (1981: 16).

The law in practice

If in its formal provision the criminal law potentially protects although fails to compensate victims of 'wife assault', its practical operation has given rise to considerable criticism. In its report, the House of Commons Select Committee on Violence in Marriage concluded:

> If the criminal law of assault could be more uniformly applied to domestic assaults there seems little doubt that it would give more protection to the battered wife [1977: xvi].

The social processes through which an incidence of assault is (or more frequently is not) transformed from an act of private terrorism by a man on a woman, with whom he is in a 'relationship', to a violent crime statistic in the criminal court are complex and uncertain. Initially they involve a decision on the part of the injured woman to call for official intervention. Many women, fearing either violent reprisals, the break-up of the family unit, homelessness and poverty on the one hand, or humiliation and degradation by the police on the other, choose not to take this course of action.

Assuming, however, that the woman decides to call for police intervention, whether an attack on a wife subsequently surfaces in the criminal court or not depends now on the police's attitude towards domestic violence and their perception of the specific incident.

The notorious reluctance of the police to intervene in 'domestic violence' has been documented by Women's Aid. Their official attitude is reflected in the following extracts from evidence to the House of Commons Select Committee:

> Whereas it is a general principle of police practice not to intervene in a situation . . . between a husband and wife in the course of which the wife had suffered some personal attack, any assault upon a wife by a husband which amounted to a physical injury of a serious nature is a criminal offence which it is the duty of the police to follow up and prosecute. Police will take positive action in every case of serious assault and will prosecute where there is sufficient evidence [1977: 375–6].
>
> Whilst such problems take up considerable time . . . in the majority of cases the role of the police is a negative one. We are, after all, dealing with persons 'bound in marriage' and it is important for a host of reasons to maintain the unity of the spouses. Precipitate action by the police could aggravate the position to such an extent as to create a worse situation than the one they were summoned to deal with [1977: 377].

If even at the level of official statements, the police attitude towards wife assault is hesitant, that their practice is characterised by an inactive non-interventionism is not surprising or anything new. In 1976 the Parliamentary Select Committee concluded: 'Chief Constables should review their policies about the police approach to domestic violence' (1976: xvii).

The question of policing families has been discussed elsewhere and involves the much wider debate as to the appropriateness of the criminal law as opposed to the family law, as advocated by Erin Pizzey as more appropriate for such matters.

Although the issue of wifeslaughter has to be contextualised with reference to domestic violence, the terrorising and killing of women, we argue definitively, does not fall into the category of crime for which decriminalisation can be advocated. In fact, it is our view that the freeing of Gordon Asher constitutes a dangerous precedent towards decriminalisation of wifeslaughter, thereby withholding state protection from married women.

The argument for decriminalisation of this form of crime turns on some notion of 'victim precipitation', i.e. that the victim was 'asking for it'. Press coverage of this case brings out many parallels with

rape trials. Both parties, the prosecutor as [...] focused on Jane Asher's behaviour, referrin[g...] had had lovers – points celebrated by the p[...] 'two-timing' wife. Jane Asher, it appear[...] 'Yorkshire Ripper' victims, did not conform[...] chastity and loyal wifeliness and thus '[...] sentence of the court predictably added su[...] dominant male double standards. Kathlee[n...] salience of the rape paradigm:

> Where the victim of sexual assault is [...] own victimisation – as leading the ratio[...] of other forms of enslavement, where[...] have 'chosen' her fate, to embrace[...] courted it perversely through rash or [...] 1979].

The extent of serious offences of vi[olence...]

Crimes of violence, we are frequentl[y...] chiefs and other right-thinking person[s...] society. Considerable measures are [...] society from violent criminals. The Pr[...] are told, unfortunately curtails our c[...] rid society of the menace posed by [...]

Examination of the official crim[e...] strates that homicide (a collective c[...] manslaughter (womanslaughter) an[d...] a family matter (see table belo[w...] insufficient evidence to determine [...] 'family' violence is in fact male vio[lence...] woman-killing (or feminicide). I[...] that a new table appeared in the [...]

This table demonstrates that [...] violence, it is overwhelmingly m[...] are the facts regarding 'serious' [...] There are no equivalent figure[s...] which anyway would be unreli[able...] hidden crime masked by the v[...] and the police attitude to do[...] seen that in relation to seriou[s...] men as husbands – who di[...] violent men and their wives [...]

Unfortunately official statistics regarding sentencing are not presented in such a way that this latter question can be answered. (John Browne, MP for Winchester, has agreed to raise this question in the House of Commons.) The sentencing figures with reference to homicide are presented as follows. These figures indicate that apart from murder, which carries a mandatory sentence of life imprisonment, the majority of those convicted of homicide do serve some time in prison. There is, however, considerable disparity in the length of sentences awarded and, furthermore, significant numbers serve no time at all.

In the British legal system judicial discretion in sentencing (with the exception of murder and treason which carry mandatory life imprisonment and death sentences respectively) is very broad. Judges in determining sentences make reference to an eclectic mixture of different, even incompatible, penal philosophies – retribution (punishment), individual deterrence, general deterrence, rehabilitation and protection of the community. In part, sentencing disparities may be explained by their differential commitment to these ideologies and their assumed appropriateness to different offenders and offences, informed by varying definitions of seriousness.

Feminists have found the question of sentencing for offences of violence against women difficult. We are in danger of having our anger towards male violence appropriated by the forces of reaction – the 'hang 'em and flog 'em brigade'.

Number convicted		Sentence		
Murder	124	Life imprisonment	124	Mandatory
Manslaughter	96	Life imprisonment	26	
		Over 10 yrs imprisonment	–	
		4–10 yrs imprisonment	62	
		4 yrs and under	80	
		Borstal	4	
		Sub-total	172	
		Restriction order	22	
		Hospital order	6	
		Probation	29	
		Suspended sentence	19	
		Others	10	
		Total	258	

Source: Home Office, 1979.

We must demand a penal system which accepts that violence against women is a serious crime, but without allowing ourselves to be used as part of a repressive law-and-order campaign. Our difficulty is the centrality of the crime and punishment issue to the working of the social order, a fact long recognised by the fascist Right.

It is only by analysing existing philosophies and dispelling a few myths that it becomes possible to look towards a constructive policy.

The myth of deterrent sentencing

Research indicates that neither at an individual nor a general level is deterrence effective, except to the extent that imprisonment does temporarily remove the offender from circulation. On a longer-term basis, there is no evidence that sentences of imprisonment are followed by a lower reconviction rate than for those sentenced to non-custodial measures – or even as reported in 'self-report' studies – in respect of those who are never caught or convicted of offences. (In self-report studies, random samples of the population are interviewed about their law-breaking activities in confidence.) At a general level, exemplary sentences (those which are exceptionally higher than is average for a certain type of offence) are not followed by any reduction in that type of offence. As an example, in the past exemplary sentences have been given and publicised in relation to football violence or 'muggings' without any noticeable reduction in those crimes. Stan Cohen concludes, 'There is no evidence that the rate of crime rises or falls with such changes in penal policy as the intensity of punishment' (1979: 27).

The rehabilitation myth

In the post-war period a philosophy of reform or rehabilitation was popular in liberal penal thinking. Disturbed by what they saw as the negative nature of punishment, liberal penologists identified reform through 'treatment' or 'corrective training' as the aim of the penal system. Innovations in the prison regimes and in non-custodial measures were introduced to secure this end. Again, research, including that undertaken by the Home Office itself, has demonstrated the ineffectiveness in terms of subsequent reconviction rates. The Mays Report on the Prison System reflected official disenchantment with the rehabilitation ethic.

A closely related philosophy remains current amongst many involved with domestic violence. Erin Pizzey, for example, suggests that the criminal law is inappropriate for matters of domestic violence. She advocates a forward-looking approach concerned with the welfare of those concerned rather than a retrospective blame-apportioning criminal law. Her context is that of 'wife-battering' rather than 'womanslaughter' – the issue here. It has been suggested that in the Asher case it was the judge's concern for the well-being of the survivors that in part prompted the suspended sentence.

Whose justice?

This individualistic welfare philosophy may have some legitimate claim as a humane approach, but we suggest that it is also, on many levels, problematic. In non-fatal cases there is no evidence to show that leniency deters subsequent attacks. In terms of justice, a lenient sentence is taken to indicate that the court does not view the offence as a serious matter. In terms of attacks on women, lenient sentencing of male offenders gives substance to the feminist claim that the law is made by, and for, men.

Lenient sentencing of violent men overlooks the welfare of women in the wider community. Since the Asher case the Winchester Women's Group has heard from several women whose husbands have used this ruling to threaten their wives: 'Look, I can kill you and get away with it', or 'It's easier than divorce'.

It is accepted here that criminal law cannot resolve the things that give rise to violence, nor in non-fatal cases can it prevent repeated assaults. Neither should the advocacy of the use of criminal law inhibit the development of measures to support the battered wife, like, for example, the development of crisis shelters fought for by Women's Aid groups. We do argue, however, that violence against women in 'domestic situations' should be defined as criminal violence and justly punished as such. With the failure of the rehabilitation ethic the only legitimate response to behaviour we define as unacceptable is to have confidence in that definition and punish accordingly.

This raises the basic question of what forms of social action or behaviour should be defined as unacceptable. As feminists, we argue that any behaviour which threatens the freedom, well-being and dignity of women is unacceptable. We demand no sexist privilege. The same definition should be applied to the male population. Thus all crimes of violence against the person should be defined as such and punished justly, fairly and consistently in the same way as violent crime. Punishing the aggressor is a clear statement of recognition of an offender's responsibility for his (and we mean 'his') actions. Furthermore, it is a statement of society's condemnation of violent behaviour.

This, while part of a 'back to justice' philosophy, is not part of any repressive law-and-order, bring-back-hanging campaign. Its starting-point is a re-examination of society's fundamental value system. When shoplifters are imprisoned for small thefts, when sentences of imprisonment are passed on those who take odd jobs in an effort to stretch state supplementary benefits or unemployment pay, and yet wifekillers are allowed to go free, then it is surely time to question society's values and priorities. As feminists we have no wish to see our prisons any fuller, or the law more repressive, rather the reverse is the case. We accept that prison serves no useful purpose for the vast majority who can be released tomorrow without detriment or danger. What we are demanding is the punishment of, and protection from, the 'men of violence' as an immediate short-term demand. In the long term, we look forward to an ending of violence against women through radical cultural change. We are looking forward to radical changes in the male-dominated culture that tolerates and trivialises violence against women.

In offering this quotation from Stan Cohen we suggest that violence can be used interchangeably with his concept of 'crime'.

It is of course possible to isolate the factors which have something to do with conventionally defined crimes . . . overcrowding, slums, poverty, racism, deprivation, degrading education, unhappy family life – but eradication of such conditions should not have to depend on their supposed association with crime . . . crime is connected not just with these evils but to society's most cherished values, such as individualism, competitiveness and masculinity [Cohen, 1979: 26].

In looking towards an end to violence against women it is to the last of these 'cherished values' that our attention must primarily be directed. All celebrations of masculinity constitute a denial of humanity and a degradation of women. All forms of male aggression from the sale of toy guns, violent sports to the sale of arms and threats of nuclear war must be defined and punished as inhumane. All assaults on the freedom and dignity of women from the routine harassment of women in the streets, the sexist cracks of the television comedian to degrading pornographic film must likewise be defined and punished.

Note

With thanks to Winchester Women's Group for their supportive tolerance.

References

Barry, K., *Female Sexual Slavery*, Englewood, Cliffs: Prentice Hall, 1979.

Cohen, S., *Crime and Punishment; some thoughts on theories and practice*, London: RAP, 1979.

Criminal Injuries Compensation Board, *Victims of Violence: A guide to the compensation scheme*, London: HMSO, 1964.

Home Office, *Criminal Statistics England and Wales 1979*, Cmnd 8098 London: HMSO, 1979.

Home Office, *Inquiry into the United Kingdom Prison Services (May Report)*, London: HMSO, 1979.

Maidment, S., 'The Law's Response to Marital Violence: A Comparison Between England and the USA', *Family Violence an International and Interdisciplinary Study*, J.M. Eekelaar and S. Katz (eds), Butterworth, 1978.

Pizzey, E., *Scream Quietly or the Neighbours Will Hear*, Harmondsworth: Penguin, 1974.

Rich, A., *Compulsory Heterosexuality and Lesbian Existence*, London: Onlywomen Press, 1981.

Select Committee on Violence in Marriage, *Report*, London: HMSO, 1977.

JEAN GARDINER

Women, Recession and the Tories

This article first appeared in full in *Marxism Today*, March 1981; and was reprinted in *The Politics of Thatcherism*, Lawrence & Wishart, 1983.

Mass unemployment and the right-wing policies of the Thatcher government are having major effects on the relationship between men and women at work, in the home and in the labour movement. Much of the progress made by women in recent years is now threatened. The opportunity this poses for the Left to set about winning the political support of masses of women in this country has, in large part, been missed. Instead, many women on the Left have felt pressure being brought to bear on them to drop their feminist demands in face of the common threat posed by Thatcherism. A united opposition to the Tories cannot be built by ignoring the very different ways in which men and women have experienced recession and Tory rule. Still less can such an approach result in broadening the base of support for the Left and the Labour Party amongst women. The emergence of the SDP–Liberal Alliance must make this doubly apparent.

There were a number of important changes in women's lives in the twenty years after the second world war, including the expansion of job opportunities for women. These changes gave rise to growing aspirations amongst women and increasing awareness of the limits of advances that had been made. This new consciousness was voiced most clearly by the Women's Liberation Movement but has also been reflected throughout the labour movement and women's organisations in the 1970s. Its impact was felt in a number of social reforms. Yet within the last few years the progress made by women has appeared increasingly limited and vulnerable. Steadily rising unemployment culminating in the present deep recession poses a special threat both to women's jobs and to women's expectations more generally. This threat has been reinforced by the economic and political philosophy of the Thatcher government and the attacks on women that this has produced. In many respects

152

women are in a stronger position to resist these attacks than was the case in the comparable period of the 1930s. However, weaknesses in the women's movement, in the relationship between the women's movement and the labour movement, and in the Left's alternative strategy all work against the development of an effective resistance.

The impact of the recession

Since 1974 in the capitalist world there has been lower economic growth and higher unemployment than at any time since the second world war. The recession of 1974–5 was followed by a brief boom in 1976–8. Since 1979 a new and deeper phase of recession has been entered. Britain has suffered more than most industrial capitalist countries from the effects of the recession because of its relative industrial weakness and decline. Moreover, since 1979 the British government has been particularly committed to sharply deflationary policies. For both reasons unemployment has risen more quickly and to higher levels in Britain than in most other industrialised capitalist economies.

There are a number of ways in which a recession such as the present one undermines the limited progress women have made. Because women are a particularly vulnerable group within the labour market their jobs are more readily threatened and their unemployment less visible than men's. High levels of unemployment greatly reduce training and job opportunities that make it possible for women to enter traditionally male-dominated fields. Moreover, the divisive attitudes that unemployment gives rise to can undermine the past progress women have made. In addition the relative pay of women tends to deteriorate in a recession. Finally, cuts in public services associated with the recession both reduce employment opportunities for women and increase the burden on women in the home.

Women, particularly married women and part-time workers, can be used as a more flexible reserve army of labour than men, being drawn in and out of employment in accordance with the demand for labour. Women move in and out of the labour force more than men because of the birth of children or the need to care for children, and sick or elderly relatives. Female employment can therefore often be reduced rapidly by means of natural wastage and without the need to make redundancies. Part-time workers (two-fifths of all women employed) are particularly vulnerable because they lack many of the minimum legal rights of full-time workers and have lower levels of unionisation.[1] Firms in many industries have used part-time employment as a temporary and cheap means of meeting demand.

For example, firms have rarely found difficulty in recruiting or laying off workers for the twilight evening shift, popular with married women who have children.

Men and women are, of course, mainly concentrated in different jobs and this occupational segregation has not diminished as a result of the growth in the female labourforce in the last thirty years.[2] The increase in employment opportunities for women that took place was the result of a growth in demand for labour in typically female occupations, especially in the expanding service sector. The relative vulnerability of women and men therefore also depends on the extent to which different jobs are at risk in the recession. Because women tend to be concentrated in relatively unskilled jobs they are again more vulnerable than men. Offsetting this to some extent is the concentration of women's jobs in service industries, e.g. finance, distribution and catering, which in the past have tended not to be as adversely affected by recession as the production industries in which men's jobs are concentrated.[3]

However, the introduction of new technology has begun to have a major impact on women's jobs in the service sector. This has led to job losses in many service industries which in the preceding period experienced steady growth, e.g. banking, insurance and finance. Clerical jobs in particular will be adversely affected by the introduction of the new microelectronic technology. It has been estimated that by 1990, 17 per cent of the secretarial workforce will be displaced by the new technology.[4]

It is difficult to assess the overall impact of these different tendencies. However, the employment statistics covering 1981 indicate that men's jobs have continued to disappear more rapidly than women's in the economy as a whole. This is mainly due to women's employment being largely concentrated in service industries. Between 1978 and 1981 male employment in Great Britain fell by about 7 per cent, whilst female employment declined by 2 per cent.[5] Part-time female employment actually increased by about 2 per cent. The loss of women's jobs was therefore concentrated amongst full-time workers.

Within manufacturing industries the picture is rather different because women's jobs disappeared at a faster rate than men's. Moreover, part-time women's employment in manufacturing shows a greater reduction (23 per cent) than full-time women's employment (18 per cent). Nevertheless, in all service industries except for public administration and defence, there was a small increase in female employment and most of the increase involved part-time jobs; on the other hand, there was a slight loss of men's jobs in the service sector.

Thus, despite the greater vulnerability of women in the labour-force, typically male jobs appear to have disappeared more rapidly than typically female jobs, at least until the beginning of the 1980s. However, the continuing trend for part-time employment to increase relative to full-time employment for women confirms a pattern of deteriorating pay and conditions for women in the workforce. It is likely that in some circumstances new jobs are created at the expense of some women workers elsewhere whose jobs are disappearing, e.g. staff agencies which substitute casual and unorganised workers for permanent staff.

Female unemployment is less visible than male unemployment. Unemployed women are less likely to register than men because lower national insurance contributions or the need to find part-time employment disqualify them from receiving benefit. In addition, when unemployment is high and job opportunities scarce, many women are discouraged from seeking work and therefore do not even consider themselves as unemployed.

Less visible

It is, therefore, difficult to estimate the overall impact of unemployment on women. The number of women registering as unemployed has been increasing since the mid-1970s faster than the number of men registered as unemployed. The rise in registered unemployment amongst married women has been particularly rapid. The gap between the official unemployment rates for women and men has therefore been narrowing. In February 1982 the rates were 15 per cent for men and 9 per cent for women.

However, if unregistered unemployment is taken into account, the gap is reduced. About 28 per cent of all unemployed women and 43 per cent of all unemployed married women do not register, as compared with 11 per cent of unemployed men.[6] The actual unemployment rates are therefore about 18 per cent for men and 12 per cent for women.

Finally, we should add to the unemployed those who give up seeking work and drop out of the labourforce altogether when jobs are scarce; there are twice as many women as men in this category, most of whom are married.[7] After a steady rise in the labourforce participation rates of women for some thirty years there has been an abrupt reversal recently. About half a million women dropped out of the labourforce between 1977 and 1980, discouraged by the lack of job opportunities.[8]

A recession affects not only the total number of jobs but the availability of training opportunities and access of women to traditionally male occupations. As firms cut back on training and men's jobs are threatened there are fewer and fewer opportunities for women to acquire new skills. Divisive attitudes, as illustrated by the following example, are on the increase:

> I believe a vociferous and militant minority is fostering the discontent among women about equal pay and jobs. A woman wants her man to be in work, not unemployed. Jobs should be first and foremost for him not her. A woman can and should get fulfillment from having and bringing up children.[9]

The restriction in women's access to skilled employment together with the trend for casual and unorganised female labour to be substituted for stable and better-paid women workers both necessarily have adverse effects on women's relative pay. In addition, the weakening in the overall bargaining position of labour has tended to make men within the unions fight more fiercely for male interests and the preservation of differentials. For the most part unions have acquiesced in this backlash in the absence of any effective campaign against it by the Left.[10] It is therefore not surprising that the limited progress they made in narrowing the differential between men's and women's pay after the introduction of the Equal Pay Act has been halted and even reversed since 1977. Women's average hourly earnings rose from 63.1 per cent of men's in 1970 to 75.5 per cent in 1977. Since then there has been a slight decline to 73.9 per cent in 1982. Any widening of the still considerable gap in pay between men and women creates further pressure on women to accept that their jobs are secondary.

Thatcherism and women

All the adverse effects of the recession on women discussed above have been intensified in two ways by the Thatcher government. The sharp rise since 1980 in the rate at which jobs have been disappearing is largely the result of the intensely deflationary monetarist policies the government has pursued. Moreover the Thatcher philosophy attempts to provide an ideological legitimation both for the attacks on women that result from the recession and for policies that take those attacks even further.

It has already been pointed out that a recession encourages the development of a right-wing, anti-feminist revival. The idea that women should accept that their place in society is to be at home caring for their family appears to make sense to more and more people when jobs are scarce. It is therefore not surprising that these ideas were gaining some popularity in the late 1970s and beginning to be expressed all the more vociferously in response to the impact feminism appeared to be having on society. At that time the major campaign to attract the support of those opposed to the advances women had won was the anti-abortion campaign. Many of the anti-abortion lobby would not, of course, be opposed to other aspects of women's rights. However, the more generalised anti-feminist stance of many of its constituents is a clear and important aspect of the shift to the right in British politics that the Thatcher government reflects.

An example of the way in which this government is acting to reinforce already existing trends in the recession is the pilot scheme introduced in 1982 to limit further the numbers of people entitled to unemployment benefit. Forms issued to claimants include more detailed questions than before, such as 'Would you take any full-time job which you can do? Do you have any children or anyone else who needs your care during working hours? Will you do night-work/shift work?' The question on childcare is particularly insidious for women. Parents may even be asked to supply evidence from a 'responsible' person that their children will be cared for.

However, when it comes to the place of women in their philosophy, the path the Tories have to tread is a delicate one, not necessarily helped by blatant anti-feminist outbursts like the notorious Patrick Jenkin quote: 'If the Good Lord had intended us to have equal rights to go out to work, he wouldn't have created man and woman.'[11]

Tories and the family

It is important to remember that appealing to women in the electorate continues to be a part of the Tory political appeal which must therefore recognise those changes in women's lives and aspirations which are irreversible as a result of experiences in the last thirty years. Moreover the Tories' position on women is not as explicit or united as their approach to some other issues, e.g. trades unions. Some Tories have campaigned actively for sex equality in some areas. A commitment to women's equal rights can coexist with moral beliefs about the family which give rise to policies that go against women's interests. The Tory government is neither explicit about its attacks on women nor even probably aware that its policies have this effect.

However, the role of the family and traditional values have been given much more emphasis in Tory philosophy and policies than equal rights. The philosophy stresses the need to return responsibilities and choice to the family, both of which it claims have been eroded by the growth of the welfare state.

It is a philosophy that seeks to legitimise savage attacks on the social services and welfare benefits upon which women and children particularly depend. The Tories have allowed the value of those payments to the family which directly benefit women and children, e.g. child benefits, to be eroded. Policies which claim to favour the family as a unit gloss over the structural inequality within it. For example the Tory objective of switching from direct taxation to indirect taxation works against women and children in families where income is not equally shared. This objective has not been achieved in practice, however, since the deflationary policies pursued by the government have entailed rises in direct as well as indirect taxes.

The cuts in public services which had begun as a regrettable expedient under the previous Labour administration have been pursued with vigour and ideological commitment by the Thatcher government. As well as withholding cash from the public sector, the government has carried through legislation reducing local authority obligations.

What was previously a very weak statutory requirement on the part of local authorities to provide nursery education has now been removed altogether by the Education Act 1980. In a context of massive cuts in local government expenditure this will ensure a further deterioration in the existing totally inadequate provision. The government's own White Paper forecasts a drop in the proportion of under-fives receiving nursery education from 40 per cent in 1980–1 to 33 per cent in 1984–5. The attack on the school meals service involves another reduction of mostly female paid labour at the expense of female unpaid labour in the home. Where the school meals service has been retained there has also been a trend towards replacing local authority staff with private contractors employing women on inferior wages and conditions. One local authority, Dorset, has even been considering introducing continental-style shorter opening hours for schools.

Such cuts in services for children have the direct effect in most cases of tying women further to the home, and of further reducing their opportunity and availability for paid work except for very short hours and very low pay. All these pressures have been reinforced by the policy of restricting maternity rights which was incorporated in the Employment Act 1980.

Developing the resistance

Whilst a complete reversal in women's position may be unlikely, the conditions for developing an effective resistance to present attacks do not yet exist. Within the women's liberation movement and on the Left there is a real need for an honest appraisal of the weaknesses that hold us back as well as the strengths that can take us forward.

The women's liberation movement has had a very great impact on society, not just through the social reforms it has helped fight for and defend, and the thousands of women who have been directly involved and influenced by it, but also through its influence on the attitudes and consciousness of many more people who would not directly identify with it. People have been forced to think about relationships between men and women to a much greater extent than before and there are now reminders in the language for those who might otherwise forget (sexism, chairperson, etc.).

However, there are also problems which feminists will have to tackle if women's liberation is to be kept alive as a movement and an ideology over the coming years.

From the earliest days of the women's liberation movement there has been a tension between fighting for women's own interests on the one hand, and asserting the needs of mothers and children on the other. Many of the women who started the first feminist women's groups in the early 1970s were in fact mothers. Throughout the history of the women's liberation movement feminists have played a key role in fighting to improve the quality of nursery provision for children, and to place children on the Left's political agenda.[12] Feminists have also emphasised the links between women's and children's oppression. If women are unwilling mothers or feel frustrated by the way in which their lives are totally circumscribed by motherhood, children are bound to suffer. The campaign for legal and financial independence for women has also stressed the material impoverishment that can arise for families from women's dependence on men.

However, feminists have stressed that the interests of women and children are separate and that women need to be aware of their own interests and be able to assert them. They have fought for a woman's right to choose whether or not to have children and for the right of mothers to decide how their children should be cared for. In this process of asserting women's needs feminists have sometimes failed to project a concern for children and an awareness of the positive role that children play in women's lives, and this failure has led many women to be wary of feminism. It has been exploited by those opposed to feminism, many of whom have demonstrated less concern for children in their own practice than those committed to women's liberation. In the face of a government which claims to support the family whilst implementing policies which go directly against the interest of women and children, feminism will only survive if it is seen to be defending the interests of children as well as women. In this way Tory rhetoric about the family will be exposed and a mass movement of women against government policies can be developed.

Mass action

A movement's ability to develop forms of mass action is crucial not only because of the power such action can have but also because of the confidence it can generate in the movement itself. Without it demoralisation can easily take over, particularly when the government of the day is set on a course of action in total opposition to the aims of the movement. There must be ways of showing that there is widespread support. One of the problems of the women's liberation movement is that often the knowledge of its influence has been confined to the women directly involved within it. The fact that they have taken many of its ideas and methods into other organisations like trade unions and campaigning groups has not always been apparent.

Where mass action in support of one of the demands of the women's movement, the defence of abortion rights, has been organised it has been successful in both achieving its aims and demonstrating a very wide basis of support in and outside the labour movement. What is needed now are other initiatives like the Women's Right to Work Festival that can mobilise large numbers of women as well as the labour movement in opposition to the attacks being mounted. Small-scale localised action is no longer sufficient.

The support of the labour movement will only be mobilised if there is an active campaign to oppose divisive and anti-feminist attitudes within it. This will only happen if more men on the Left resist the trend towards seeing feminist demands as expendable in the current difficult period.

A democratic alternative

Resisting current attacks, however difficult a task, is not enough on its own and probably will not succeed unless alternative policies that relate to the present and an alternative philosophy that makes sense to masses of women and men can be offered. Whilst the Left's alternative economic strategy, as a set of economic policies, is an important advance, the fact that it has nothing directly to say to women is a major weakness. There is as yet no recognition that major structural changes will be necessary for social and economic progress to mean something genuine for women.

The alternative strategy will have to tackle the whole relationship between men's and women's work and between work and home. It is not enough to say that the economy will be reflated and more employment created. Steps must also be taken to equalise employment opportunities for men and women. This will depend ultimately on reducing hours of work to make it possible for the present division between part-time and full-time employment to be gradually eliminated. In the shorter term moves in this direction could be made by reducing the hours that parents (fathers as well as mothers) are required to work as well as introducing parental rights to paid leave for family sickness. Positive discrimination will also be needed to break down the occupational segregation of men and women.

In committing itself to an elimination of some of the gross inequalities in Britain today the Left as yet has nothing to say on the inequalities that exist between men and women. Inequality is structured into not only the wage payment system but also into taxation and social security. It is no use responding to these issues by merely pointing out how far removed the Left alternative must be from a society in which the community principle of 'from each according to his/her ability, to each according to his/her need' can operate. If genuine egalitarianism is our long-term aim, there must be steps, however small, in the short term that can be taken towards it. If none can be found then doubt will necessarily be cast upon the Left's long-term aims.

New priorities

Given the pace at which British industry has been declining, any Left government that came to power in the future would be likely to inherit an extremely weak industrial base lacking the capacity to expand quickly to provide goods for private consumption. Any reflation that takes place would depend initially to a large extent on expanding public services and the social wage whilst increases in take-home pay would be limited. This would provide the opportunity for expanding many services that would be of particular benefit to women, e.g. nurseries and other forms of childcare. It is therefore crucial that the Left's plans take account of criticisms of existing services that have been made by feminists, and by workers in the public sector. Alternative plans must be more than a commitment to restore cuts. They must highlight what changes in priorities are required and indicate how services can be democratised.

There are many other issues that a democratic alternative strategy would need to tackle in order to satisfy women's aspirations, many of them concerned with attitudes and values rather than economic changes. The alternative strategy will have to be more than a set of economic policies. It will also need to embody a political philosophy concerned with transforming relationships between men and women at work, in the home and in all democratic organisations. Such a strategy will only emerge if the women's movement is actively involved in its development.

This will only happen if the Left can overcome its tendency to see the women's movement as a luxury in the present crisis period. Without the support of the women's movement it will go on failing to reach the mass of women. To get that support will require positive steps to involve women more effectively in decision-making and the development of strategy. Equally, without the support of the Left and the labour movement, and willingness to examine its own weaknesses, the women's movement will also find itself increasingly isolated and ineffective. If an alliance of this kind can be developed it will represent a powerful political force capable not just of resisting Thatcherism but also of showing masses of women and men that the Left has the only credible democratic alternative strategy to put in its place.

Notes

1. Hurstfield, Jennifer, 'Part-time pittance', in *Low Pay Review*, no. 1, June 1980.

2. Hakim, Catherine, 'Occupational segregation', *Department of Employment Research Paper*, no. 9, November 1979.

3. Elias, Peter, 'Labour supply and employment opportunities for women', in *Economic Change and Employment Policy*, Robert M. Lindley (ed.), 1980.

4. 'Communication Studies and Planning Ltd, Information technology in the office: the impact on women's jobs', Equal Opportunities Commission, 1980.

5. 1981 Census of Employment, *Employment Gazette*, December 1982.

6. *General Household Survey*, 1980.

7. McNay, Marie, and Pond, Chris, 'Low pay and family poverty', *Study Commission on the Family*, 1980.

8. *Cambridge Economic Policy Review*, April 1981, p. 41.

9. Power, Susan, 'Opinion column', *Sunday Times*, 28 December 1980.

10. Campbell, Beatrix, 'Women: Not What They Bargained For', in *Marxism Today*, March 1982.

11. *Guardian*, 6 November 1979.

12. Campbell, Beatrix, and Coote, Anna, *Sweet Freedom*, 1982.

6 Sex and Sexuality

Introduction

There has not been much internal debate about sexuality in the past three years, although two interesting anthologies have been published[1] which include articles by feminists on subjects that five to ten years ago would perhaps have been discussed only in internal publications. Women are now prepared, it seems, to make public issues they would previously only have discussed with other feminists. But this move into the public arena has left a gap in debates internal to the women's liberation movement that has yet to be filled. Articles published in, and written for, books do more to sum up particular positions than to feed into and stimulate debate.

What are the reasons for the lack of debate in the women's movement about our sexuality? Has the demand for the right to a self-defined sexuality meant that women have not been looking critically at their sexual practice? Has sex been relegated once more to the private sphere? Is it simply that other issues seem more important? Is the silence of heterosexual women a defence against criticisms that they have received in the past from lesbians who see men as the enemy and heterosexual practice as a form of collusion? If so, why?

In fact, talk around lesbian sexuality was briefly opened up at the conference on Lesbian Sex and Sexual Practice held in London in April 1983. This conference was called partly to forestall the kind of bitterly polarised debate that has taken place in the United States and in Europe around the issue of lesbian sado-masochism – between those who see sado-masochism as an essentially personal yet radical practice, and those who see it as perpetuating forms of dominance and submission only too prevalent in the heterosexual norm. The conference did open up discussion around the positive aspects of lesbian sexuality, and certainly no comparable exchange has taken place among heterosexual or bisexual feminists. In the past, much discussion went on at the overcrowded 'sexuality' workshops at conferences, which were sometimes the sole reason for a day's gathering.

Over the last ten years sexuality has been written about

predominantly by white women in their twenties and thirties – a debate that has grown out of the painful and often difficult attempts to make the personal political in the early consciousness-raising groups.

But again, as in other areas, the dominant voice has been challenged recently, and while we notice that there has been much less internal debate on sexuality than previously, a tradition has now been established for women to speak about their own sexuality more publicly than would before now have been possible.

Note

[1] *Sex and Love*, ed. Cartledge & Ryan, The Women's Press, 1983; *The Left and the Erotic*, ed. Phillips, Lawrence & Wishart, 1983.

JUDITH WILLIAMSON

Seeing Spots

First published in *City Limits*, February/March 1983

Despite all our troubles, we live in a time of great discovery.

In each of the last four decades, a book has been published that has greatly altered our understanding and knowledge about human sexuality. The pioneering works of Kinsey, Masters and Johnson, and Hite are about to be succeeded in the 1980s by *The G Spot and Other Recent Discoveries about Human Sexuality*. Never before have the facts been explained so thoroughly and convincingly, within the context of other sexual discoveries throughout history. Scientific and statistical evidence is included to substantiate the pioneering work of the authors . . . Bound to be widely read and hotly argued, *The G Spot* is the perfect guide for millions of people who want to explore further the pleasures of their sexuality.

Thus runs the jacket blurb; and inside, the authors' own message:

This book is about important newly discovered facts that are crucial to our understanding of how human beings function sexually. We believe that the information presented here can be used to help millions of women and men lead more pleasurable and satisfying lives and avoid a good deal of unnecessary suffering and frustration.

In this one field, at least, the endless red carpet of Progress unfurls faster than we can run down it, discovery succeeding discovery on the path to true 'understanding and knowledge about human sexuality'. For those of us who have grown up under the artificial light of positivism, believing that science and society march forward into the future hand in hand like the children in the Start-Rite ad, there is still one area where technology, medicine and statistical logic can offer riches, in the midst of general devastation. That area is physically small, but in the alchemy of science, its power and effects are magically limitless. It appears to be, on the one hand, a small area the size of a bean located on the inside wall of the vagina, and also, simultaneously, 'sexuality', that mystical substance denoted by a word which only came into existence in the nineteenth century.

Evangelism

That access to 'human sexuality' should be afforded through such a small and specific spot is a mystery to unravel later. But as long as we understand 'sexuality' to be as old as the hills, and only our understanding and knowledge of it to be new, we miss the point that in the modern era, 'sexuality' has been set up precisely *to be understood*. The relatively recent use of the word itself shows that it is a particular *concept* of sex which characterises our own time, not the revealing of sex itself which, after all, has always been known to people.

For what is so interesting about these twentieth-century 'discoveries' about sexuality – a context in which this new book quite rightly places itself – is not the actual findings, which are always either statistical or clinical, but the evangelical nature of their demystifying, in fact the belief that they are indeed demystifying anything. A mystique is created in the very act of ostentatiously knocking it down. A glance over the last few issues of *Cosmopolitan* – a key product in this era – shows this most simply: 'Sex myths exploded' (what myths?); 'Sex – the new realism' (what was the old idealism?); 'How I stopped worrying and put sex into perspective' (*were* you worrying?); and finally, the ultimate modern dictate, 'Be true to your own sexuality'. The real point about this endless, obsessive speech about sex is that it claims over and over again to destroy some previous notion, it is a knowledge that parades a cast-off ignorance before it like a shadow. Our society speaks insistently of what it doesn't speak of, relentlessly finding things that no one had lost in the first place.

And the territory of the great march forward into sexual knowledge always seems to be the *female* body. It is *our* bodies the pioneers search for clues into 'the understanding of human sexuality' – yet another case of 'they've got it, she wears it'. Far more revealing than anything *The G Spot* could reveal about our bodies is the claim that:

these findings constitute an important step in demystifying

Freud's 'dark continent', which is not quite as dark as it was when he coined that phrase in connection with female sexuality one hundred years ago. But much more research remains to be done.

The missionary zeal with which this colonisation of the dark continent takes place is one which holds up a light, precisely to reveal darkness; an empire on which the sun never sets, but is always rising. Maybe the dark continent is no longer 'quite as dark' – but there can be no slacking, 'much more remains to be done'.

So what are the new facts that further this cause? The G spot itself, called after Ernst Grafenberg who 'discovered' it in the 1940s, is a small, invisible area of sexual sensitivity 'usually located about halfway between the back of the pubic bone on the front of the cervix . . . the exact size and location vary. It lies deep within the vaginal wall . . .' – like the Sleeping Beauty, waiting for Prince Science to awaken it from centuries of oblivion.

The clitoris, located outside the body, is easy for every woman to discover and enjoy by herself. The G spot, located inside the anterior wall of the vagina, is more difficult for a woman to find on her own.

But why now? The G spot was not, in fact, 'discovered' but only cashed in on, in the 1980s. The particular significance it acquires in this book comes from its association with the 'dramatic discovery' of female ejaculation. The G spot is found to be the equivalent of the male prostate gland, and its stimulation produces an ejaculation similar to men's. The excitement of finding this analogy also hands us something we might not have felt – that we were missing something because we were different. Now we know we are up to scratch: we have an equivalent for the penis (the clitoris) and the prostate (the G spot) and we can also come like the boys. The relief of the specialists at finding these precise analogies measures the unease, perhaps, aroused by sexual *difference*. But for women, the endless reassurances which accompany each 'discovery' are merely the gift-wrapping for more anxieties. It is *perfectly normal* to ejaculate a quantity of fluid through the urethra in orgasm – but what if one *doesn't*? The sexual tasks pile up like homework on a Sunday night.

Enlightenment

The authors claim that 'the G spot is what specifically frees us from the either/or thinking of past decades', i.e. the clitoral *vs.* vaginal orgasm debate. They begin the book with a tour through Freud, Kinsey, Masters and Johnson and others, leading up to their own discovery as if on an inevitable escalator to enlightenment:

> . . . these four discoveries, the Grafenberg spot, female ejaculation, the importance of pelvic muscle tone and the continuum of orgasmic response, unify the findings of the Freudians and other sex researchers into an understandable and consistent whole. Our dilemma is resolved. We now have a new synthesis that validates the experience of both vaginal and clitoral orgasm.

They parade their work as the solution to an enormous dilemma. (*Our* dilemma?) But why was it a dilemma in the first place? In claiming to solve it, they actually confirm that there *was* a problem to be solved – the 'problem' of the female orgasm. Although *The G Spot* is so superbly liberal in allowing both sides of the debate to be true, it also confirms the categories of clitoral/vaginal orgasm even further than before, with its diagrams showing the difference between the 'Tenting' (clitoral) and 'A-Frame' (G spot) effects – which make one's vagina sound like a camp-site.

The point about the clitoral/vaginal argument, whether seen from one side or the other, or 'both', is that it presupposes an incredible faith in the truth of scientific categorisation – a truth which one would think would be questionable simply on account of its so frequent up-dating. It is a strange assumption that we need our experience of orgasm validated by research, as if it were not valid on its own. Clearly there is an enormous range of sexual experiences, and obviously sex feels different having something inside you. *The G Spot* mistakes trying to name the wheel for inventing it.

This is exemplified in the opening chapter, where the authors remind us that Kinsey *et al.*

> certainly brought into the open a whole range of human behaviour that had previously been discussed only in whispers behind closed doors, if at all.

Oh, how they love those whispers, which confirm their own imagined shout! Those closed doors, which they believe they are the first to open. But historically, this is nonsense. Sexual theories sold well long before the twentieth century. A popular sex manual, bizarrely titled *Aristotle's Masterpiece*, which ran through hundreds of editions over the sixteenth to eighteenth centuries, was most graphic about the identification of the clitoris as 'the seat of venereal pleasure' in women, and the female capacity for multiple orgasms, and such works as this were, as an eighteenth-century observer wrote, 'sold openly on every stall'.

No, what is modern is the idea that sex is such an explosive subject.

> Three times in this century, great pioneers in the field of human sexuality have shocked, informed and transformed our world. The people responsible for these seismic changes are Sigmund Freud, Alfred Kinsey and the team of Masters and Johnson.

And this seismic shock – 'Tenting', perhaps – is nothing to the global, 'A-Frame' orgasm triggered by *The G Spot*. Its main selling point is not, in fact, its discoveries, but the controversy and violent storms it claims to have already aroused. The publishers themselves suggest that the truth of the argument is far less important than its impact:

> As expected, publication of *The G Spot* has set off fireworks amongst sexologists – some wholeheartedly agree with the existence of the spot, whilst others fault the authors' research. One thing however is quite certain – no other book has ever prompted such a response from the public.

The repeated emphasis on this flood of response carries over-tones not only of sexual eruption, but also of the confessional, in which 'hundreds of case histories and personal testimonies' pour through the grille to our high priests of modern sexuality. Sex and confession have always been intimately linked, but with *The G Spot* this is hardly metaphorical: one of the authors, John D. Perry, MDiv, PhD is 'an ordained minister, psychologist and sexologist, specialising in vaginal myography and other innovative applications of bio-feedback, the inventor of the Electronic Perineometer which measures the tone and health of pelvic muscles'.

The chapter devoted to Minister Perry's device, headed 'The Importance of Healthy Pelvic Muscles', suggests it is a moral duty to keep your pubococcygeus muscles in tip-top shape through constant vigilance:

> You can encourage yourself by placing some kind of reminder where you will see it. For example, affix a brightly coloured dot to your briefcase, the telephone, the refrigerator, a clock or lamp. Every time you see the dot, contract your PC muscle several times.

Then there is the case history of an extremely religious woman whose husband

> threatened to get a divorce if she did not get medical help for her weak muscles. According to the therapist 'she was the best patient I ever treated. She was literally motivated by the fear of Hell and Damnation . . . She practised like mad . . .'

The peculiar machines for measuring the strength of your contractions look like a dog-bone attached to a battery charger and are on mail order at the end of the book, with the footnote: ' "Electronic Perineometer" (patents pending) is a trademark of Health Technology Inc. . . . "Femtone Isometric Vaginal Exerciser" is a trademark of J. & L. Feminine Research Center . . . "The Vagette 76" is a trademark of Myodynamics Inc. . . .', and so on. There is money to be made from pelvic contractions.

Think positive

The obsession with sex as health follows directly from Reich and his excessive belief in the social power of orgasms. But it takes on a sinister edge here, since 'undiagnosed chronic pelvic tension . . . can also contribute to more serious problems' like, guess what, cancer, the punishment of our time for a failure to THINK POSITIVE. Your *attitude* is all-important: *The G Spot* bullies with the voice of a games mistress or brisk nurse. It prescribes sexual healing as if it were a form of Savlon.

For the most striking aspect of the whole G spot enterprise (and others like it) is the way it manages to de-eroticise sex. Our bodies become a form of fruit-machine, to be played on for pleasure: women can have different kinds of orgasms, multiple orgasms, plateaux, climaxes, ejaculations, you name it. But how about desire? – without which the G spot is as useful as a hole in the head, and which, equally, can turn the nape of your neck or the back of your hand into a sexual explosion. But it is always as if men have desire. Women have 'pleasure' – usually given by a man. You can bet that hordes of heterosexual couples will be up all night searching for *her* G spot, not *his* prostate gland (which the book also locates).

Underlying the very earnestness of this search are two mistakes. The first is a tendency to overestimate the power of sexuality, which in recent times has taken on a pseudo-radical role. In modern jargon sexuality 'frees' us; it has become part of a discourse of 'liberation' which makes repression, rather than oppression, the enemy of human happiness. But is 'sexuality' really the arena in which our well-being is determined in the power-structures of modern societies? And if, indeed, we overestimate its power, what effect does this have? What is the function of an ideology that keeps everyone looking for the meaning of life up their own or someone else's vagina?

But the second mistake is the assumption that 'sexuality' can be conjured up through anatomical locations: the G spot plays the part of Aladdin's lamp, with female sexuality as the genie. The whole drive of books like this is one that simultaneously sets up 'sexuality' as unfathomable, while purporting to fathom it through de-sexualised clinical information. When will they stop searching our bodies for new sources of pleasure, and allow us desire?

ANON

Grab Yourself a Hunk

First published in *Shocking Pink*, no. 1

The aim of every young girl aged between eight and twenty is to grab herself a guy. Why is this? The answer is simple: they are told that this is how the normal, average young lady behaves. Unfortunately, no one has yet told them that there is no such thing as a normal young lady.

The first signs of the Miss Average syndrome begin when the girl in question starts to spend several hours at a time in front of the mirror, combing her hair and trying to catch her image out by jerking erratically and clicking her fingers at odd moments to the music on her radio. Then the usual symptoms follow – the avid collection of certain magazines which shall remain nameless, a nervous giggling when any one of the male sex over twelve is present. This syndrome progresses to a nervous fever until the girl may spend up to two hours in front of the mirror every day, making herself up to go out to the shops.

Soon after the girl decides that she must find a hang-out where she can meet boys and, as suggested by one of her favourite nameless magazines, she picks on the disco. Discos are the most active abomination since the Mafia-controlled speakeasys. They are generally run by 'do-gooders' of the local community who hire themselves a DJ, advertise in the local paper and make themselves a tidy profit, better than any church bazaar, for the new village hall by charging a 'small' entrance fee. For this small fee, the girl enters the disco to the sound of pulsating music and gyrating multi-coloured lights. In her disco-dazzling boob-tube the girl joins the crowd of boogieing adolescents already grinding their hips and shaking as much or as little as possible. Anyone standing around the room not dancing is referred to as a 'wallflower'. The 'wallflowers' spend their time hoping that they will not have to make fools of themselves. But don't think for a moment that these girls do not want a boy of their very own. They need to prove themselves as much as their friends.

This nervous fever is due to the lack of interesting light reading available to this group. The only magazines which do fill this gap in the market are written by adults. Is this why teenagers are forced to react to boys in this way?

BRONWEN

Life is Just a Phase I'm Going Through

First published in *Spare Rib*, no. 115, February 1982

In retrospect, I've always known I was a lesbian, since I was about four – that's when I first remember 'falling in love' with a woman. I kept on falling in love with them from then on. I did get a crush on a boy when I was about ten – except he looked like a girl, and anyway, I was still into various women at the same time. At about twelve, I went to my mother and said, 'Do you think I'm a lesbian?' I was beginning to think it was a bit strange that I never fell in love with boys. My poor mother, who'd been thinking, 'I wonder if she's a lesbian?' said, 'Oh no, of course not, it's very normal at your age, most girls get those kind of crushes.'

About that time, around twelve or thirteen, when I was busy ignoring any of my own feelings for women, the idea of lesbianism actually made me feel sick. Because what I thought lesbians were was big butch women doing strange things, which didn't have anything to do with what I felt, or with any of the women I was falling in love with.

At fifteen I was having to deal with feelings for one of my women teachers – corny but true. I kept telling myself, 'This is just a crush, I'll grow out of it,' when in fact I didn't think she was 'wonderful' and 'unobtainable' – like a pop star or something – but felt very attracted to her, almost as an equal (except of course she was much older than me). At the same time I was noticing a couple of girls around the school and thinking, 'What *is* it about them?' One of them was in the fourth year. But – when you're in the fifth year, you don't speak to the years below unless it's to tell them not to do something, so I decided to speak to Melanie, the one who was in my year (but whom I'd never spoken to before, since it was such a big comprehensive). We got on straight away. So well that I went to her house that weekend. We went for a walk while I was there, and started talking really easily, as if we'd known each other for years.

She was telling me about a friend she had in London, called Fiona, talking a lot about her – she seemed to be really fond of her. Eventually I said, 'Sounds like you really love her.' She didn't bat an eyelid, just said, 'Yeah, I do.' I was struck by how easily I'd come out with the question, and how easily she'd replied. Normally I wouldn't have said anything like that – anything which would give someone a chance to say, 'Ugh, what do you think I am, a lessie?'

The next thing I was going to ask was, 'Do you get a chance to see her often?' but for some reason I paused after, 'Do you . . .?' Almost instantly she said, 'Go on, why don't you say it?' I was completely confused – I really didn't know what she was getting at. She said, 'What you mean is, do I sleep with her?' 'I wasn't going to ask *that*!' I was genuinely shocked. 'Oh,' she said. There was a painful silence. 'Do you?' I tried to make it sound casual. 'Yes,' she said, trying to be equally casual. Aha! I thought. *That's* what it is about Melanie . . .

The fact that I now knew that Melanie and Fiona were *lovers* crystallised a lot of the things that had been churning about in my head, but a lot of the confusion continued. I now knew for sure I was a lesbian, but I still couldn't identify myself with the 'popular' image of lesbians wanting to be like men. I certainly didn't want to be like a man, and neither did Melanie. Maybe I was bisexual . . . and so the confusion continued.

As a result, I did eventually start having a relationship with the girl in the fourth year, Anne. (I figured, *that's* what it must be about her, too.) That makes it sound dead easy, but in fact it took months of scheming and plotting. However, after the initial euphoria had worn off, I realised that in many ways our problems had only just begun. OK, so we were really into each other, but where could we meet, and how could we meet without people finding out? – because obviously no one must. That hit me very hard – if anyone found out we'd both be in a lot of trouble. I felt locked in some kind of sick joke, and there didn't seem to be a way out. Suddenly I knew what it was like to be 'queer'. Maybe Tom Robinson had a point.

Whenever we did find somewhere to meet, we'd be in terror all the time that we'd be discovered. Once we met at the end of a very dark street, where there were no houses, and we were pretty sure we wouldn't be seen. What we didn't realise was that we weren't the only ones to think it was a good meeting place. We'd been there about fifteen minutes when we saw two friends of mine, a boy and a girl, coming up the street from the other end. We just froze. Fifth years didn't *talk* to fourth years, let alone go up dark alleys with them in the middle of the night, let alone ones of your own sex. How were we going to get out of this one? In the event, we didn't have to, as they stopped a few feet away from us, and because it was so dark, and they were otherwise occupied, they never saw us. I had real trouble trying not to laugh. The whole situation was crazy. Things like that happened all the time.

Meanwhile, I'd started talking to another fourth-year girl, Sue, who gradually hinted that she thought she might be a lesbian, but was going through all the same confusions that I had done. She wrote to me, saying that talking to me had helped her to sort out a lot in her mind, and that she now knew she was a lesbian. I wrote back to her, saying there was nothing wrong with being a lesbian, in fact it was wonderful (OK, so I was over the top – I was trying to cheer her up) and making it quite clear that I was one too. And then her mother found my letter. And ran waving it in screaming blue fits up to the school. However, I knew nothing about that, and so I was surprised to be called to my housemistress's office. This was right in the middle of my O-levels, so I thought that's what it might be about. Wrong. She asked me if I didn't think I was seeing too much of Sue. Again, total confusion reigned: I'd seen her exactly twice out of school, when she'd come round to borrow some records. Did she mean Anne? Shit, what *did* she mean? This conversation went on for a few minutes at completely cross purposes, until she finally asked me if I was coming back in the sixth year to do my A-levels. She knew I was – what was she getting at? She said that she felt it would be better if I didn't, and that everyone (who was everyone?) felt that I'd be better off doing them at technical college. This was in mid-June – I couldn't possibly have registered for college then – you have to register in February, she knew that. I said all that, and said I wanted to come back to school, anyway, as a lot of my friends were. In that case, she replied, she'd have to write to my mother.

Before she got a chance, I went home and talked to my mother myself, having found Sue first, and realised what it was all about. I was really pissed off when I found out. So was my mother. I'd already told her I was a dyke (she'd said, 'Oh, I know *that*, dear' – I'd given it such a build-up I think she thought I was going to tell her I was pregnant or something), and I was luckier than most, she was (still is) totally supportive. She phoned my housemistress, who said they didn't want me back. (I was a 'disruptive influence on the younger girls' blah blah. No one mentioned lesbians.) It seemed easier not to fight it. I didn't feel I'd be exactly welcome if I went back.

I used my extra year to do a secretarial course, and planned to take my A-levels the next year, although I never did in the end. It seemed a bit pointless by that time. But at least I wasn't wondering if I was a lesbian or not any more.

Fury Over Bid to Make Sex Under Sixteen Legal

First published in *Shocking Pink*, no. 1

About a year ago a report by the National Council for One-Parent Families came out, calling for the abolition of the age of consent laws for heterosexuals. This led to some wild reporting in the press.

You probably know that under these laws it is illegal for a man to have intercourse with a woman if she is under sixteen years of age. I think this is ridiculous and am against the age of consent laws for both heterosexuals and homosexuals, because I believe that all people who give their consent to sex, both young and old, should have the right to determine their own sex lives.

At the moment, if a woman under sixteen decides to enter into a sexual relationship, it means she can be placed in care on the grounds that she is in 'moral danger', to herself because of her – wait for it – 'abnormal sexual appetite'.

It is only the man who can be prosecuted, not the woman, as the law says that whether she wanted sex or not is irrelevant. We, as women, are not taken seriously. When these laws were thought up, our sexual desires were ignored, in fact it was thought that we didn't have any. An example of this is that there is no age of consent for lesbians as Queen Victoria didn't think it was possible for women to have fulfilling sexual relationships together.

Maybe a few of you are thinking that this law protects young women, for example from rape. In fact, there are very few prosecutions under this law and when they do happen they are against young people who have *both* consented.

I talked to some women, all of whom are under sixteen, about what *they* thought about the laws:

It's stupid, no one takes any notice anyway, if they want to

179

sleep with people they will do it regardless of the law.
Have you slept with a boy?
Yes.
Are you taking any precautions?
No.
Why not?
'Cause I don't want to go to the doctor as he'd tell my Mum.

It's all right but people should be allowed to do what they want, they shouldn't get prosecuted.
Do you think that the law would stop you?
Probably, but I don't want to sleep with anyone yet anyway.
If the laws were abolished, would it make any difference?
No, people do it when they want, but I think that when they do they should be able to get contraception.

I don't think that it is a good idea.
Why?
Everyone should be able to do what they want to.
Have you ever slept with a boy?
No.
Is it the law that's stopped you?
No, I just don't want to do it.
You think it should be lowered to twelve? Why not get rid of it altogether?
If it was any lower people would get forced into it.
Why?
'Cause men are men.
Why twelve?
'Cause you know what you want at that age.

These laws are a result of a society which punishes consenting young people, while turning a blind eye to a lot of cases of rape and violence.

We as young women get the worst of it all round. Some doctors won't give contraception to women under sixteen years, and a lot of young women are frightened to go and obtain contraception, or to tell a doctor they are pregnant in case the doctor tells their parents.

I believe that all women should have the right to abortion on demand, free contraception, and we should be able to get info. on these things at any age.

I'm not saying that we should all be having sex before we are sixteen. What I am saying, however, is that at the moment the law decides when we should have sex, *not us*; the law says when we should get contraception, *not us*; the law says whether we can have an abortion, *not us*.

We should not have our sexual relationships made illegal and should not be punished for them. We must have the right to determine our own sex lives.

SANDRA McNEILL

Age of Consent

First published in *York Feminist News*

Power imbalance

The Home Office are reviewing the age of consent, currently sixteen. A 'liberal' lobby is intent on persuading them to reduce/abolish it. We as feminists must consider the issues involved. What will the consequences be? Who will benefit?

We know there is a power imbalance between men and women in society. Men are the dominant group. One of the ways they benefit from this is that their views, their definitions, are seen to be 'everyone's' – as feminists we must fight to change that. Because men and women are not equal, individual men have advantages, in status and money, over individual women.

We also know that adults as a group have power, physical, economic and psychological, over children and young people. Thus an individual adult has authority/power over a younger person. (We may wish this was not so but the way to change it is *not* to pretend it does not exist.)

I believe a mutual non-oppressive relationship is the only base for sexual relations, otherwise the dominant person is exploiting the other. What chance is there in this society that a sexual relationship between an adult male and a young woman or child will be mutual and non-exploitative of the woman?

Age of consent

Currently women under sixteen are considered unable to consent to sex. So a man who has sex with them is guilty of unlawful sexual intercourse (USI). When a woman under sixteen does in fact 'consent' *she* is not breaking the law; the man who has sex with her is. Reducing the age of consent means therefore reducing the age of women men can *legally* have sex with.

Age of consent refers to sexual intercourse, defined in law as penetration of the vagina by the penis. Men can also be convicted of indecent assault, and the penalties for that are higher if the woman is below the age of consent. This does *not* mean that boyfriends of women under sixteen get convicted for 'heavy petting' (mutual masturbation). Consent has been most clearly defined in the rape laws. It is not rape if a woman is coerced into agreeing to penetration by threats, except threats to her life. Threats such as 'losing a job' or losing a boyfriend do not count. If a woman gives in to such threats, she has consented to sex.

How does the law affect men?

It does not affect males under fourteen, as they are not *legally* capable of intercourse. And the law-enforcers (police/courts) are not interested in young (male) teenagers 'experimenting with sex' as they call it. The only boys convicted are those having sex with even younger women – under thirteen. In practice, *the law is only concerned with older men – adults – who have sex with women under sixteen*. And although the penalties are potentially the same for all men over eighteen, in practice the larger the age gap the heavier the sentence.[1]

I believe it is not so much the threat of prison that deters adult men from coercing young women into sex, but fear of social disapproval. Such disapproval will go if the age of consent is abolished/reduced.

What effects will the law changing have on women?

(1) Rape. We do not know what proportion of the cases that reach court are due to parents objecting to an older man having a sexual relationship with their daughters, and how many are in fact rape cases. Under what is known as plea-bargaining, a man may agree to plead guilty to a lesser charge rather than stand trial for rape.

The victims often agree to this, especially if young, to avoid the harrowing experience of a rape trial where it is notoriously difficult to prove non-consent. In the case of women under sixteen, the man pleads guilty to USI.

Such cases seldom receive press attention. One I do recall from California, where the law is similar to ours, involved ageing film director Roman Polanski. A woman of fourteen was invited to one of his parties by a friend of his. He told her she would meet film stars, which of course she did. She also met Polanski. He dragged her into a bedroom and raped her. Accused of rape, he threatened that all his friends would say she had consented, so she would lose and her name become public, etc. The prosecution continued until he agreed to plead guilty to 'statutory rape' (equivalent to USI).[2]

If the age of consent is lowered many young women will have to face the trauma of a rape trial who currently do not, as their assailants plead guilty to the lesser charge.

(2) Incest. Incest laws only cover fathers, brothers, uncles and grandfathers. They do not cover stepfathers. With increasing divorce and remarriage, more and more young women have stepfathers, that is, a male in the power/authority position of a father but legally entitled to have sex with her if she is over the age of consent. The lowering of the age will make many women – not entitled or able to leave home – more vulnerable.

Once over the age of consent, the woman as well as the man (e.g. father), is legally guilty of incest. If the age is lowered the young women involved will be prosecuted too, so they will be less likely to report it, and will become more vulnerable to incest.

(3) Lowering age of consent and girls being 'taken into care'. These are not, as one might suppose, directly related. The Sexual Law Reform Society, for example, has proposed that the age of *consent* be lowered to fourteen, but the age for 'taking into care' be raised to eighteen. Now we all know it is only girls who are 'taken into care' for having sex, not boys. So this proposal means that *any* man, of any age, could have sex legally with a woman aged fourteen to eighteen, but the woman would be liable to be taken into care if she consented. (Double standard alive and well in Sex Law Reform Society.) To advocate retention of the age of consent does *not* imply we agree with the current practice of putting young women into care but never of course the boys, because of 'promiscuity'.[3]

What proposals are there for changing the law?

(1) Abolition. The International Marxist Group, Gay Activist Alliance and the National Council for Civil Liberties (the latter 'in principle') want the age of consent abolished. Yes folks, just because your four-year-old daughter has a sexuality that means she can consent to intercourse with adult men. Or as the Paedophile Information Exchange put it, vaginas can stretch wider than most people think. In fact this is medical nonsense as doing that to a child can cause bone dislocation, haemorrhage and death. But the principle seems to be, if it's big enough for a penis she can be fucked. Here we meet again male definitions of sexuality. *They* define having a sexuality as wanting 'penetration of the vagina by the penis'.

(2) Abolition in law – but the courts will decide, case by case. The National Council for One-Parent Families have suggested *no fixed age*. That is, every young woman concerned would be individually subject to examination/cross-examination, to see if she was mature enough to have consented (something not advocated for driving tests) – not something any adult would wish imposed on themselves before being able to do anything. This would be particularly humiliating in a rape case. To get off, the rapist would first of all argue she was mature enough to have consented (she would have to 'prove' she was not) before going on to make the usual allegation that she did consent, thus putting the victim on trial twice.

(3) Home Office Report on Consent and Sentencing. Currently higher penalties are imposed for USI with a woman under fourteen. This report considers this might be reduced to twelve since 'a large number of twelve-year-old girls have already attained puberty and may not only be willing to take part in sexual activity but may actually initiate it'. Again, note the equation, this time between having a period and desire for 'sexual activity'. (A coy phrase used to disguise what they mean – penetration.) They also claim when the age of consent was sixteen that was the *average* age of puberty, which I doubt. But anyway, what basis is that? If puberty (i.e. menstruation) comes on at ten does that mean a ten-year-old wants sex – with an adult male?

(4) Other bodies have suggested it be lowered to fourteen. What arguments are there for its continued retention at sixteen? If we are agreed it must be an arbitrary age, rather than subject women to the humiliation of proving their maturity/immaturity, *why sixteen not fourteen*?

(i) Sixteen is when one can leave school, and thus earn an independent income. Before then a woman is dependent on her parents. She is at an extreme disadvantage versus men. She may be under direct control of a stepfather, and is more vulnerable to pressure from a teacher. Currently heavier sentences (i.e. prison) are reserved for those men 'in authority positions over the girl'. To reduce the age gives legal and social sanction to those men to exploit that authority.

(ii) Women will become more vulnerable to incest (see above) and liable to prosecution for it.

(iii) We must consider the effect this will have on *younger* women. Just as currently sex with a fourteen- to fifteen-year-old is viewed relatively lightly as being *just* under the age of consent ('I thought she was sixteen, Your Honour'), so, if it is reduced to fourteen, will sex with twelve- to thirteen-year-olds be seen. And just as sex with a twelve-year-old is seen as borderline between a serious offence, so will sex with a ten-year-old be seen. (Currently 19 per cent of USI with girls under thirteen is with a stepfather.)

(iv) Marriage. It is unlikely that sex will legally be allowed before marriage is. Thus the age of marriage will have to be reduced to fourteen.

(v) Prostitution. The 1885 law raising the age of consent from twelve to sixteen was introduced, as a result of feminist pressure, mainly because of prostitution. Fourteen years for the age of consent means legalising fourteen-year-old women becoming prostitutes, or, as we would put it, being coerced into sexually servicing men for money.

Conclusion

On balance I think we must conclude that the age of consent must stay where it is, at sixteen. We are fed up with men defining sex as penetration. We are fed up with male images of our sexuality as exemplified in porn mags and 'Page 3'. We have demanded the right to a self-defined sexuality – something we don't yet have. Is it in our interests for even younger women to come under more pressure from men to become their sexual servicers, than they already do?

Yes, having the age of consent at sixteen does inconvenience many young women: but many more will be more than inconvenienced if it is lowered.

Notes

1. *Sexual Offences, Consent and Sentencing*, Home Office Research Study, no. 54, HMSO, 1979.

2. Polanski skipped the country when given a six-month sentence.

3. Smart, Carol, *Women, Crime and Criminology, A Feminist Critique*, Routledge, Kegan Paul, 1976.

See also: *Working Paper on the Age of Consent*, Policy Advisory Committee on Sex Offences, HMSO, 1979; NCCL, Report 13, *Sexual Offences. Evidence to the Criminal Law Revision Committee*; *Pregnant at School*. National Council for One-Parent Families/Community Development Trust. From NCFOPF 255, Kentish Town Rd, London NW5.

MADHU PATEL

The Struggle to be Accepted as a Person

First published in *Spare Rib*, no. 136, November 1983

It is hard to survive as a woman and harder as a lesbian, but to be an Asian lesbian is much, much harder still.

I 'realised' my sexuality at sixteen, and suppressed my feelings due to confusion and life's prejudices. I went to a gay counsellor and talked over my feelings and inhibitions. I felt stronger and ready to cope, and realised what changes had to be made in order for me to lead the life that I wanted to lead. The first step was to accept my sexuality, the second was 'coming out'.

The loss of friends, noticing society's hostile attitude to gays (for instance, in the media), feeling hurt and guilty, made life difficult. I often asked myself, 'Why pick on me?' and though it helped to talk to another lesbian, my strong feelings often gave way to feeling weak and crumbled. At school they said that I was just going through a phase; others told me to think about it carefully as it was a big step to take, but no one really took me seriously. Some even joked that they had never known a gay person before!

Telling my parents

Losing friends at a time when I needed them most was very hard to take, and though I made new friends through gay clubs, it didn't help. The more I thought about it all the worse I felt; my feelings were churned about to suit other people, and the hardest part was yet to come – my parents. My parents are typical Asian parents, wanting the best for their daughter, especially as I was the only daughter they had, and I was the eldest in the family. They were in the process of arranging a marriage for me, and I got fed up of having to lie every time I wanted to go out, so it became urgent to tell them.

My father was told first as I can communicate better with him and feel close to him, and I'll never forget the look in his eyes. The look of failure, the fear of what people would say. He immediately thought that I was ill and arranged for me to see a psychiatrist through the family doctor. My mother was totally shattered; she cried for a month continually, not once looking me in the eyes or speaking to me. Their hopes of me being an ideal woman, getting married, having children and holding a respectable position in the community were shattered, and I had to pay for it. That terrible feeling of guilt will never leave me.

I was torn. What was I supposed to do? Should I return to their expectations or lead my life my way, or find a compromise? Why should I lead a dual life? Why should I 'change' for the benefit of others? Compromise seemed impossible.

I became more and more distanced from my family, those feelings of guilt kept creeping back and hurting, and every time I saw my parents I could see the hurt in their faces. I made my decision, I 'chose' to live my life my way – as a lesbian – and I started to explore the great big world. I went to various clubs to find companionship, but all I got was prejudice. I was seen as a museum piece, as if nobody had seen an Asian lesbian before. I was asked the same questions over and over again, 'How can you possibly be a lesbian, you're Asian?' and 'Does your family know?', 'What did they say?' and 'Are you going to have an arranged marriage?' and so on. By the end of the evening I felt very alone and isolated.

Making a fresh start

I felt it was time for me to leave all this and make a fresh start. I decided to come to London as I had the offer of a job and a place to stay. My parents were not pleased, but they did not try to stop me. I arrived in London in November 1982 and felt relieved to be away from all that had happened before, but this feeling did not last long. In the clubs in London I had to go through the same channels as I had had to go through in Birmingham. I was very unhappy but worked hard at the job and kept myself alive. The contract for the job ran out in April 1983 and I was jobless and homeless. I felt like going back to my parents but decided not to in the end, having thought about it a great deal.

I enjoy my independence in London and find it more of a challenge to live in new surroundings with new people. And all the time I am trying to find myself – which somehow got lost between Birmingham and London.

My parents are my biggest worry now. I think that I have found my meaning and purpose, things have settled down now and seem to be calm. I have found excellent accommodation in a lesbian shared house and I will soon be going to college.

I hope that other *Spare Rib* readers will learn something from my experience. I would also like to thank *SR* for putting me in touch with other Asian lesbians – so now I know that I am not the only one in the world!

LINDA BELLOS

For Lesbian Sex, Against Sado-Masochism

Paper for Lesbian Sex and Sexual Practice Conference, 1983

As a feminist I have found it relatively easy to write about what I don't like about male sexuality and more recently about lesbian sado-masochism. But it is far harder to talk positively about lesbianism. I suspect that the silence around the subject of positive aspects of lesbian sex has led many women, and particularly men, to accuse those of us involved in anti-male violence campaigns of being anti-sex. It should not have to be necessary for lesbian feminists to have to assert that they are into sex. But the fact is that if we remain silent, at least publicly, the only space to talk about sex is within the growing sado-masochism lobby.

I've had lots of arguments and discussions with other lesbians about books like *Coming to Power*, a book promoting lesbian sado-masochism. Most of the argument has centred on whether, because women are doing things with each other, those things like whipping, torture, bondage, etc. are different solely because it is women. Another highly arguable point is about power. Because sex is about power, then sado-masochism is argued to be only an extension of that power, and anyway, where do you draw the line?

In this paper I want to try and make some kind of distinction between sexual practice which is compatible with our feminism, and that which is not. I am not trying to lay down a 'line' or impose on other women what they should do or think. Instead I want to try, at least for myself, to understand what the difference is between the two, because I want to continue the fight against male violence and I don't like being confused about lesbian sado-masochism.

Sex and power

I think sex is about power, it is for me an exchange of power, making myself vulnerable, but also receiving another woman's vulnerability. Through sex I feel close to another woman, but if I

190

refuse to make myself vulnerable, by which I mean both an emotional openness and physical openness, I am playing a power-game with that woman. So it seems to me the sexual exchange that makes sense and is most satisfying is the one based on equality, each sharing and exchanging. Through my own experience of heterosexuality, and particularly years of marriage, I know that I don't want to do anything that resembles those years of sexual oppression and domination. If I wanted to be dominated, I could have stayed married. When I discovered lesbianism it was an amazing revelation to find a reciprocal love, sex which was at last equal, in a way which it never was – or at present under male supremacy – could be with a man. With other lesbians I questioned the things I did within sex, whether, for example, penetration was OK or not. There were lots of questions which for me were, and are, crucial about sex with women. But it's all very well having these private conversations; few of us have dared to make those ideas and answers public. I feel a personal reluctance to do so myself, but I feel I can't expect other women to do it if I'm not prepared to do it myself.

I don't think that it's the things that we do in sex, so much as the context that's important. My starting-point in saying that though is the assumption that I will not hurt another woman, or use sex to gain power over another woman, neither do I want to be hurt or have another gain power over me. If I thought sex was about rules of what you can do and can't do, apart from what I've just said about not abusing another woman, I don't personally think that I'd want to do it. I do not want to act out sex 'consciously', instead I want to respond to another woman. I feel that sex is created by two women, and each time it's different depending on how you each are feeling – happy, quiet, energetic, sad, depressed, or whatever. If I consciously had in my head a list of 'things' I could do, it seems to me that sex would become mechanical, and the 'things' – whatever they are – could be done with any woman, instead of that particular woman.

The 'acts' of sex themselves are, for me, hardly the point, since sex isn't just a thing – a list of activities. I do not want to make sex into an object, but instead I want, with another woman, to create it. If, out of joint feelings, we want to be gentle, we shouldn't feel ashamed that we are into 'Bambi' sexuality, as some gay men have called gentle sex. Similarly, if we want to be rough, then that doesn't make us into sado-masochists. If the context is love, respect, caring, then it seems to me it is OK. Many women have argued, particularly Pat Califia in an article, 'Sado-masochism and feminism', that sado-masochism is about an exchange of power, and many of the things that I have said above about sex. But there are different kinds of power, institutionalised power that already exists, like race, class, age, money, etc., as well as the power which a woman might have by her personality. There is the power that exists by making oneself vulnerable, but I wonder whether power is the right word to use to describe it.

Sado-masochism reintroduces institutionalised power into sex in order to get off on it – ritualising and eroticising it. If the power between women is roughly equal, e.g. they are both white, middle-class, then acting out those roles based on dominance and submission puts back the power imbalance that is missing. I would argue that it is the quality, or at least the belief that we are all equal, which is the basis of our lesbian feminism. Power imbalances do not have to be introduced into our sex to make it exciting.

Pat Califia describes sex which is based on acting out dominance and submission. She argues that it is equal because each woman has agreed in advance that she wants this, she has contracted into a situation freely. I don't want to get into the argument, are women being really free to want to be tortured, although I suspect that they are not. The point is that the proponents of sado-masochism see the acting out of fantasies based on dominance and submission as liberating. The scenarios she and others describe are of one woman acting the part of Nazi, the 'top', the other acting the part of Jew, the 'bottom'. One woman being master, another slave, etc. She claims that the acting out of these scenarios based on the fantasies most of us have is not harmful, it is only fantasy.

An essential part of the sado-masochism cult has been the codes for women who are into particular practices to indicate to each other that they are keen. The handkerchief code, where women wear different-coloured handkerchiefs to indicate, for example, that they are into fist-fucking, bondage or whipping. Which back pocket you wear your handkerchief in indicates whether you're into doing it, or having it done – whether you are top or bottom. I mention this because it shows me what is basically wrong with the whole sado-masochism argument, and how it is different from the lesbian sex that I want. The codes – and there are more presumably than the handkerchief one – allow women to separate sex from feelings towards another woman, all that becomes important is the particular act of sex, irrespective of whom you do it with. In other words you use another woman, even if she agrees to be used, in order to satisfy your own individual needs. For me that is exactly what men have always done to women, use us for their sexual gratification – turn us into objects on which they 'act out' their wishes.

The sex that sado-masochism promotes is a sex of limited responses. It is not spontaneously created by two women; if it was they wouldn't need to write books about it, or draw up elaborate codes. Neither would they form support groups to learn new acts to play. They are constructing a sexual practice which has been adopted directly from gay men, and before them heterosexual men. Where sado-masochism comes from is not exactly the point, although I can't ignore the fact that the Marquis de Sade, from whom the term sadism comes, and Sacher-Masoch were both aristocratic white men. The point is, what does sado-masochism do to us?

It allows us to exercise power in a way not allowed in any other aspect of our lives as women. It allows the masochist to indulge in feelings she has learned to enjoy because she is a woman – without guilt. Sado-masochism is about power, and so is the lesbian sex that I want. But sado-masochism is about the abuse of power: power which is itself the erotic charge. Those of us who are not biological determinists have always known that women can do the things that men do. We have argued that we don't want to. The sado-masochist lobby is telling us that we should want to. But I became a lesbian both in reaction to men, and, more importantly, because lesbianism was, and is, different. It was the positive alternative that lesbianism is that made me give up my heterosexual privilege. Sado-masochism seems the very opposite of an alternative to male sexuality, it is instead embracing it with open arms.

Is sado-masochism between women different from when it is done by men?

It is argued that the meaning of sado-masochism between lesbians is different from the male meaning. That because all women are relatively powerless, the acting out of fantasies, rather than repressing them, is liberating. Pat Galifia implies that sado-masochism is, in fact, a revolutionary practice for lesbians. It would be all too easy to dismiss this argument, but I think that it does have to be addressed.

Women are not the same as men, and when one woman, for example, is violent to another in a relationship it is not the same as when men are violent to us, although the woman violated might find it hard to believe. The violence *is* coming from somewhere different and I don't want to pretend that it is exactly the same. But because women do not have real power doesn't alter the reality of the inequality of power that exists between women. The scenarios which are acted out within sado-masochism are based on real situations – master/slave, Nazi/Jew, teacher/pupil. That power relationship hasn't gone away, but still exists. Women playing with them are making a mockery of real suffering.

Just because sex is the issue doesn't mean that we suspend all our objections to the abuse of power, or the trivialising if physical suffering. I might feel differently towards the whole issue of lesbian sado-masochism if I were not a black woman. I don't know. But seeing black women in bondage as part of a sex game never strikes me as amusing. Women may get an erotic charge from acting out Nazi/Jew scenes, but then so did the warders of Auschwitz and Belsen who tortured my relatives. It's not just my problem because I happen to be a black Jew. I am not a 'victim' of these oppressions, I want political responses to my objections, which are surely shared by other women?

As feminists most of us have challenged role-playing, we have also argued very strongly that we do not want to be dominated by men. It makes no sense to me to say I do want to be dominated by women. Either domination is wrong or it isn't. Sex is connected to the rest of the world, and if some lesbians are promoting a form of sexuality learned from men, which oppresses, we only reinforce their power. The meaning of one woman sexually dominating another, or of one woman wanting to be dominated, is different from when men do it to us, it comes from different places within us. We are not, after all, men, but the effect of sado-masochism on us must be to view other women as sexual objects.

Role-playing

I said earlier that I wanted, when making love with a woman, not to have a scenario, or pattern of 'things' to do that are called sex, but given my demand that sex is not based on pain or hurting, there are a range of responses to a woman I may feel, dependent on my mood. One way the responses could be described is as role-playing, either being passive or dominant. But is it role-playing? A role is a fixed, at least for the duration of the relationship, set way of acting. If, briefly, I feel that I want my lover to make love to me it doesn't follow that I am playing the role of the 'passive'. If, on the other hand, passivity was my only sexual response to my lover, then I would be role-playing. I would be stuck in the passive role, rather than exploring a range of sexual responses and actions. It seems to me that it is the fixed nature of roles that is wrong, but being sexually passive of itself may not be, if that's what I feel like at times. The same naturally goes for wanting to make love to your lover. It's only a problem if that's all you want to do. I'm not trying to prescribe what is 'correct' sexual behaviour amongst lesbian feminists, but instead clear up for myself the confusion I've felt about so-called role-playing.

The democratic mode, as I call it, is all very well, but if I did that all the time I would feel that I had restricted my responses to the one particular kind, so I no more want that than I do a fixed role.

Sex as part of our identity as lesbians

We don't need to be sexually involved with a woman to define ourselves as lesbians, but we do define ourselves in relation to sex with women. A lesbian is a woman who loves other women. Many lesbians, however, may never have had a sexual relationship with a woman due to a whole host of circumstances. They are no less lesbians for it. Or what about women who are celibate for years or months between relationships, do they cease to be lesbians in these periods? I suggest not.

Lesbianism, like heterosexuality, is more than just whom you sleep with. Being woman-identified, giving space and support to women, are parts of the things it means to be a lesbian. It is also about our life-styles. But being a lesbian does have quite a lot to do with sex. We do relate to each other sexually. I don't mean that we see all other lesbians as potential lovers, but many friendships are developed by having sexual relationships, and sharing the friends of lovers. I'm not suggesting that this is the only way we get to know other women. And anyway, sex is not simply a short-cut to friendship. There are some very positive things some of us get from sex, which many other lesbians get from women in other ways. Strength, validation, joy, pleasure, to name but a few. I don't want to feel guilty about enjoying sexual relationships, on the other hand I don't want to suggest that sex is the only thing that matters to me as a lesbian. It's just that I feel sex does play a part in how I am. I neither want to deny sex nor elevate it.

Passion

Trying to question our sexual practice as lesbian feminists doesn't mean for me that sex has to be dull and unexciting. I know nothing more exciting than getting to know a woman, both socially and sexually. The first tentative moves towards each other, each woman taking a step nearer to the other. And then, when the messages and signals are positively responded to, what is created is such an emotional intensity that often it feels unbearable. That I call passion, it comes from emotional honesty and openness. It is also dangerous and perhaps out of the danger of making yourself vulnerable to another woman comes the excitement. Not only the fear of rejection, but finding out whether you both want the same things. One of you wanting an uncommitted relationship, the other a more committed one, or both wanting the same thing.

Perhaps what I'm describing as an ideal is no more than a romantic illusion. It seems to me possible that two women can have similar needs and wishes and satisfy each other's needs in a relationship. It is possible because I know that I've done it. Whether it reproduces, or approximates, heterosexual, romantic love, I don't know. I feel it doesn't because I am not expecting all my needs to be met by a relationship with one woman, but that within the relationship there is an equality of need, and an equal ability to satisfy each other's needs.

I think that it is risky to admit emotional needs, in loving and being loved, but that risk is the price one pays for closeness and intimacy. We all have different needs and perhaps few other women share my particular needs so I'm not trying to lay down the law on what passion means. I can only speak for myself. But in reading the stuff on sado-masochism I suspect that some women are trying to put the excitement and passion back into sexual relationships artificially. They are doing so by short-cutting the problems of getting to know each other, or being emotionally close, and just doing the sex bit. The codes and the scenarios which accompany sado-masochists consist, by their own admission, of 'playing' either roles or fantasy. But playing is not being. Personally, I would rather be with the woman I am making love with rather than have her playing at being someone else.

I don't hate myself or feel guilty any more, so I don't want to be hurt or punished. I have had those feelings. I think they came from an internalised reaction to my oppression. I remember masochistic fantasies during my heterosexual past, but also occasionally since I've been a lesbian. I have dealt with them by talking with other lesbians about them, in order to understand and reject them. I'm not trying to pretend I'm a better feminist or more 'right on' than anyone else, but just that I know it is possible to reject the crap in our heads; that is hard, and I don't think that I have finished yet. In order for women not to feel guilty about our masochism, those of us who experience, or have experienced it don't need to validate it. Masochism and sadism are insidious because we get pleasure from our humiliation and degradation. Learning to love it is not the answer, and is no substitute for the good things that can happen between women.

I feel I want to be free to enjoy making love with my lover

without a checklist of 'right-on' behaviour and especially without guilt. And I feel optimistic, indeed I know it is possible to analyse lesbian sex critically and continue to enjoy it. It doesn't have to be a choice between an acceptance of sado-masochism or dull lesbian sex. Am I the only one?

JAYNE EGERTON

The Goal of a Feminist Politics . . . The Destruction of Male Supremacy or the Pursuit of Pleasure? A critique of the sex issue of *Heresies*

First published in *The Revolutionary and Radical Feminist Newsletter*, Autumn 1981

The attack on Women Against Violence Against Women (WAVAW)

The American feminist journal *Heresies*, no. 10, gives room to the kind of libertarian, pleasure-seeking sexual politics which justifies paedophilia, pornography, sado-masochism, trans-sexuality (female imitators) and the institution of heterosexuality. The sophisticated and relentless pushing of sexual pleasure which is to be found in the majority of the articles is coupled with a hostility to feminist anti-porn and anti-male violence groups in the States.

The accusation that feminists who campaign against or condemn anybody's chosen form of sexual expression and recreation are censorious and narrow-minded, is hardly new. What is new is the extent to which we are hearing these familiar male put-downs from within our own supposed ranks. The fierce debates taking place in the American women's liberation movement about sexuality (see the on-going discussion in *Off Our Backs*) are beginning to find echoes and sequels in British feminist ideas. At the recent Communist University of London (CUL) annual event,[1] several women in both the Sexual Identity and the WAVAW workshops seemed to regard pleasure as politically unproblematic and good in and of itself. But I think we must challenge and oppose any feminists who seek to legitimate those sexual practices and preferences which are detrimental to *all* women. If the experience of CUL is any indicator, we may soon have to contend with political attacks on WAVAW groups in this country. Therefore, I think we should look very carefully at the dangerous implications of the pro-pleasure arguments and begin to state forcefully and clearly why we do not think feminists should adopt such a position.

I believe that a feminist sexual politics necessitates strategies for exposing and fighting the techniques and propaganda men employ in order to maintain their power over women. I cannot see this perspective as being synonymous or compatible with the pursuit of pleasure, given that we live under male supremacy and may have internalised male sexual values to the extent that we 'enjoy' and gain pleasure from being humiliated. What gives us pleasure may not always be in our own best interests.

The politics of Heresies

The politics of Sex Issue are a curious and contradictory mixture. There are elements of Freudianism, Marxism, libertarianism, hedonism and anti-feminism all sitting uncomfortably together. The editorial collective insist that 'it is not necessarily true that women share a uniform relationship to sexuality, sexual identity, fantasy and sexual practice' without realising or acknowledging that this is a profoundly anti-feminist statement. This emphasis on the diversity and plurality of women's experience contradicts the basic first principle of feminism, i.e. that we are *all* sexually oppressed by men. It sees us as atomised individuals struggling towards a 'self-generated' sexuality according to our particular choices and desires. Feminists spent years endeavouring to de-privatise sex and put it into the arena of feminist politics. These women wish to take it out again.

Some of the collective even 'suggested that there was something intrinsically different about sex which might preclude it from being modified by the word "feminist". This something could be its privateness, its roots in infancy, its unique connection with repression.' So sex is not political at all. Another aspect of the anti-feminism is the constant and savage attacks on feminists who do not wish to see every sexual fantasy and desire liberated. We are accused variously of being moralistic, anti-sex and uptight. (Does this sound suspiciously like the guilt-tripping rhetoric of the male sexual revolution?) Our politics are caricatured and misrepresented. Paula Webster in her article 'Pornography and Pleasure' (which condones porn, needless to say) and Pat Califia in her piece 'Feminism and Sado-masochism' (which condones sado-masochism) both claim that their opponents are trying to celebrate and eternalise feminine virtues such as passivity but the alternative which they posit is no more than role reversal and playing men at their own game. As a rebellious alternative it looks remarkably conformist and non-threatening to the male *status quo*. It is simply perpetuating male sexuality amongst ourselves and can only serve to indirectly reinforce our oppression. But Califia and Webster do not seem to care much about women's oppression. Their anger and vitriol is reserved for feminists, and not for men. Indeed none of the many articles analyses or attacks male sexuality.

> There is little objective difference between a feminist who is offended by the fact that my lover kneels to me in public and sub-urbanites calling the cops because the gay boys next door are sunbathing in the nude [Pat Califia].

Libertarianism and Marxism

Libertarian and gay male left attitudes to sex are promoted throughout *Heresies*. Apparently women are oppressed by conventional, bourgeois morality, and not by men at all. The libertarian strand of thought focuses on the sexual freedom angle and the Marxist on the revolutionary potential of sex. Libertarian politics tend to conflate the struggle for women's liberation with the struggle for sexual freedom. The main sentiment in *Heresies* is that it is sexuality that is repressed rather than women who are oppressed and therefore it is people's right to free sexual expression which must be defended even if this may prove antithetical to women's liberation.

> We believe that all people, whatever their sexual preference and predilections, have an unalienable right to freedom of sexual association with a consenting partner, regardless of whether others approve of their behaviour. We therefore support the right of individuals to practise consensual sado-masochism and to use pornography for sexual gratification [Rosalyn Baxandall, Barnie Bellow, Cynthia Carr, Karen Dunbar, Brett Harvey, M. Monk, Alix Kate Shulman, Ann Snitow, Katy Taylor, Ellen Willis [a group of 'feminist activists']].

Pat Califia's belief in the inalienable rights of the individual lead her to support lowering the age of consent and legalising prostitution. Men must have the legalised right of access to girl-children and paid sex. As she (like the rest of the women writers in *Heresies*) does not have any concept of male supremacy, she cannot recognise that a liberalisation of the sexual climate can only increase men's sexual control of women. She switches to gay Left arguments when it suits her and trots out the old chestnut about non-procreative forms of sexuality undermining the nuclear family and thus hastening capitalism's decline. This line is also implicit in other articles, particularly Paula Webster's. There is a major contradiction in the simultaneous insistence on individual rights *and* people's rights. I think Marxist and libertarian arguments are introduced randomly because these women are quite desperate and hell-bent on justifying what they like best in whatever arbitrary political terms seem convenient. How they can reconcile the libertarian and Freudian emphasis on an innate sexuality which is being repressed with the Marxist belief in the social construction of sexual identity is a problem they leave unexplained.

Sex issue of Heresies – or why should men have all the fun?

It seems ironic that I should have spent so many hours reassuring women that feminists do not want to be like men and along come the *Heresies* women insisting that that is precisely what we do want to be like. The kind of sexuality which is encouraged by these women separates sex from emotion, objectifies women in pornography, justifies power relationships which are based on the giving and receiving of pain (lesbian sado-masochism) and supports the very male sexual minorities (trans-sexuals and paedophiles) who are most in the vanguard of oppressing women. The institution of heterosexuality is left unexamined and lesbianism is treated as no more than a sexual preference. Claiming to be moving towards a goal of sexual pleasure, what these women are really doing is sanctioning and abetting male sexual tyranny over women. I do not oppose these women because I am some sort of matriarchal, back-to-nature feminist who believes that women are naturally mothers or healers with a tender, nurturing and passive sexuality. I believe that women have been sexually controlled and colonised by men and that therefore we cannot celebrate our present sexual characteristics (with their predominant element of masochism) as essential and eternal. Similarly, I don't attack male sexuality because it is nasty, crude and unfeminine in an unchanging and fixed way, but rather because it is the crucial instrument of our control, and has developed in ways suitable to this purpose. It is not a question of saying that men are bad and women are good and I feel sure that the *Heresies* women realise that anti-porn and male-violence feminists for the most part are not claiming this. But it is easier for them to attack us if they represent our politics as reasserting Victorian and conservative morality.

Dogmatism, moralising, and censorial mystifying tended to dominate the anti-porn campaign . . .

One viewer for example asked why the photo of a young girl about to have anal intercourse was described [by Women Against Pornography] as 'the violent rape of a child'. The reply was that she was obviously under-age, so at least it was statutory rape. The lecturer added that anal intercourse was 'very painful'; therefore it was unlikely that this 'tiny young girl' could have been anything but *brutally injured*. I thought this reply indicated certain biases about pain and pleasure and preferred positions [Paula Webster].

What is sad, but perhaps inevitable, about the direction the pursuit of pleasure has led these women into is that for all its claims to be innovative and daring it really only demonstrates the extent to which some women have internalised male supremacist values. All the so-called alternatives are, in fact, modelled on the dominant male sexuality. But we cannot select aspects of male sexuality (i.e. the need to dominate and objectify sexual partners) and somehow neutralise or subvert them. They cannot be used for feminist purposes because their sole function is to oppress women. Reproducing and emulating the forms male sexuality has taken can only facilitate its development as the instrument of our oppression.

In the process of fighting male power the extent to which we can speak of an authentic, self-defined female sexuality is limited, although I do believe lesbianism as a political strategy and sexual practice to be the beginning of this self-definition. Our needs, desires and preferences have all been constructed under male supremacy and our subjective responses to our powerlessness and subordination cannot be prioritised if they further enslave us. The logical conclusion to arguments in favour of the pursuit of pleasure is best and most frighteningly expressed in a letter I read in *Off Our Backs*. The woman writes, 'I would like to see the end of violence, especially violence towards women and children, but I am not ready to see it at the cost of my own freedom.' Personally, if I had to choose between sexual 'liberation' and women's liberation, I would choose the latter every time.

7 Our Bodies

Introduction

Although not much has been written about the politics of women's health recently, much practical work has been done. Women have fought the cuts in a crumbling health service, encouraged self-help activities, and there has been increasing interest in alternative forms of healing.

Attention has focused nationally on the National Health Service; the services it provides, its racist nature and the employment it offers to women, have all come under scrutiny. Daytime abortion clinics and special health services for women, including women's hospitals, have been threatened with closure, and this has met with massive opposition. Although there has been no direct legislative attack on abortion since the Corrie Bill, the implementation of cuts by local health authorities may well increasingly restrict access to NHS abortions.

The emphasis on self-help activities continues. Many women's centres now provide pregnancy testing and women are learning to practise self-examination to detect infections, chart their menstrual cycles, and inseminate themselves. Women are turning to therapy and co-counselling more and more; indeed, we could draw the conclusion that therapy is fast replacing consciousness-raising. Osteopaths, naturopaths and acupuncturists are in increasing demand, especially as previously accepted concepts of western curative medicine are challenged. These remain private services and accessible to few women, but they offer a more holistic approach to women's health.

Various networks of women have been set up. The Women and Mental Health Group recently held their first conference; disabled women have formed self-help and campaigning groups; radical midwives are organising; and a support group for lesbian nurses now exists. A Women's Health Information Centre has opened in London, and a black women's health centre will open later this year. *Spare Rib* is always a source of informative articles on health, and some of these will be published as an anthology by Pandora in 1984.

Abortion rights are one aspect of the fight to control our own fertility, but as has been realised, other aspects of this must be fought for, too. Black and white working-class women have frequently been sterilised against their will, and the injection of dangerous contraceptives, notably Depo-Provera, continues. A conference in October 1983 led to a split in the National Abortion Campaign, and a Reproductive Rights Campaign encompassing all aspects of fertility control will now take up these issues. The headquarters of the International Contraception, Abortion and Sterilisation Campaign (ICASC) is in England, and has made the sharing of information and solidarity work between women from different countries much easier. Support groups offering practical help for women in other countries provide valuable assistance.

This section includes personal accounts of women up against a health service that neglects our needs, as well as some challenges to feminists to examine our own acceptance of sterotyped images of ourselves.

BARNEY BARDSLEY

The Incurable Illness

First published in *Catcall*, no. 12, April 1981

In the summer of 1980 I was very ill. It was the most wretched experience of my life, and was made so by one body of holy men, the medical profession. I was talked down to, dismissed, and mistreated. But because of the power wielded by doctors I was reluctant, even after such bad treatment, to write about them in derogatory fashion. Somehow they seem untouchable and above reproach. But with some persuasion I have written down my experiences and have tried to break that taboo. Many women will identify with my story. Many doctors are guilty of what I shall describe. It is unforgivable behaviour, which has no place in the twentieth century. Once the code of silence is lifted, we can go some way to stopping the abuse inflicted on our bodies, and can reclaim what is ours to cherish – our health.

At the hands of several doctors last summer I suffered profound self-doubt as well as illness, a real feeling of being threatened and misunderstood, which makes me think that some doctors have a totally warped perception of the female mind and body. This is something often made worse when the doctor is female, since under this system 'she' so often slips into the starched paternalistic role played by many male GPs.

All this meant that three months after starting to be ill, and after visits to three doctors, I was still unable to drink alcohol, stay up later than about 10 p.m., do anything remotely energetic, sometimes even to think straight. Sure, it's got better, but I've had to fight to get it that way, without constructive aid or advice, and at the same time fight off medical blunders designed to sap my already battered strength and peace of mind.

The whole thing started at the end of May. I had been back on the pill for two weeks, after a year's break, and against my better judgment. I suddenly started to feel very ill, soreness all over, including my throat, and an overpowering weakness and tiredness. It was an effort to move. Any exercise left me breathless, aching and sweating, so that even walking down the road to the shops became a major ordeal. Immediately I thought it was the pill, and went back to the family planning clinic to ask the doctor's advice. With calm detachment she said that I seemed to have some water retention (in two weeks I had put on over a pound in weight, unprecedented for the skin and bones creature I've always been) and must cut down on salt the week before my period. When I protested that I was quite prepared to be fitted with the cap, rather than put up with this torment every month, she shouted me down, and told me to persevere. It was early days yet, and my body would probably adjust. Anyway, the sore glands were definitely not due to the pill. (No explanation as to what they *were* due to.) Come back in six weeks, please. Already the easy way out had been taken, at the expense of *my* body and *my* health, even my eating habits. I was outraged, and stopped taking the pill immediately.

Two weeks later the water retention had disappeared, but all the other symptoms remained. Other people at work had complained of aching limbs, so I thought it was something going round which would clear up of its own accord. But when I could not get up at all one Monday morning, I realised that medical help was necessary, and reluctantly dragged myself to the local surgery. After a perfunctory examination, focused mainly on my eyeballs – the only parts of me by this stage that were not painful – the GP sent me for a blood test, gave me a week off work, prescribed nothing. Come back next week, please. Which is when it all got out of hand.

'I've come about the blood test you had taken a week ago. The name's Bardsley.'

I rubbed my hands together anxiously. It had been a week, and I'd been in pain, and I wanted finally to know what was wrong. His eyes fixed beadily on the involuntary action.

'Oh *yes*, Miss Bardsley.'

Tone dismissive, condescending.

'Well, the tests showed up nothing at all. No glandular fever.' (I have since been told it takes fourteen days before glandular fever shows up on any tests.)

'Blood count normal. I suppose you must have had a virus – we didn't test for that.'

(Tiresome. Yet another patient who hadn't fitted the one-symptom, one-cure, textbook bill.)

'Well, how do you feel now?' he muttered as an afterthought. Shamed into feeling guilty for feeling ill at all, I stammered out a few things about still being tired, sore and aching. In fact, the symptoms were exactly the same as they had been a week ago. A look down my throat. A quick feel behind my ears. Another glance at the hands clasped together in self-defence.

'You're very nervy, aren't you?'

Silence on my part. Shocked at that cool and hostile stare.

'You are. I think you are. So [small resigned sigh], I'm going to give you some tranquillisers.'

I went cold inside at the word. Mental confusion – I couldn't have heard it – I was a sick human being for God's sake, not a racehorse to be drugged out of the running. Then he said it again, and this time I managed to interrupt, albeit timidly.

'Tranquillisers. Do you really think I need them?'

There was a flicker in his eyes that might even have been doubt. Then he continued.

'*I* think you do. I would not have prescribed them otherwise.'

And he scribbled it down with relief, the very act of making a decision giving it for him a cast-iron validity. Once again my body was being abused – and this time my mind with it – for the sake of an easy life. Easy, that is, for the doctor. Finally, he shot the two standard questions at me, to which I replied that I was sleeping all right (all the time, in fact) and, although I had bled a little longer than normal after my period this time, I thought it was because I had just come off the pill. He seemed interested in this, and I could see him make the instant connection: come off the pill, row with her boyfriend, bit strung up: let's dose her up and quieten her down. It would not have occurred to him that I could have come off the pill due to well-founded concern over my body, for that reason and that reason alone.

He concluded with a sober little lecture.

'Now I'm going to give you another seven days off work, and I want you to come back *with the bottles* [a token bottle of iron tablets was included] next week.'

He might well have added: 'Just to make sure you've taken the week's supply, like a good girl, but not taken too many, and begun to enjoy the drug.' I just nodded, like the helpless little child he was treating me as, no longer taking it in, no longer even scared of the dangerous wrong turning this 'consultation' had taken. Just numb.

Only when I got outside did the madness of it hit me. I sat, drinking tea and discussing it with a friend. He found it as crazy as I did, but couldn't understand why I hadn't protested about the superficial examination and the hasty conclusion. Why had I behaved so meekly, even though my health was being abused in this way? There are two powerful reasons, both of which will be familiar to many women.

First, the overpowering awe of doctors that we have had instilled in us since birth. I have always been afraid of them, and I have always been encouraged in that fear. Ironic, is it not, that we should have such a horror of those who are supposed to heal and tend sick bodies? And yet my mother tells me that she feels the same way. For years, she says, she has quietly taken the pill bottles handed over to her, even when these pills have failed to help her pains. The GP is a father-figure and fathers are *not* to be disobeyed. I still remember the Smarties I was given as a child for being good by the visiting family doctor. Nor does the memory fade of sharp reprimands when I was not brave enough and cried in pain. So even now, at twenty-four, I am shy of the doctor, so shy as to sit – like a child – and accept even the unacceptable.

The second reason is of far more recent origin and is far more disturbing. The word 'tranquilliser' has particularly nasty connotations for me, because I was once in a state of nervous depression while I was a student. Then, as now, sympathetic doctors were thin on the ground, and the experience of tranquillisers is mixed up with repeated humiliation in front of GPs who refused to believe there was anything the matter with me at all, although, as one medic finally realised, I was on the brink of a nervous breakdown.

It was the anguish of that dreadful time that came flooding back as I sat and listened to the London doctor. I *knew* what it was like to be in a nervous depression, and I *knew* it wasn't what was wrong with me now. But he was bringing it all back, with his glib assumptions and easy answers, which left me totally out of account. (He didn't even have records of my one-time depression by which to prejudge the case.) He was creating in me the very thing on which doctors blame so many wasted surgery hours: the neurotic female. That same night I went to stay at my parents' home for some rest. In a last-ditch attempt to get proper medical aid, I made an appointment to see a local doctor, tried and trusted in the past. He listened gravely to the whole saga, examined me, and then ruined his credibility for me when, in an attempt by me at lighthearted conversation, I said, 'London isn't all bad you know. Parts of it are very good indeed.' He replied smilingly, 'Depending on which boyfriend you have at the time?'

And there you have it. Woman seen through the eyes of man, treated always with the male as a reference point, even when diagnosed (wrongly) as having a traditional female complaint. He had carefully picked on the most peripheral of the information I had given him – my coming off the pill – and voiced the unspoken opinion of the London doctor, that I was unstable, nervous, depressed, all because of a man.

I have since been told that I was probably suffering from glandular fever, or something like it, all those miserable months.

Were I a man, that conclusion would have probably been drawn without recourse to three doctors and a specialist. Health-service time and money have been wasted, not to mention *my* time, health and peace of mind. Of course, I am by no means the only one. In the past I used to hear stories about women being fobbed off with Valium so often that they became addicted. I know vaguely about 'mother's little helpers', sung of so despisingly by the Rolling Stones. But, like so many Mick Jaggers in this world, I blamed it on the women for being neurotic, or shrugged it off as a wild exaggeration. When it happened to me, my opinion changed, and I began to talk to other women about their experiences.

First, I heard about a friend's mother, who had stomach pains and was given Valium for nerves, until she insisted finally on seeing a specialist, who treated her for what she had – a stomach disorder. Then I commiserated with a friend who was ill with a virus similar to mine. She had been prescribed 'vitamin tablets', which, she later learned from the chemist, were in fact tranquillisers. (At least my doctors did not actually lie to me.) I realised then that women are often faced with dangerous prejudice when they go to the doctor.

Ask your women friends about bad experiences with GPs and you will be amazed at the dreadful stories that nearly every woman has to tell. In fact this consciousness-raising exercise is a valuable first stage in breaking the pernicious secretiveness that surrounds the doctor's surgery. Write to people involved in medical associations. Let people know that the doctor is *not* a god, but *is* answerable to his patients, the women just as much as the more demanding and less put-upon men. My flatmate says she only goes to the doctor when she knows what is wrong with her, so she can tell him what to prescribe! That is one solution. But what happens when, like me, you *don't* know what is wrong with you, and you go for professional advice, not sexist diagnosis and drugs that are far too often only too unnecessary, and addictive? Our bodies are too precious to be used in this offhand way, and only when we ourselves start to fight back, will things start to change.

Black Women – What Kind of Health Care Can We Expect in Racist Britain?

First published in *Sheffield Women's Paper*, Autumn 1981

Black women in Britain are under attack from state racism which takes the form of successive immigration laws, the proposed* Nationality Act, harassment by police and immigration officials on the street, in the home and at work. The Nationality Act, combined with the new DHSS rules about who can and can't use the National Health Service, has serious consequences for black women. It limits even more the choices that black women have about our bodies and our health. Already, entitlements to benefits are being denied on the basis of skin colour. Hospitals have been demanding passports from black people they 'suspect' may not be eligible for treatment:

> Ms Lulu Banu, resident here for fourteen years, was refused treatment in Fulham and Dr Farideh Shira was refused ante-natal care at a London hospital till she produced a passport.

More recently it has emerged that a Department of Health exercise is to begin, involving the questioning of patients about their nationality and residence qualifications. So, as black women, our right to any kind of health care under the NHS is under threat before we even start to talk about what kind of health care we want.

Our choice doesn't come into it

Black women are frequently sterilised without their knowledge or consent, or offered abortion on the condition that they agree to be sterilised. At the same time as white women are finding it harder to

---

* This Act is now on the Statute Book.

get abortions, black women are often being pushed into them, as an attempt to limit the numbers of black children being born. Our choice does not come into it.

It's the same story when we come to contraception. The major objective seems to be reducing the number of black children rather than giving black women an informed choice about methods and side-effects. In fact, despite the growing literature on the dangers of both the pill and the coil, women's fears are dismissed as old wives' tales and a product of their 'inferior' culture. More leaflets have been produced in Asian languages on birth control than any other health topic, yet it is rare to find hospital handbooks or information on health rights (how to complain, get a second opinion, etc.) translated into Asian languages, and the provision of interpreters is not taken seriously in hospitals or family planning clinics.

> Asian women are very rarely offered the cap. Sometimes they are denied it even when they ask for it, because it is assumed they won't use it properly.

> A Bangladeshi woman was given Depo-Provera[1] over a two-year period with side-effects of bleeding, nausea and headaches. According to official records the clinic she attended does not use Depo-Provera.

Racist attitudes in hospitals

When we go into hospitals and clinics we face racist and hostile attitudes from the staff.

> After a two-hour wait in an ante-natal clinic it transpired that two Asian women's notes had got muddled up because they had the same second name. The comment from the receptionist was: 'Some of these women don't even know their own names.'

> A pupil nurse in a London hospital had this to say: 'The problem is that Asian women don't look after their own babies, they just feed them and their mothers and sisters do all the rest, like bathing and changing them. It is really bad because it discourages bonding.'

> West Indians – I can't figure them out – the woolly-cap brigade – I can't fathom their minds. They don't attend ante-natal clinics, can't be bothered . . . they just collect money at the Labour Exchange [a senior nurse in charge of the maternity department at Central Middlesex Hospital].

Rickets campaign – what is it really about?

There are never enough interpreters, there is never any recognition of our own cultural needs. Instead, the health service is used against us to control us and intimidate us. All efforts at health education are on the state's terms and not ours. They are not concerned with giving us more and better informed choices, but with reinforcing racism. Recently, for instance, there has been a lot of publicity about rickets, vitamin-D deficiency and Asian diets. The impression that all the propaganda gives is that Asian diets are unhealthy. In fact, Asian diets are very healthy and the incidence of rickets amongst Asian children living in Britain is to do with there being less sunshine here than in their country of origin.

One of the reasons why white children avoid rickets is because the British government supplements margarine with vitamin D. The problem could be overcome very simply by also including vitamin D in chapati flour or other Asian foodstuffs, and black organisations have repeatedly asked the DHSS to do this over the last few years. The DHSS refusal stems from anxiety that this would constitute the 'thin end of the wedge', setting a precedent for the recognition of other cultural needs. White mothers are no better informed than Asian ones about the need for vitamin D in the diet, yet all the publicity about the inadequacy of Asian diets creates the impression that Asian mothers do not know how to feed their children properly. The extent of the prejudice and ignorance generated by the publicity that the vitamin D/rickets issue has received continually surprises us. Bluntly, Asian children, adolescents and pregnant women get rickets because of government racism, but what all the advice on diet (often beautifully produced in Asian languages) does is to imply that it is Asian women who are to blame.

Note

1. An injection of Depo-Provera consists of a massive dose of a synthetic hormone. It is manufactured by an American company. As in the case of the pill, and many other drugs, thousands of Third World women were used as guinea-pigs for D-P.

JASSY KOWALSKI

Fat Liberation . . . Some Facts

First published in *Irregular Periods*, Bradford Women's Paper, no. 3

The stereotypes which are attached to women who are fat are all lies. We have all swallowed the myths put out by medical 'experts' – even those of us who are sceptical and even downright disbelieving about what the NHS says is best for us wimmin. The oppression of fat wimmin is based on looks and looks only. Yet everyone has their own particular pet theory as to why we should lose weight – the fact is we can't – fat wimmin are biologically fat – I'm a fat woman and I do know what I'm talking about!

Anyway, I'd like to say something about the myths which are put out about us. I'd also like to point out that I'm talking about wimmin who *are* fat, not wimmin who *feel* fat. We know who we are, don't we, girls!

Fat people eat too much – that's why they're fat

In studies that have been done in America of the amount fat and thin people eat, there rarely was any difference in food intake. There are thin people who eat a lot (she eats like a horse and never puts on a pound!) and there are fat people who eat a lot. Likewise, there are thin and fat people who have small appetites. The average fat person eats normal amounts. Fat people are made to feel very uncomfortable about eating in public – for years I used to eat tiny plates of food and then finish my meal when no one was around. We are made to feel ashamed every time we put food to our lips, because it's always assumed that we're stuffing ourselves.

Fat is unhealthy and unnatural

This isn't true. So far all studies which have been done on fat people have been done on those who are continually dieting. Dieting kills. A diet of 1000 calories a day is practically starvation level – but nobody thinks fat people are starving because they don't *look* malnutritioned. 95–99 per cent of fat wimmin who diet will regain all their weight, plus extra. Diets only have a 1 to 5 per cent success rate. They have been shown, in medical research, to be the cause of diabetes, strokes, kidney disorders and heart attacks.

A study was carried out in the USA on a group of blue-collar Italian-Americans in Roseto. These people were very fat. They ate hard, worked hard and played hard. Fat was socially acceptable inside their community. They had excellent health and the rate of heart attacks and strokes was lower than the national average. These same people were studied as they left their community and went to places where fat is hated and fat people are oppressed. The rate of heart attacks climbed right up to the national average for fat people.

Diseases thought to be caused by fat are also stress-related (like high blood pressure and heart attacks) and are more likely to be caused by the stresses of fat hatred in this culture.

So-called 'cures' for fat people – like intestinal bypass operations (in which most of the small intestine is disconnected) and stomach stapling (where a 12-mm hole is left at the end of a row of staples near the greater curvature of the stomach) – have high death rates. They also cause stomach perforations, liver damage, kidney failure, diaorrhea and malnutrition – that's if you're lucky enough to survive the operation! In one year in the USA 2700 wimmin died from these operations, about 15 per cent of the operations carried out. Are we really hated and despised so much that society considers such a death rate acceptable?

Fat people are lazy – they should exercise more, then they'd lose weight

If every time *you* ran anywhere, someone laughed at you, made jokes about how comical you looked, maybe you'd think twice about setting off at a brisk pace. Fat people are told they *can't* run – our culture is so steeped in these myths that we believe them ourselves. Yes, we do look different to you 'thinnies' – fat is more mobile, it changes position as we move. So what? If a woman with short legs is having a race with a woman with long legs, chances are that the long-legged woman will win. Do we then turn around and tell the short-legged woman that she is unhealthy and should get her legs stretched? It is oppression which stops fat people from running, swimming, learning karate, etc. We *can* do it – just leave us in peace! In the States, there is a Fat Dyke Karate troupe. These wimmin weigh mainly between 12 and 20 stones and very many of them have black belts. Who says we are lazy?

Fat people smell

Some thin people smell, some fat people smell. Oppression stinks. Which is worse?

Fat people are always so happy and jolly

There is nothing funny about being fat. We are jeered at, reviled, spat upon, physically and mentally pushed around and joked about to our faces. Where is the humour in a life like that? Fat people learn they must laugh first – at least then they have some sort of control over deciding *when* people laugh. Unfortunately, fat people will then find out that we outwear our use when the 'life and soul' of the party routine fades out and the dancing starts. We do not consider our bodies to be funny and it is *not* amusing in the slightest when we can't walk down a street or through a shop without people looking at us in disgust and laughing at us.

As fat wimmin, we have learnt the lies and have crash-dieted our way up and down the scales, laughing all the way, praying at the same time that some day we would be treated as people and not monsters or ugly mutations.

Fat is ugly

The WLM screams blue murder about stereotyping wimmin as sex-objects. We all demand the right to define ourselves. Yet, even by their sisters, fat wimmin are defined as ugly, physically repulsive. We are written out of the human race just because of how we look. Thin wimmin have to stop making judgments about our bodies. They're all right as they are!

RUTH ELIZABETH

Deprivatising Pain

First published in *Catcall*, no. 14, August 1982

This was written for my radical feminist group which had been meeting for some time, but had not addressed these issues. I had felt unable to talk about what was obviously an important aspect of my life, and also a central issue politically for all of us. It was my first attempt to break the silence. Since I wrote it, I have actually experienced a 'bout of depression', and for the first time felt able to bring it to the group. The support has altered not only how I dealt with this, but the nature of the experience itself.

The group has had to change. This gives us hope.

This is something I have never tried to say before. In fact, I didn't even know that this was how I felt until I sat down to write and it all poured out along with a lot of tears. It took many hours to write and cost a great deal in hurt and anger and the flooding-back of many excruciatingly painful memories which I would in many ways have rather left undisturbed. The result is not at all what I expected. I hadn't really known what sort of thing I would end up writing but I suppose I thought it would be fairly detached and academic-sounding, referring to present and past pain without really expressing any of that pain. But it is not really possible for me to talk about 'mental illness' in a detached manner, so I began to think about why I felt that I should try. And it began to seem ridiculous that I had been in this group for over a year and only now was talking about all of this for the first time. I realised how little any of you really know me – apart from Jackie that is – because a very big part of my life, my experiences of despair, pain, depression (I don't know what to call them), has always been kept out of the group. So I decided that it wasn't enough just to refer to those experiences in a detached way – that the only really honest thing to do was to let some of that pain speak for itself.

I want first of all to talk about the wall of silence surrounding this sort of experience of pain, where it comes from, how it is maintained, and what we might do to try and break it down. Although women ourselves have not been responsible for the building of walls between us, for the intense privatisation of our experiences of pain, we can exercise a choice about whether to allow these walls to continue to separate us, or whether to use our combined strength to bring them down. This obviously applies to lots of barriers – those of race, class, sexuality, and so on – as well as to those related to mental illness. I have never really thought of it in this way before, but I really do feel separated off, behind some sort of enclosure, from most of the women I know. Partly, this is the result of having been labelled 'mentally ill', of having been locked up, unfit to mingle with the rest of the world, so that it is very, very hard for me now to believe that I am acceptable, that I have a right to be here. But it is not just a problem with my self-image resulting from my experiences in mental hospitals. I believe this sense of separateness is perpetuated, perhaps unwittingly, by other women who distance themselves from me.

Ever since I was very small, I felt, in some fundamental way, different from everyone else. I don't know how many other women grew up with this feeling, but I suspect it is an inevitable part of growing up female in a patriarchal world, *knowing* you are not *really* what you are supposed to be – a male-defined woman. I no longer feel the only unfeminine failure in a world of successfully feminine women, but I still feel very much apart. Now, I feel for most of the time like someone who 'cannot cope', in a movement full of women who can. Perhaps it is unrealistic to expect that in our individual lifetimes we can do away with those basic feelings of alienation and otherness that are so basic to our experience of ourselves as women under patriarchy. But I can't accept that it is necessary for me, when I am depressed, to feel so utterly alone and freakish that I often wish I could go back into hospital because that is the one place in my life I have ever felt I really belonged.

Let me describe some of the ways in which I feel other women distance themselves from me and from the despair that is such a large part of my life. One way in which women have responded to my trying to talk about it is with silence, accompanied by looks of incomprehension. This happened in one women's group where, it seemed, no one else had experienced anything like it. Can this be true? I have no way of knowing.

Another reaction, fortunately one I haven't met within the women's movement but have often met outside, is a kind of morbid fascination. I am asked questions about padded cells and suicide attempts, what mental patients are like, whether I've ever tried to hang myself, and so on. I'm sure you can imagine how that makes me feel.

Then there are the women who want to help, the patronising social worker types who get some sort of kick out of 'looking after' me. Other women feel they ought to warn me about the dangers of taking medication and want to explain that mental illness is really all a patriarchal plot and that what I should really be doing is fighting to change my situation. How helpful to have further feelings of guilt and inadequacy heaped on those I've already got! Do they think I don't worry about poisoning myself? And how do you change your situation when you can't even get out of bed? Besides, I *have* changed my situation. I am *here*, not in hospital, despite all the predictions doctors made about me. No one but my closest family knows what sort of struggle, what sort of achievement that represents.

A more seductive reaction, but still a distancing technique, is the idealised view of madness as a breakthrough into an unmapped, forbidden territory. One particular woman put me on a pedestal in this manner and treated me like a sort of prophet. Although I resented this treatment, some good things did come out of it in that I began to see some of what are traditionally held to be weaknesses as strengths. There *are* situations in which 'not coping' is the healthiest thing to do. And it is good if through my 'not coping' other women have been made aware of the price they have been paying in numbness, blinkeredness, rigidity, and especially in not communicating with each other, for their ability to sail or muddle through horrendously destructive situations. Hence, I have more than once been the cause of a group of women drastically changing a situation because my 'not being able to cope with it' forced them to look at what was really happening and how much bad feeling, tension, or whatever, they were all blocking out. These were all good insights and strengths that I would like to keep and develop, but the glamourising of despair and depression was not helpful. It is simply another way of distancing ourselves from the reality of it, the *agony* of it. And being able to choose to refuse to 'cope' with a situation is very different from simply not being able to cope with it whether I want to or not.

A more common distancing technique is the trivialising one: 'Oh yes, I get off-days too, isn't it *awful*.' Or people who have never been with me when I've been depressed tell me that of course we *all* experience these kinds of things.

A more complete silencing takes place when women pretend that my depression doesn't exist. So they never ask about it and somehow communicate that it's not the sort of thing they're interested in talking about. This is something which I feel has been happening in this group. I'm not trying to blame anyone for this – I'm probably as responsible for it as anyone else – but I want to talk about the effect it has. It makes me feel split, as if I lead a double life. An important part of me remains hidden, privatised, a personal problem I have to deal with on my own. When I am unable to keep this unacceptable part hidden, under control, I have to hide *myself* away, stay away from the group. It makes me feel inadequate that I don't do all the active and outgoing things that other women do. I feel ashamed, and unable to admit, for example, that parties terrify me and that I get very anxious if I'm away from home for any length of time and therefore cannot just decide to stay overnight with people unless I'm psychologically well-prepared and feeling exceptionally strong. Because very few people appreciate the amount of energy I often have to put into doing very basic, daily things, I feel often misunderstood, seen as unreliable, erratic, and so on.

So, what is it that I want other women to do? This is much more difficult to know than what I *don't* want from other women! First of all, I want to be able to stop feeling like a freak. I want to hear other women talk about *their* experiences of anguish, despair, pain, rejection, insecurity, whatever, so that we can make connections. One way in which we could get away from the divisions caused between us by using medical definitions might be for us to relate the experiences of patriarchal violence that I suffered in the form of 'treatment' for mental illness to other women's experience of other forms of patriarchal violence – such as battering, physical pain, surgical mutilation, rape, heterosexuality, and so on. I'm sure my experiences of abject powerlessness, hopelessness, humiliation, agonising guilt and self-hatred, if not my experience of clinical depression, have been shared by other women in the hands of other male institutions. Perhaps what happens is not that I am particularly prone to these feelings but that most women block them off in order to survive, or that, feeling them, they choose not to talk about them, so that they remain private and unutterable.

I have often said that we need to re-conceptualise those experiences which men label as 'mental illness', so that those of us who have been so labelled can cease to regard ourselves as 'ill'. I have struggled for years to abandon that conception of myself as 'ill' and have been unable to do it, and I have only just realised why. It is because I've been trying to do it on my own. If I am to integrate myself so that I am no longer split between the 'normal' me and the 'ill' me, then that 'ill' me must be acceptable not only to me but to other women as well. In fact, I cannot accept it until others do. And for other women to accept it I think means that those women must examine their *own* unacceptable, inadequate, frightened, vulnerable parts of themselves. Then together we can try to find words for these experiences, to explore their origins, and understand them in order to *do* something about them. What I am advocating is decidedly *not* some form of therapy. It is precisely the experience of pain as an illness, a privatised, personal problem that I want to get away from. I'm not asking for support so much as a sense of mutual recognition, a door through which I can come in from the cold, or through which you can come out into the storm. For if mental illness *is* a patriarchal plot then it concerns all of us, it needs to be examined as a mammoth patriarchal institution that does violence to us all, not only in the way I have been affected by being labelled as 'ill', but also in the way that the rest of you have been affected by male-defined standards of normality, of health.

If I broke down and sobbed uncontrollably what would you do? If it makes you embarrassed is that my problem or yours? What exactly is happening when women behave 'normally'?

Perhaps we should ask not only why some women crack up after they've had a baby, or why some women have 'nervous breakdowns' while they're at university, but why other women don't. When women 'cope' with, get through, and even get on and succeed in unhealthy, destructive patriarchal institutions, what is happening to them? In other words, we need to examine mental *health* as well as mental illness if those of us who have been labelled mentally ill are going to be able to stop seeing *ourselves* as the problem, as victims of an unfortunate personal failure setting us apart from all the 'normal' women around us.

I'm fed up with feeling always on the fringe of women's things, a sort of emotional cripple who cannot fully take part – I want my struggle to be seen as important too, as something which affects all of us in a fundamental way, something which is an integral part of the building of our movement.

ANGELA CHEETHAM WILKINSON

Alopecia: courage to be yourself

First published in *Spare Rib*, 122, September 1982

Dear *Spare Rib*,

I am an artist. Female. Thirty-three years old. Largely ignored. I am divorced. I have two sons aged thirteen and a half and nearly nine. I am living (?) on supplementary benefit. Prior to my divorce I had given six days a week support to my husband in his business. Any time left I painted pictures. Then my husband ran away to Canada when his business was in great debt, sending a note and a bunch of keys from the airport. The business was closed. My house was sold to meet the debts. I had previously signed a second mortgage agreement with the bank. My children and I now live in a council house on the very edge of Taunton.

I worked for my husband for nine years and during all that time I managed to keep my own work going. When I first went to the DHSS I told them I drew and painted pictures. The reply was:

'That's OK, if you have a hobby on which you spend four or five hours a week like other people may knit for instance, that's fine. But if you are working on these pictures daily then you are self-employed and will not be eligible for supplementary benefit.'

It seems strange to me that I am allowed to perform perpetual housework and receive SB, but I must not work to try and improve my situation.

As a result of the problems *vis-à-vis* my marriage I have not much hair left. I am going to talk to you about this because I think it is a problem which many women suffer in silence.

Let me explain – when a woman loses her hair and the specialist pronounces 'no hope' she is then given the most dreadful wig courtesy of the NHS. My wig was given to me in a dark cupboard of a room by a man with a suitcase of wigs. There was a tiny mirror. I wore the wig until I could afford a better one. For two years I hid under my acrylic hat until I could stand it no longer.

I think it is probably impossible to describe the difficulties which arise from wearing a wig to hide the fact that you have no hair – the overwhelming feeling of 'falseness' – this is not me – I am not like this – of being a split-person, the image presented to the public and the real me in the mirror, in private. There is always a very real fear of having the wig knocked off – in a pub, for instance, as someone raises their pint to their lips. You are at home, there is a knock at the door – is it a friend who knows you are bald, or a stranger whose face will show immediate shock as you open the door? Maybe your wig is upstairs and you have to creep past the front door to rush upstairs and don the ghastly lump of plastic which makes everyone else feel uncomfortable.

Of course, before a woman takes to wig-wearing her hair is extremely thin and when she wears the wig and goes off to the shopping there is always someone who sees her and exclaims:

'God, what *have* you done to your hair, it doesn't look like you at all, I never imagined you to be a person who would spend hours in the hairdresser's.'

You see, it is impossible to purchase a wig which looks like ordinary, messy hair with all its wonderful imperfections. Wigs are for 'feminine' ladies and if you are most definitely not one such person it's quite horrid to go around looking like one. One's usual jeans and T-shirt look ridiculous topped by this obscene nylon creation.

Women suffer dreadfully concerning their sexual attraction. Of course I could write much more.

One year ago when my husband escaped all responsibility and left me holding the baby I took all my wigs and burned them – yes, I think it was when the bras got dumped too. Jesus, it took some doing. It was some time before I felt brave enough to venture forth unaccompanied. It has made all the difference to my life and freed me from all the anxieties I experienced whilst wearing a wig. There have been new difficulties to face. Wherever I go I am laughed at, often quite openly, some people actually wind down their car windows for a better look. There is no hiding as there is with a wig and going out always requires a moment's squaring of shoulders to face the giggles, gawps and sneers.

Taunton is a town of 40,000 inhabitants and I am able to perceive that there are many women with the same problem. Some of them are poor and with an NHS wig only available at the rate of two a year, it makes them look tatty and ridiculous.

Then, a few weeks ago, I advertised a sofa for sale. One evening a woman came round to look at the sofa. She became nervous and agitated. The deal was done but she did not appear to want to leave. Suddenly she said, 'I am so relieved to meet someone with the same problem.' It took me some moments to realise what she was talking about, her wig was so good and well-fitted to her well-dressed image. She wept. She came back the following day and wept some more. She told me she was happily married and that for four years she had been wearing a wig.

Her husband had never seen her without it, nor had her children, not even her sixteen-year-old son, so sure was she that she was totally unacceptable. She wears a headscarf in bed, secured tightly with yet another headscarf. Sex is a wash-out. Her young children never have the pleasure of sharing her bath. She lives in a perpetual state of anxiety.

I think alopecia is a feminist issue. Men are allowed to go bald. They may walk the streets without being jibed at. The image many women feel they must present, their belief constantly reinforced by a media so strong with its urging of physical 'perfection' in women, is threatened to the core by baldness.

Any advice would be most welcome and you are more than welcome to print this letter.

Good luck for the future,

In sisterhood,

Angela.

A True Story: cystitis

First published in *Shocking Pink*, no. 2

Once upon a time there was a sixteen-year-old woman who was once told she was beautiful. Unfortunately, she had been prone to umpteen ups and downs that teenagers have to put up with and found this fact very hard to believe, and only very nearly believed it when the sun was shining and the wind was in the right direction. Like many of her friends she had a boyfriend and also like many of her friends she had been told by popular magazines and media that unless she had sex with him, he would disappear into the sunset riding with another girl. So off she trotted to her family doctor and promptly started taking the pill.

Now it was here that our heroine's troubles began. At first, sex with her boyfriend was OK, but shortly, she began to itch a bit around her vagina. Thinking nothing of it, she found that it was relieved by friction when she had sex, so she had it more often. Then one sunny Sunday (when her family had gone out for the day) she felt an urge to pee, and again thinking nothing of it, she tried to go. *And the only things that came out were a few drops of blood!*

Cancer! She knew it was cancer! Blood in the urine meant cancer in the kidneys! or bladder! somewhere inside her! She almost fell over with fear and she started moaning out loud oh no, oh no – whom could she turn to? Family gone – doctor's closed – boyfriend? Boyfriend's mum!

She promptly pulled up her pants and ran to her boyfriend's house where she collapsed in a heap of tears and fears. Wonderful-ly, his mum took control and took her to the casualty unit of the local hospital, where our heroine was told she was having sex too often and she had not got cancer, but cystitis.

This became a regular occurrence in her life. She began to feel bad about sex, that it would always hurt afterwards, that more activity meant more pain (so she became very passive), and she avoided sex when she could. She also knew that she was not beautiful, but in reality ugly, disease-ridden, and her insides were crawling with worms.

Each time our heroine had sex, a visit to the doctor's ensued.

Act 1. Scene 2.

Stage divided into two by a partition with a single door in it. One side is a doctor's surgery; a cluttered desk, a comfortable chair on one side in which doctor sits, and a hard upright chair on the other side. Other side is a waiting-room, several chairs arranged in rows, one occupied by a woman, a few old magazines scattered around. Woman squeezes legs together. Painful tense look on face.

Woman: (to herself) Well, doctor, I think I have cystitis and thrush and these are the symptoms: pain when I have intercourse, followed by an uncontrollable urge to pee; I usually spend four hours on the toilet during which I drink liquid constantly; it burns when I pee; I have diarrhoea; I have cramps in my stomach; I get feverish; and I completely empty myself of all food or liquid. Also, I itch unbearably around my vagina. This is causing problems with my sex life, I don't like sex any more.

(Pause. Door opens.)

Doctor: Next please.

(Woman stands up, walks through door, closes it, and sits on chair facing doctor.)

(Long pause while doctor writes).

Doctor: Well, who are you?

(Woman mumbles name.)

Doctor: And what can I do for you? (still writing).

Woman: Um, I er have cystitis.

Doctor: Oh, take this (slaps prescription in hand). Five times a day – and this (slaps prescription in hand). After every meal. Oh. And drink plenty of liquid – about five pints a day. Goodbye.

Act again six times, changing actor who is doctor.

Meanwhile, this woman's life was becoming unbearable. She was often away from work or college because of cystitis. She very definitely had sex problems with her boyfriend. She lost her self-respect. She spent a greal deal of time sitting on the toilet since she had become incontinent during attacks. She often had to cancel outings with her friends for fear of being away from a toilet, and she constantly thought she might wet herself in public, and a creeping doubt came into her mind that she might have an advanced case of VD.

A few years passed, and our heroine is now twenty-one. After the last bout of cystitis, she realised it was long past time to have tests done so she asked her doctor. He promptly laughed in her face and reduced her to tears.

So she independently went to the Housewives' Clinic at Westminster Hospital where she met the doctor of her dreams. He was sympathetic, concerned, asked lots of questions, medical and personal, and made lots of tests. Within the hour he was able to tell her there were lots of things wrong with her, he explained what they were and said that he was going to make her better. For once, she knew she could trust him, and that in this case, she would live happily ever after, and she actually began to believe she might be beautiful inside.

Moral: Doctors are often a load of shit who given half the chance will dismiss our problems as unwarranted 'silly women's problems'.

WE HAVE THE RIGHT TO DEMAND TREATMENT!!

DOROTHEA

Sickle Cell Anaemia:
women speak out

First published in *Spare Rib*, 126, January 1983

A student nurse's story

As a student nurse in a London hospital I met two women suffering a 'crisis' of their sickle cell anaemia. I became friendly with one in particular, J. She explained to me about her illness and her pain. On reflection both of them knew as much as the nursing staff, more than the juniors, like me. I learned that J. had been in hospital often; some of the nurses had met her before and warned that she could be 'difficult'. They put the rest of the staff on their guard. I tried to keep an open mind.

The 'difficulty' became clear when J. needed Pethidine to relieve her pain. They all thought she didn't really need too much of it, and hinted that she was over-reacting, just so she could have the drug. Being new to the situation I didn't know what to think. Most of them just humoured her.

They kept stressing that the drug was addictive, and that she had been on regular doses before, so we had to be careful. At first, J. was on a standard dose which they all felt was enough. So when she still complained of pain they were doubtful; they had been warned about this. Once as I was going off duty I sat to talk with J. hoping to take her mind off the pain until her next injection. Her doctors came, and together with the senior nurses asked her a lot of questions – trying to catch her out.

The doctor did ask her if she'd prefer stronger medication, but she refused. This only confirmed their idea that J. just 'liked' Pethidine. But as I tried to explain to the doctor afterwards, she had had violent, and in one case nearly fatal, reactions to a number of stronger drugs, so she was scared to change. They gave her an injection after they'd kept her talking. They took me to one side, trying to make me see that although their actions might seem harsh to me, they were much more experienced. But the doctor admitted to me that he hadn't much experience with sickle cell anaemia, only of pain, and she didn't seem to be in pain!

With the help of her haematologist they did increase her dose, but added Valium to 'relax' her. She began to irritate some of the nurses. They got tired of J. always watching out for her next injection. Sometimes she'd ask me to go and remind them. Sometimes I wanted to avoid her, so I wouldn't get caught up in it, but she didn't have that option. It might have been then that a staff nurse thought she'd make J. 'pull herself together' by telling her to 'stop wasting everybody's time'. This nurse had decided right from the beginning that J. was going to be 'difficult'. J. reported her. The whole incident didn't make life any easier. The sister advised me not to get involved, and that I shouldn't let J. take advantage of my inexperience. She suggested to J. it might be best if she transferred to another ward.

J. told me she didn't trust any of the staff, except her haematologist. She knew they were just waiting for trouble from her. Finally she did ask for a transfer. The sister had said it would be easier for everyone. But it didn't change much, as she was still under the same doctors who took their attitudes to the ward, and also her file contained comments from the nursing staff.

The other woman with sickle cell anaemia was quiet and unassuming compared to J. She was the sort of woman who would lie there until the pain was unbearable before she would 'disturb' the staff. They even told us to make sure we asked her regularly! The staff liked her, she wasn't any trouble. Her doctor seemed to be more understanding, as she was prescribed Pethidine at regular intervals, then PRN (whenever required). She knew exactly what she needed, and was given it.

But they still showed their ignorance. After they'd taken her off Pethidine, they kept her in for almost a week, to bring up her fluid intake. Her doctor was on holiday. She kept saying it was OK to send her home now but they wouldn't listen. As soon as her doctor got back he discharged her immediately, apologising for wasting her time. He couldn't understand why they hadn't realised.

I'd be a liar if I said I believed J. from the start, but at least I kept an open mind – I didn't have all that 'experience' clouding my vision. I could appreciate how she was being forced to behave the way she did. That the majority of the staff were white and middle-class, was I feel a contributing factor to the problems that these black women endured.

Interview with Elizabeth Anionwu

E: You asked me if there was any difference between the incidence of Sickle Cell Disease amongst men and women. It's equally distributed. What is interesting is that studies in the United States, and my own experience in this country, seem to show that women cope more with the illness. They don't seem to be admitted as frequently. Amongst our group, off-hand, I can think of more women who are working, studying, bringing up families, despite the illness and appear fairly well 'adjusted' to the fact they have a chronic illness. Whereas men don't appear to have adjusted so well. This does affect the nursing care they get. It is the men who are having much more difficulty, classified as 'problem' patients. Your interview with J doesn't accord with this though.

D: Could you say something about Pethidine, as this is where her trouble began.

E: In talking about Pethidine we have to talk about pain as the main problem in this illness. The pain is commonly experienced in the long bones of the body, but also the abdomen, chest and back are frequently affected. The major problem is the professionals! I don't think they understand why there should be pain – what type of pain. Pain is a very difficult thing to judge and yet when I give lectures to student nurses about it, I ask them would they accept that a person having a heart-attack has pain? Oh, and there's total acceptance; everybody's sympathetic.

But when it comes to Sickle Cell Disease, there's no doubt in my mind that nurses do not believe the patient is in pain! Also there is an incredible amount of fear amongst health-workers that they are going to make drug-addicts out of patients if they give them Pethidine as frequently as the specialists, who are geared up to Sickle Cell, would like. A black student nurse told me of a patient who had been given water by injection, based on the assumption that this patient really didn't have the pain and was just playing up! This is a frightening indictment of nursing and of the care of black patients, because underlying all this is, firstly, the ignorance of the profession about Sickle Cell which affects black people. Secondly, although there is quite a lot of literature in the medical press now, how come we still find this degree of ignorance? Overriding this are attitudes towards black people as a whole which all jumble up in the care of Sickle Cell Disease. What nurses and doctors have got to accept is that the pain involved can be very severe. Most patients, if you take the trouble to ask them, are frightened of the battle of words and thoughts between the patient and the medical staff that is going to take place once they are admitted. That battle is about whether prople believe them.

According to some nurses you get the 'clock-watching' syndrome, when a patient is prescribed pain-relief four-hourly, and the patients find that they're needed that frequently, or even *more* frequently. Some specialists will prescribe drugs 'PRN' (whenever they're required). This causes eye-brows to be raised because of fear of drug-addiction. But once the patient trusts that the staff believe she has pain, our experience is that less drugs are prescribed during the hospital admission.

Patients with this illness are in and out of hospital. They know the situation on the ward, that the student nurse may not be the best person to approach, but they also know that possibly the only way they can get any relief is by being a 'problem' patient, making very loud, aggressive demands on the nursing staff. They don't come in acting like this! It's the constant experience of not being believed.

I, and a lot of medical staff involved with Sickle Cell Disease, are deeply concerned about this, because pain is pain and why should the profession have this position of power and control in relieving such a distressing symptom!

ANON

Abortion: one woman's horror story

First published in *Breaking Chains*, 20, January 1981

We were recently sent this account by reliable friends of ALRA within the movement. It is a horrific story of one girl's humiliating experiences, gained whilst attempting to obtain a health-service termination. It poses a lot of questions – we hope the people involved will be able to provide some answers.

My period was a week late when I first went to see the doctor at the university Student Health Centre, on Tuesday 22 July, partly because I needed antihistamine for hayfever and partly because I had been feeling run-down and tired. The doctor suggested that I might be pregnant. I said I thought not, but my symptoms were classic and I use the cap. He then asked me how I felt about termination (not how I felt about having a child). I had not at this stage thought about it but told him that I considered termination preferable to having a child, given my unstable circumstances. He was very sympathetic, said that he hoped I'd menstruate before the following week, and if not to see him for a pregnancy test.

On Tuesday, 29 July, I went for a pregnancy test. The doctor told me it was positive and that I'd better get some money together fast. He booked me in to see him at 9.30 the following morning. When I said that I'd like a TOP (termination of pregnancy) in a National Health hospital, he became quite angry and told me that my reasons had better be good.

Wednesday, 30 July: I explained to my doctor my social reasons for wanting a TOP. I was unemployed, I lived on my own in a flat I was to vacate the following March as my landlord was selling up, I did not have a stable relationship, I could not foresee the possibility of using my recently gained degree whilst pregnant or after the baby was born, I had no support from my friends or my family, I was already in debt with an overdraft of over a £100 – I felt desperate. I also feared foetal damage since I'd taken drugs known to risk chromosomal damage after I had conceived but before I knew I was pregnant. This was the most important reason for wanting a TOP and the real deciding factor – I felt the risks were too high and I could not face seeing a pregnancy to full term with that sort of psychological pressure.

It was quite obvious from the doctor's attitude from the week before that he was not against TOP in principle, but he became quite nasty when I insisted that I had a right to one on the NHS. I was given what I term a 'horror story'. I would have to wait until I was sixteen weeks pregnant, when I would be induced and give birth to a 'live and screaming' foetus. I was sickened by this, at six weeks (at the very most) I did not believe this doctor. He then phoned (having sent me out of the surgery) a Mr —, consultant at the General Hospital, for an appointment.

Friday, 8 August: (10 days after the pregnancy test) I was seen by Mr —, consultant at the local General Hospital. He was short and sharp, telling me how irresponsible I had been, that I must go on the pill, asked me which I thought was more important, cancer of the womb or TOP, and did I not consider his feelings about TOP. After examining me, the consultant concluded that I'd 'obviously damaged the baby' and he had no choice but to terminate. I was told that I would be admitted within a fortnight, 'as soon as there is a bed free'.

Thursday, 28 August: I was admitted to Ward 2 of the General Hospital at 9.15 a.m. (four weeks and two days after my pregnancy test and my doctor's referral). The Registrar, a woman doctor and the head sister came to see me. Their attitude was hostile; I was told again how irresponsible I had been, that I was bigger than my dates predicted, and accused of lying about the date of my last menstrual period – and I therefore could not be trusted. Their moralising and obvious hostility towards me put me on the defensive. I pointed out that it was not my fault that today's society could put men on the moon but had still not yet developed 100 per cent safe contraception, and that I'd used contraception responsibly for seven years. I was then accused of being a narcotics addict. I have never taken narcotics in my life.

Having re-examined me, the Registrar, head sister and woman doctor stood just outside the open door of my small ward discussing which TOP method to use. Although I was only just within earshot and cannot quote exactly what was said, the words 'blood', 'pain', 'hours of contractions', and how awful it would be for me, in serious tones, carried clearly. I lay on my bed, frightened, in tears and half disbelief at what they were saying.

Although I had expected some resentment and a few nasty

comments from anti-abortionist staff, this sort of scaring tactic was hard to believe and I cried with anger at how they'd deliberately frightened me.

At about 11.00 a.m. I was examined by the woman doctor and had a blood test taken. She was cold and detached but not unpleasant. She told me I was eleven weeks pregnant and would go into theatre at about 3.30 p.m.

I was then told by one of the nurses to have a bath. I explained that I did not have a towel or soap. I was reluctantly given a towel (along with NHS expense comments) but no soap.

At about 12.30 p.m. two nurses came in to dress me for theatre. One of them pointed out the 'fairy-tale' rubbish I was reading and that it was time to face up to reality. (I had deliberately brought a light novel to read with me.) The other nurse complained about the waste of NHS money on people like me as she had to use half an 'expensive' bandage around a bangle on my wrist (which does not come off). I was then given some tablets which I presume were tranquillisers (the 'pre-med').

Upon examination by the consultant, I was told that I was 'borderline' and had a very tight cervix. He added that for all he knew I probably had 'two in there'. He made remarks about the possibility of me never being able to conceive again and that he didn't think they'd be able to cope with the blood loss. He indicated the size of the foetus's head with his hands and asked me if I really wanted him to crush 'your baby's head'. At this point I was very distressed and a little confused by his medical terminology (and presumably the tranquillisers were beginning to work), so that I cannot say for sure what else he said to me. However, throughout the interactions, the consultant, Registrar and head sister all referred to my 'baby'.

I cried myself to sleep and was later awakened by an auxiliary nurse who asked if I wanted a cup of tea. I said 'no thanks', since I was going into theatre that afternoon (I had been fasting since the night before). She looked surprised, and then very sorry for me, asking me had I not been told. I asked what she meant as at this point I was not sure what was happening to me, and told her that I was confused. She said she would send the head sister in to explain. It was only at this point that I realised the doctors were really serious about inducing me and were not going to operate that day (I was still dressed for theatre).

The head sister came in and was very patronising, saying that TOP was not like the media said it was; it was a very complicated, dangerous and ugly thing, etc., and explained about the drip in my arm, catheter through my cervix into the womb dripping a hormone, etc., from 9.00 a.m. the following morning through to early evening when I would go into contractions, experience labour pains which they could not give me anything for. The earliest it would be over would be twelve hours but it could be longer and I would probably stay in hospital till Sunday.

At this point, I resigned myself to accepting everything the doctors did and said, since they obviously knew best. Had I not been so sure that my decision to have a TOP was correct, I most certainly would have changed my mind, as going through an induced miscarriage in such a hostile environment sounded so traumatic and painful I wasn't sure I could go through with it.

After my tea at 6.00 p.m., which consisted of one sandwich and a jam tart, my only meal throughout the day, a friend who had by then heard about my treatment phoned me. He suggested that I discharge myself, since even if it was necessary to have a TOP by the most complicated method, at least I could have it in a more supportive environment. He had already booked an appointment at Birmingham's British Pregnancy Advisory Service (BPAS) and offered me the necessary money. At 6.40 p.m. I got dressed when my friend arrived to collect me and walked into the main ward. One of the nurses smiled at me (for the first time), saying, 'Oh, you've changed your mind.' I said, 'No,' that I had not changed my mind, but was going elsewhere. There was no surprise that I was discharging myself and I had the feeling that this was not the first time it had happened.

Before leaving the hospital at 7.20 p.m. I called in to say goodbye to the young woman, twelve weeks pregnant, who was already on the drip, being induced. Her left arm was swollen and hung in a sling (they had missed the vein). Her right arm was also in a sling, attached to a drip and a bleeping machine. The sheet under her arm was blood-soaked. She had been lying like this, with a catheter inserted into her womb, since 12.00, waiting, on her own, to go into contractions. A friend whom I asked to visit her the following evening reported that she was still like this, suffering a lot of pain, thirty-one hours later. She told me that all the nurses were extremely unsympathetic, had made nasty comments all day, and that the head sister had even gone as far as saying something about teaching her a lesson.

I left the hospital feeling like a convict just escaped from prison. I was my own person again and convinced I'd just escaped the risks and consequences of staying.

My 'conspiracy theory' was confirmed on Saturday morning, 30 August, when I saw two BPAS doctors in Birmingham. They were very sympathetic and supportive. They concluded I was between eleven and thirteen weeks, small enough for the simple suction method and certainly not big enough for TOP by inducement. I was booked into Wistons Nursing Home in Brighton for the following Thursday, 5 September. There I was given a TOP by the suction method.

Within half an hour of coming round I was up drinking tea and eating sandwiches with other women in the ward. Our ages ranged between fifteen and forty and we were all a great support to each other. All the doctors and nurses were kind and reassuring. We were treated like human beings. The contrast between the two experiences is obvious. The more subtle psychological differences were those between seeing smiling faces of caring staff and frowns, serious looks, from staff who resented you; between being called Mrs — and by your first name; between the terms 'pregnancy' and 'baby'; the difference between being made to feel mature and responsible (doctors' letters, charts, etc. were quite open) and small, foolish, and bad; the difference between leaving hospital confident in having made the right decision and leaving hospital with regret and guilt. I say this last point because I'm convinced that the combination of several days of such sophisticated psychological pressure and the natural depression following would certainly leave my head very unstable.

I've made this statement because I see an urgent need to prevent this sort of experience happening to other women. The questions I ask are:

(1) Why was I kept waiting so long?

(2) Why was everyone who took care of me in the General an anti-abortionist?

(3) Why did the consultant decide to induce me when three independent doctors decided it was safer to use the suction method?

(4) How many women have needed anti-depressants, tranquillisers, or psychotherapy after a TOP under Mr —, consultant at the General Hospital (and others)?

(5) How many other women have discharged themselves before going through with it?

Hospital records will reveal the answer to the last two questions and also the number of TOPs by the induced method relative to the simpler, safer, cheaper suction method.

I believe that the belittling nature of the experience has prevented many women coming forward to complain.

The lessons drawn must be that there is a desperate need for the provision of daycare abortion clinics, manned by sympathetic staff, and a mechanism to ensure that anti-abortionists in the medical profession never work in these clinics.

NAC: The Case for Change:
two views

The following two pieces outline the area of debate at the Eighth Annual Conference of the National Abortion Campaign, held in October 1983. They were circulated throughout NAC and published in *Outwrite*, 17, September 1983. At the conference it became obvious that opinion was deeply divided; it was finally decided that NAC should continue as a single-issue campaign and that a separate reproductive rights campaign should be launched early in the New Year.

View 1
Supported by Glasgow NAC, Dundee NAC, and the Scottish Abortion Campaign

Free abortion on demand is one of the original demands of the Women's Liberation Movement because it was recognised at the outset that, without the right to control her body, a woman cannot control her destiny. Naturally we feel that the fight for the improvement of women's health care is crucial in all aspects of our lives, and that, without the right to freely available safe abortion, we remain prisoners of our biology.

Why abandon the original demands of the campaign, when we have not yet won them? It is relatively easy to obtain an abortion in London, but in many other areas of England, and in Scotland and Wales, we have great difficulty getting the limited provisions of the 1967 Act implemented.

In Northern Ireland abortion remains illegal except in very extreme circumstances. It is recognised that women with money have always been able to obtain a safe abortion, unlike women without, who have had to go on the backstreets.

One of the biggest problems for NAC has been the way in which it has always been forced on the defensive by restrictive Bills and

Amendments, by devious, but legal, back-door methods such as Statutory Instruments, and by the smear campaign of our enemies, the anti-abortionists. Ironically these very attacks have served in many ways to concentrate the energies of the campaign on the single issue of abortion. Through the constant pressure of the Women's Liberation Movement, and with the support of women in the labour and trades union movement, we have managed to force the issue of abortion not only on the agenda of trades union conferences, but onto the streets.

Without this support we would not have defeated the Corrie Bill. *It was to be the only notable defeat of Tory policies since 1979.* With more of the same policies in store, can NAC seriously consider abandoning what has been up till now our single-minded determination to counter all attacks on our abortion rights, whenever they occur?

NAC has consistently tried to promote improvements, like NHS outpatient abortion clinics, and positive legislation, e.g. Jo Richardson MP's Ten-Minute Bill in 1981. However it would be unrealistic to expect NAC to win these improvements in the next five years. *On the contrary, we expect the attacks on our abortion rights to be more frequent and varied.*

The large anti-abortion rally on 25 June 1983 in London, organised by the Society for the Protection of the Unborn Child (SPUC), and their subsequent full-page adverts in national newspapers and in *Private Eye*, mobilising support 'to get the law changed', heralds a huge no-expense-spared campaign. The most obvious and dramatic next step would be a further Private Member's Bill to restrict the 1967 Abortion Act. This would have massive government and Tory back-bench support with a much depleted opposition in parliament. Even if all opposition MPs voted against such a Bill, the responsibility for organising the campaign would necessarily remain with NAC.

Even without a Private Member's Bill, certain aspects of the law could be changed by using Statutory Instruments (a parliamentary device to change the law without a vote). We witnessed this in 1982 when the wording was changed in abortion notification forms, thereby challenging social grounds as a reason for abortion.

Perhaps the greatest threat to abortion facilities lies with government intentions to dismantle the National Health Service. Even now, abortion is the only operation more commonly performed in the private sector than in the NHS. We already know that most area health authorities put the very lowest priority on abortion facilities. *We would have the prospect of a woman's right to choose – so long as we could pay.*

To broaden our campaign out into the wider issues of reproductive rights would diminish the importance of abortion as the central issue. By dropping the word abortion from the name of our campaign we would be shirking our responsibilities to those who look to us to lead the fight on abortion rights. We have not yet succeeded in our aims, but the fact that we have never failed is a tribute to the single-minded determination with which the aims of the campaign have been pursued.

View 2

Supported by Jane Marshall, Julia South (Merseyside NAC), Dianne Grimsditch, Marge Berer, Sarah Vickerstaff, Julia Goodwin, Jo Mussen (NAC Steering Committee), Helen Minett, Cathy Manthorpe (Leeds NAC), Isabel Ros (Norwich Abortion & Reproductive Rights Campaign)

NAC's main aim has been 'Free abortion on demand – a woman's right to choose' since 1975, when the campaign began. All of us remain committed to that aim and we are far from achieving it. But some of us feel we have become complacent about what 'a woman's right to choose' means.

We are deluding ourselves if we believe that women in this society *can* make choices about having children or not, when there are over four million unemployed, when the wages most women earn (if at all) are still abysmally low, when being married or not makes so much difference, when there is such a lot of unchallenged racism on both an individual and institutionalised level, and when we are faced with virulent anti-lesbianism. Our experiences both in NAC and in the women's movement generally since the 1970s have made it clear that to focus exclusively on abortion rights is not enough.

Abortion is not an isolated event in women's lives. It means something different to a woman whose doctor is discouraging her from having a third child by suggesting sterilisation; to a woman whose husband has just been made redundant; to a young woman involved in her first sexual relationship; and to a woman who has decided never to have children.

As women, we all share a lack of control over our own bodies especially in terms of when and if we want children. But we experience that lack of control in different ways, and it is not only through abortion that control over our reproduction is felt.

There is an entire climate which promotes certain women having babies and which does not favour others, on the basis of prejudice and oppression to do with colour, class, marital status, sexual preference, disability and notions of the 'fit/unfit' mother. We come up against these notions when we go for contraception, if we need an abortion, if we want AID, if sterilisation is an option, if we need tests for infertility, or if we are pregnant or want to get pregnant. We come up against them precisely at the point where we attempt to make whatever limited choices are open to us, given our individual circumstances.

Abortion rights are still being attacked and eroded now, much more insidiously and successfully than five years ago. The struggle to protect those rights remains crucial in a right-wing and repressive atmosphere.

But so much else is also threatened that to continue to focus on abortion means ignoring too many other, equally important and totally related, issues on *reproductive rights*. If we continue to do this in NAC, we are excluding and making invisible those of us who experience these other problems.

For example, closure of family planning clinics has begun. If it continues, our choice of contraception will narrow because not all GPs have the training or time to provide all the methods, and many women do not want to go to their GPs for contraception.

Contraception has only been a right – free on the NHS – since 1974. It could well become a right on paper only.

There is an increasing backlash against whatever sexual freedom we can be said to have, especially for young women. Policies such as routinely fitting IUDs after an abortion and routinely giving Depo-Provera with rubella vaccinations after childbirth lump us together as passive receivers of contraception 'for our own good'.

Contraceptive failure is defined as our failure only, and there is an increasing intolerance of accidental pregnancy. We are offered – or denied – particular methods of contraception, abortion or sterilisation, depending on who we are. And we are encouraged – or prevented – from having children on the same basis.

Our politics have changed as we have learned all these things, and we believe NAC must change too. It has become clear to us that we ought to be campaigning for reproductive rights generally.

We are therefore proposing to the NAC Conference on 1–2 October that we dissolve NAC and start again with a new name, a new structure based on local groups, a broader perspective, and hopefully new energy and new women involved.

We feel it is the only way to continue at all as a campaign, without denying what we have learned and without ignoring the women whose experiences we have learned it from.

8 Challenges

Introduction

Not much introduction is needed here. This section brings together our many and varied voices of opposition to current ideology and practice in the Women's Liberation Movement.

No longer can we afford to pretend that the Women's Liberation Movement is a united whole; there are deep divisions between us. If these remain unacknowledged and go unchallenged, we in the WLM will lose our collective power in our attempts radically to change the world.

LUCHIA FITZGERALD

Who's a Witch?

First published in *Manchester Women's Paper*, November 1981

Everyone is being told lately not to believe all we see on TV or read in the papers, and that is quite rightly so, as there is no doubt whatsoever that in the present system we live under are the greatest liars who ever walked the earth in shoe leather, that is, the ones who run the country – the government of the day, or whatever.

If they can all sit back and decide what goes into the papers and into the TV like news, etc., debates and so on, why should we accept the history that has been handed down to us? Could it be that those old stories have been chopped, censored and in the end made to look good, or perhaps cleaned up so as not to let too many cats out of a lot of bags? We are all aware that news is kept back, well it was in my opinion kept back before today, chewed over and hashed out to make things look not quite how they seemed.

We have barrelsful of evidence on witches, some the greatest heap of trash you have ever had the pleasure of reading, like broomsticks, spells, etc. Wicked, that's the kind of stuff we were told as we were growing up. Then when we grew up, we were told of another type of witch altogether, that is, the ones that are roaming about today, doing their thing up in places like Alderly Edge, and supposedly making a fortune out of bumping people off by sticking pins in dolls for a small fortune. No wonder they can all afford to live out there, the rest of us can hop on our broomsticks I presume, anyway these are the stories that we hear.

It seems today that the word witch would be lumped together with the thing that they call the OCCULT. To be honest with the reader, I think that all this trash is just the rich with nothing else left to do, after trying everything else that money could buy. You can bet your ass that you'll never find the average working person out at Alderly Edge on Halloween, for a start off they couldn't afford their share of the lamb that they throw up on the slab for slaughter. Let's face it, no working people can afford a leg of lamb these days, but let's get back to the point.

242

It's true; we are quite sure that these women were burned to death, and that is something that they could *not* hide. Likewise there are some things today that they cannot hide either.

The question is why they had to die.

Where did the word 'wicked' come from, and 'evil' and 'magic potions'? Did they make all this up about these women because basically they knew piss-all about them, only that they existed in the community and countryside? Some say they were wise womin, maybe they were *too* wise, and needed bumping off. They lived alone – not all, but some – could it be that the ones who lived alone for years on end were seen as a bit weird, and the ones who lived in pairs were seen as even weirder, and perhaps worst of all they started getting themselves together, and talking shop? That must have been far too much, so the system started a scandal and used the women as scapegoats. The Christians were right in there with their twopence worth, to collect a few souls, by saying the womin were into devil-worship. And, let's face it, it was very easy to get people whipped up in those days. This system still gets people worked up today.

Here is scapegoating for you, here are a few examples. The system we live under makes terrible mistakes, but they always find someone to take the rap, so, at the drop of a hat, blacks are blamed for everything. Oh, you might say, it's just the National Front, but the system is in there with its wooden spoon, don't you worry. And it was in there with its spoon in the fifteenth and sixteenth centuries doing the same dirty work. Now it glorifies the Pankhursts, but says piss-all about the working-class womin who took part in that struggle, but use the token one, Annie Kenny, as the working-class heroine. It makes me feel sick to think about it. Maybe, like the witches, poor Annie Kenny had to be gagged in the end. Let's face it, there are two sides to every coin, but the system will make sure that we working-class people only ever read or hear one side of what we want, whether it be now or long, long ago. They only tell you so much, you have to guess the rest.

Well, one thing we can be certain of, like I said at the start, the womin were burned and burned alive, and that did happen. Also, just for the record, some time ago there was a communal grave found with all female bones in it. At least forty womin were said to be buried in that grave and laid beside all the bodies were double-headed axes. More graves were found soon after. Who killed all those womin, and why all in one grave, what went on then? Well, we have since found out that our Amazons were not a bloody myth but they were real people, groups of womin, who stuck together like glue and carried double-headed axes for protection.

Protection from what and whom? Like the witches they too just got wiped out, history distorted, so that we will never know the real from the unreal. All we know is that we are seeing womin killed down the centuries for reasons that the system wants us to know, or would like us to believe.

But I believe a lot of those reasons were probably cobblers, because we all know that the press and TV of today can con us all, so it must have had a field-day back then in the fifteenth and sixteenth centuries, and said what they liked about those poor womin that they slaughtered in them days. Let's face it, there are a lot of people out there who would still like to put a lot of womin in a big hole and shoot them all, all at once, to wipe them off the face of the earth. If you don't believe what I'm saying, why don't you phone the Lord Mayor of Trafford Council and ask him what he would like to do to women who live together with other women, otherwise known as lesbians, and he will tell you quite openly that he would like to shoot the whole damn lot. Maybe it was his relatives way back that killed all the women at the stake, who knows? But one thing is for sure, and that is women who pal about together and share their sexual lives together and decide that that's the way they want things to be for themselves had better watch out. Because, you see, they don't burn you at the stake today, but they have tried to cut one's brain out, the common word to use I believe is lobotomy. Oh yes, the methods are clean and quick, and you can continue your life as a cabbage, if you can bear it, that is.

On the other hand, you could get your ass holes together, all you wicked witches out there, and tell society once and for all that you are back, and this time, you are here to stay, and that you will *not go away*. You are going to fight and WIN, like everyone else you have a right to live and love and walk the earth in peace and not in ridicule.

P.S. So go out this Halloween and celebrate your homecoming, for this time we will win, or no one will survive . . .

Black Feminism

First published in *Speak Out*, no. 4

Feminism is the theory underlying the struggle against the systematic oppression of women based on sex. When we speak of the 'systematic oppression of women' we refer to the many factors which contribute to the oppression of women and maintain and reproduce our subordinate position. These can broadly be divided into the following categories: ideological–cultural, economic and political.

Ideological–cultural oppression

Ideology is a system of values and beliefs. Within each society is a dominant ideology which is linked to the economic and political organisation of that particular society. It acts by moulding people's consciousness so as to reproduce that particular way of life. In a highly oppressive system such as the capitalist system in which we live, the dominant ideology attempts to make people accept exploitation and it is successful in so far as it can make the oppressive power relations seem 'natural'. People, on the other hand, cannot be fooled by lies so easily, and there is a continual process of struggle between the dominant ideology and people's resistance to it.

Children are born male or female (determined by biology), but women and men are prepared for their different biological and social functions by the process of socialisation, which is determined by the dominant ideology. The meaning of 'woman' and 'man' in social terms is what we call gender. The female is conditioned into passivity, submission and emotional dependence, and the male into self-assertiveness, dominance and independence in the process of socialisation. As women, our consciousness is formed in the conditions of subordination and oppression. Therefore, gender for us means division, inequality and internalised inferiority.

The family, or to be more precise, the ideology surrounding the family, is an important site of women's oppression. Through the family our roles as men and women are clearly set out. We are taught how to think and *be* women and men. It is also within this concept of the family that various themes that influence our idea of gender are supposed to be fully expressed. These include such things as romantic love, feminine nurturance, maternalism and self-sacrifice for women; together with masculine protection and financial support. What this means in practice is that women are primarily responsible for all the tasks connected with housework and childcare. A woman has to service the male, has responsibility for three categories of people – children, the sick and disabled, and the elderly – and also has to look after herself. Moreover, performing this role either excludes her from earning a living or negatively affects the terms on which she does so. Both mean she has to be financially dependent upon a man.

Therefore, within the household there is not only a division of labour (women and men performing different tasks), but also the relationship between the woman and man is such that the woman is systematically dependent upon and unequal to the man. This ideology of the family has far-reaching effects on the position of women in all aspects of life.

Economic oppression

In the present-day economic system, based as it is on wage labour, women's severe disadvantage in, if not total exclusion from, the labour market is another important area of our oppression.

In earlier periods, during the pre-capitalist feudal times, the whole household as a unit was engaged in productive labour. The development of wage labour with the production of goods for the market rather than for use, meant that household needs had to be met by incoming wages rather than by internal production. The development of capitalism also brought with it the separation between home and workplace, which created a crisis over the daily care of children, the disabled and the elderly. This has, as we know, customarily been resolved by giving these responsibilities to women, thus cutting them off from equal participation with men in wage labour. This has been accompanied by the establishment of the privatised domestic area of 'the home' as the particular province of women, and of 'femininity' and maternalism as characteristic of women. Women have become dependent upon the male wage in capitalism and this is accompanied by an ideology of emotional and psychological dependence.

These ideological processes are, however, not in keeping with hard economic reality, which forces most working-class women to take up employment outside the home – just to make ends meet. So, family ideology doesn't actually keep women within the home, but it does influence the nature of women's participation in employment and ensures that women do a second, unpaid job within the home.

The division of labour in present-day capitalism involves a sharp separation between male and female workers. Women are concentrated in particular industries at particular levels, and are systematically subjected to poorer pay and working conditions than men. Despite the equal pay legislation, figures for 1978 show that weekly earnings of women comprise only 64.8 per cent of those of men. Low pay is not the only thing that characterises female wage labour. Job security and wages for part-time work are greatly disadvantaged when compared to full-time work. Yet 41 per cent of all women with jobs in Britain work part-time. Homework on piece-rate contracts (highly exploitative) is also mainly undertaken by women because of their domestic and childcare responsibilities.

Women workers are more vulnerable to redundancy in times of recession. Since 1974, redundancy among women workers has been three times higher than the rate for men. Low representation of women in senior grades and in the 'higher professions' in general, reflects the systematic discrimination that women suffer in education and training.

In general, within a particular trade, industry or profession, women occupy jobs which are lower paid, more insecure and less likely to bring promotion than men. Furthermore, women are concentrated in certain low-paid industries. Over 60 per cent of the entire female workforce is concentrated in only ten occupations: clerical work, shop assistants, typists and secretaries, maids, cleaners, nurses, teachers, canteen assistants, shop managers, and sewing and textile workers. Looking at this list, a clear picture emerges. Most of these jobs can broadly be described as service work, the 'caring' professions and socialised forms of domestic service. In other words, the distribution of women in the employed workforce bears a striking resemblance to the division of labour in the family.

Division of labour, not only between men and women, but also with regard to children and old people, probably pre-dates capitalism and is not necessarily divisive if the various tasks hold equal status. However, capitalism not only caused the takeover and strengthening of the differentiation of tasks, but divided the workforce itself into wage-earners and those dependent upon the wage of others. Capitalism did not create domestic labour, but it did create a set of social relations in which pre-existing sexual divisions were not only reproduced but solidified within the wage labour system.

It can be seen how family relations and the ideology of domestic responsibility play a large part in determining the position of women as wage labourers. As outlined earlier, responsibility for childcare forces women to be involved in the highly exploitative areas of part-time work and home. Women are channelled into categories of work such as servicing and caring, which have been established as predominantly 'feminine'. Also, the construction of a family form in which the male head of the household is supposedly responsible for the financial support of a dependent wife and children has acted against demands for equal pay and an equal right to work for women.

The fact that women happen to be the sole breadwinners in many cases, especially within the black community, still doesn't allow them to escape all the restrictions that operate within the area of women's employment. The ideology of the family also extends to family structures other than the nuclear type. For example, even in the extended family, it is the women who shoulder the responsibility for childcare and domestic work and so get excluded from equal participation with men in wage labour.

The state and women's oppression

The state plays an important role in legitimising the various dimensions of women's oppression in this society. It actively maintains the household system, where women and children are supposedly dependent upon a male breadwinner's 'family wage'. Provisions such as the 'married man's tax allowance' and arrangements for national insurance payments are reflections of a woman's financial dependence upon a man within marriage. This same principle extended to cohabiting couples results in the disgusting practice of social security officials attempting to ascertain a woman's sexual relations with men with a view to depriving her of the right to benefits. Thus, the state very firmly upholds the principle of woman's dependence in spite of the fact that the number of households fitting the stereotype of the male breadwinner/full-time, dependent housewife is, at any given time, very small.

In the area of employment, the state regulates terms and conditions of employment in order to reinforce women's subordination, e.g. banning of women from certain work (such as mining), withholding maternity benefits from unmarried women. State provision and regulation of education clearly plays an important part in structuring the different opportunities open to women and men.

The state also creates conditions within which racism and sexism are reinforced and legitimised. For example, the Nationality Act, virginity tests and the administration of the contraceptive drug Depo-Provera are all measures that are particularly oppressive to black women. Another clear example is the recent change in the immigration law which prevents black women from bringing to Britain husbands who are foreign nationals. What this means is that if you are a black woman, even full British citizenship does not give you the same privileges as those of either men merely settled here (who can bring their wives to settle), or EEC women who, even without British citizenship, can, under the Treaty of Rome, bring their husbands to settle in Britain. This law effectively makes us second-class citizens and constitutes yet another blatant breach of the European Convention on Human Rights, which denounces discrimination based on sex or race. Britain has been taken to the European Court of Human Rights on this issue and the initial proceedings have found that Britain has a case to answer.

Sexual harassment

In keeping with the state's oppression and subjugation of women, individual men – fathers, brothers, husbands, sons, comrades, friends and strangers – continue to exploit and humiliate women. In the family, where women are financially dependent on their men, we are treated as their property. As property, men feel that they can use and abuse women verbally and physically with impunity. We are frequently beaten, psychologically pressured and physically forced into having sex, and then often left to support the offspring of such encounters. On the streets we are stared at, leered at, man-handled and raped at knife point. Women, therefore, live a daily life of fear of violence from men, both inside and outside the home.

Our instilled fear of male violence then drives us to seek protection from other men (e.g. the police), giving them more power to control us. This control operates on two levels. First, on an individual basis, whereby women are confronted with individual police*men*, and are subjected to hostility, thinly disguised disbelief and mistrust, and an overall lack of support. One explicit example of this is police reluctance to intervene in cases of even the most brutal marital violence – respecting the privacy of 'the family' and upholding the idea that women are the property of men. In rape cases the police are well known for subjecting the victim to an offensive and degrading inquisition in which her own sexual history is on trial.

Individual male violence becomes male social power and is legitimised by the state. This legitimised male social power and sexual aggression is used as a tool to control and intimidate women who dare to fight back. Thus, the law itself reinforces fundamental assumptions about gender division and it is only very recently that women have been recognised as legal subjects within their own right.

The second aspect of this control has to do with the fact that the policeforce is an arm of the state. As such it is another tool by which all black people are terrorised and oppressed. As black women, we are faced with the twin oppressions of implicitly condoned male violence because we are women, and explicit violence by the state because we are black.

The images that men have of our bodies are thrust upon us. We are evaluated as sex-symbols. Pornography and all types of advertising perpetuate sexist stereotypes of how we should look and behave: this is in turn reinforced by the mass media through films, television, newspapers and magazines. Based on the notion that women are the property of men, many women are further exploited through prostitution as a commodity to be bought and sold at will, the male pimp always hovering in the background to collect his supposed 'due'.

Sexual harassment, violence and exploitation of women transcend class and race boundaries. Black and white men, regardless of their class position, align with each other on the basis of shared sexism. Black men who are victimised by racism in the same way as black women, act as sexist oppressors of black women. This points to an underlying failure on their part to understand that although sexism does transcend class barriers, it only acts in the interest of one class – the rulers. They fall for the myth of white society which says that all black women are sexually 'loose' and treat us as such. They devalue our efforts to create a better life for ourselves from which as black people we would all benefit.

As black women we are also blamed by the state for being in collusion with the black man to perpetuate our own oppression. Although this is *not* the case, we can appreciate what it means to be in a racist society where a black woman may think twice before she calls the police for violence done to her by a black man. However, as black women our struggle is not about blaming the victim, but is a struggle against the system which has allowed men to see and treat us as mindless objects, because of the fact that we are women.

Black feminism and the black struggle

To be feminist, therefore, necessitates an understanding of these forces which are brought to bear to oppress us in many subtle and not always apparent ways. To be black and feminist adds a very different dimension to feminism and involves our coming to terms with the specific implications of such a position. One important consideration concerns the issue of black feminism as a cause of division within the black community.

There is a strongly held opinion that black feminism is an assault on the black family and thus, the black community; and which further states that black women have always been sexually liberated. This argument has its foundations in slavery and is based on the so-called 'easy' life of those black women who were forced to 'service' their white masters sexually. Their condition has historically been projected as being closer to that of white women than black men. But the truth is that black women were the *most* victimised by this situation. We were raped, abused and beaten by the white masters and even by some male slaves who imitated them. We were bred like cattle. Mates were chosen; husbands and children taken away at the slavemaster's command. Black women were assumed to be the sexual property of the owner, his friends, visitors and relatives. Is *this* what they would have us call sexual liberation?

The myth of matriarchy – with its image of the all-powerful black woman – has persistently plagued the black community and forms the basis for another argument against black feminism. The reasoning behind it contends that there is no need for black women to be feminists because the black woman has always wielded power in black society. Nothing could be further from the truth. Historically, the racism of the state has denied black people their right to employment, while the interaction of racism and sexism has facilitated the entry of black women into specific jobs only. This often means that the black woman is forced to assume responsibility as the breadwinner. However, the work she does is usually menial with long hours and low pay; at the end of which she still has to care for her own family's needs. The effect of this is to create a twofold situation, calculated to produce hostilities within and thus undermine the black community; and at the same time provide a source of cheap labour for the state.

The black man, the argument goes, suffered because his position was demeaned in the eyes of the community – he was made to feel 'less of a man'. But it is the black woman who suffered most from the matriarchal myth. For not only was her labour exploited, but she had (and still has) to bear the accusations and fight against the charge that she emasculates the black man as a result of this situation. To make matters worse, some black men have seized upon this myth to blame all of their oppression on the supposedly 'domineering' black woman. We have always fought against this outrage, however, and will continue to strike out against the application of these insidious stereotypical labels to us. Further-more, in waging the struggle, it is crucial for us to remember that the only real winners in the whole matriarchal myth/mess, are the ruling classes – the state and its forces. The sooner we get rid of this issue as a bone of contention between black men and black women, the better able we'll be to concentrate our efforts against our common oppressor.

A further argument against black feminism says that for black women to speak out against sexist oppression causes division within the black community because it takes time and energy away from the black struggle. We are told that the black woman should be squarely in her man's corner, but behind him. During the civil rights movement, a time when the talents and abilities of black men and women should have been jointly recognised in the struggle for black liberation, along came Stokely Carmichael declaring that the position of women in the movement should be 'prone'. Later, Eldridge Cleaver, a prominent member of the Black Panther Party, said that black women had 'pussy power'. We were expected to contribute to the movement but only in the way the black man said we could.

So black women were left in a kind of limbo – damned if we did and damned if we didn't. Our roles for the revolution were to be as coffee-makers, cooks, fund-raisers, and, of course, willing sexual partners; while the men conducted the important business of the struggle. We were not expected to open our mouths about the oppression we suffered as women at the hands of black men, who saw women's liberation (if they thought about it at all) strictly in terms of a minor side issue – 'a white girl's problem'. What they failed to recognise, however, was that the status of black women places us at the intersection of all forms of subjugation in society – racial oppression, sexual oppression and economic exploitation. This means that we are a natural part of many different struggles – both as black people and as women.

This brings us to another issue which we as black women must deal with – the question of *autonomy*. We must begin by distinguishing autonomy from *separatism*, as there is some confu-sion surrounding the two terms. An autonomous movement creates a favourable climate for understanding and evaluating the intrica-cies involved with the question of the liberation of a particular group; which, in turn, makes it possible to expand the whole political struggle. The black women's movement in Britain should, like those women who either belong to a women's movement or the arm of a party in Third World countries, form part of the total struggle for liberation. This is quite different from women who wish to create change for women, in isolation from men. We see this evaluation of the changing position of women in post-revolutionary societies being grappled with by the women in these societies, with one striking example being Cuban women.

Black people throughout history have formed autonomous organisations, in the belief that it is those who are oppressed who are the best equipped to liberate themselves. No one else can do it for them. Given the nature of our oppression as black people and as women, this can be no less true for black women.

Having arrived at autonomy as a necessary option for black women raises the point of exactly what form it should take. There are two major and opposing views in the women's movement currently.

Radical feminism contends that the oppression of women is the major and primary oppression in all societies. Patriarchy is identified as a universal mode of power relationship and domination. Male domination and female subjugation, they argue, are achieved through (among other things) their construction of sexuality, masculine–feminine role models and the socialisation of children. Within this perspective men are seen as dominant by training, and use force to maintain control of the economy, the state and a monopoly on sexual violence. Radical feminists identify patriarchy as being all-pervasive, penetrating class divisions and different societies, and as crossing cultures and historical periods. The logical outcome of identifying men as the sole enemy leads to total separation as the only solution.

The other viewpoint is *socialist feminism*, which we in the Brixton Black Women's Group hold. To us it is clear that, while male domination goes back a long way, women's oppression today is inextricably linked with the whole system of class oppression, whereby a small group of the rich and powerful ruling class control, exploit and severely oppress the vast majority of the people, both men and women. To understand our situation properly we have to understand the roots of women's oppression both historically and cross-culturally. To achieve this, it is necessary to examine and analyse the interrelations and connections between the various factors which form the basis of women's subjugation, as discussed earlier. These areas have to be examined not in isolation, but in relation to the whole oppressive capitalist system. Likewise, the struggle for women's liberation has to be part of the concrete struggle against class oppression, for no form of liberation will be possible without the overthrow of the capitalist system.

In adopting this position, as black women we are strongly influenced by the knowledge that our countries of origin, the so-called 'Third World', having been actively underdeveloped by *colonialism* (a part of capitalism), are even now being raped and pillaged under the stranglehold of *imperialism* (yet another, and to us very relevant, aspect of capitalism). Thus, a few industrialised countries grow more and more wealthy and powerful at our expense, while our people die of starvation and our own countries fall ever deeper into dependence and poverty.

It is therefore impossible for us to consider the oppression of women separately from the international oppression by imperialism of our countries of origin, and our experience, even here in Britain, of racism which moulds the life of our whole community. Yet we are also aware that overthrowing the whole capitalist and imperialist system does not automatically bring about an end to women's oppression. It is a specific and complex issue which needs to be addressed and dealt with directly, if it is to be dealt with effectively.

Some would argue that given the immense task ahead of black people in liberating ourselves as a people, we should concentrate on that task first, before worrying about women's liberation. But this ignores the fact that as long as women are oppressed, and this oppression continues to be ignored, we cannot take our rightful place in the overall struggle which will as a result be only half as strong as it should be. Hence, in the context of the wider struggle for black, socialist liberation, it is as important to address the issue of women's oppression right from the *beginning*, as it is for women involved in the struggle for our own liberation to recognise our role within the wider struggle.

It is in this context of an understanding of our oppression based on sex, race and class and the recognition of our struggle being part and parcel of the greater black struggle for the liberation of all our people from all forms of oppression, that black feminism is defined for us.

LONDON LESBIAN OFFENSIVE GROUP (LLOG)

Anti-Lesbianism in the Women's Liberation Movement

First published in *Revolutionary and Radical Feminist Newsletter*, no. 10, Summer 1982

This is an attempt to raise some of the issues which have been emerging from our discussions in the London Lesbian Offensive Group (LLOG) about our experiences as lesbians in the Women's Liberation Movement.

LLOG was formed after the strong interest shown at the 1982 Lesbian Conference in the workshop called on anti-lesbianism in the WLM. The group comprises women with differing feminist politics, all concerned about this issue. A sister group has started in Birmingham (BLOG), and we hope to see other groups forming in different places.

All of us have come up against, and greatly suffered from, anti-lesbianism from women who identify themselves as feminists. It is time for anti-lesbianism to be identified as political oppression. We are angry that heterosexual feminists do not take responsibility for being members of an oppressive power group, do not appear to recognise or challenge the privileges which go with that, nor do they bother to examine how all this undermines not only our lesbian politics, but our very existence.

Many heterosexual feminists seem to understand that anti-lesbianism can take very violent forms (assault, loss of children in custody cases, loss of jobs, incarceration in mental institutions), but it can also take more subtle and prolonged forms, sometimes unconsciously held, which come from deeply ingrained attitudes, expectations and assumptions. These attitudes, in this country, both come from and promote heterosexuality and the small nuclear family unit. It is this set of ideas and values to which we refer when we use the term heterosexist. We want to expose heterosexism as a set of institutionalised attitudes which are fundamentally anti-

255

feminist and anti-woman, not with the aim of making heterosexual women feel guilty and behave defensively, but rather to demand of them that they cease to undermine lesbianism by making us invisible and voiceless and that they make conscious moves to undermine their own heterosexual privilege.

Many heterosexual feminists seem not to believe any more (if they ever did) that *lesbians are oppressed*. Those who do seem not to believe that we are oppressed not just by *society* (which always means somebody else) but by heterosexual people, women as well as men, feminists as well as non-feminists. Our experience of this oppression varies according to our age, race, ethnic group, class and whether or not we have a disability. Of course, in the final analysis, men benefit the most from outlawing lesbianism. Any threat to the institution of heterosexuality is a threat to male control of, and power over, women . . . and this is the political power of lesbianisn. Of course, also, women do not get heterosexual privilege without paying for it in some ways. We would not deny that women are oppressed within heterosexual relationships. But, nevertheless, they also oppress lesbians by the unavoidable use (and abuse) of heterosexual privilege and power.

How often have we heard heterosexual feminists claiming that they feel *oppressed* by lesbians in certain women-only situations, when they really mean they are outnumbered and/or threatened and/or challenged or criticised. How often have we heard lesbian oppression ignored when heterosexual women proclaim that lesbian relationships are a soft option because we as lesbians do not have to struggle in our relationships . . . because women are equal. How often have we been questioned for wanting children where, for heterosexual women, it is seen as an absolute right. How often have we heard heterosexual women describing themselves as 'normal' or 'ordinary' . . . which of course makes us freaks. Surprisingly enough, *we also* have housework to do, bills to pay, children to get to school, men and their sexism to contend with. Anti-lesbianism is taking place every time our childrearing is criticised and scrutinised in an unsupportive way, and every time it is assumed that what we want, or ought to want, is to raise 'ordinary', 'normal' children.

Lesbian oppression is fundamentally about living in a world where we are made to feel that we don't have the right to exist. Of not ever (except from each other) having affirmation, approval, recognition for our way of life from the world about us. Heterosexual privilege is about having all that in some measure (depending on how well you toe the line). Lesbian oppression is about losing our children, not having access to male money (which is most money), having fewer housing rights, getting barred from pubs, being forced to lie in order to keep our jobs. Even those of us who work in 'alternative' projects experience a vast split between our public and private lives, for example, never being able to talk about what we really feel as it is too threatening to the heterosexuals who invariably dominate. It's also the continual worries about the victimisation of the children we *do* manage to keep, being beaten up and abused, being told that we are sick and/or disgusting (and sometimes believing it), being forced into insular groups and then being despised for depending on that.

Lesbian oppression is also about being forced to remain silent about our lesbianism for fear of the reactions we know it brings. It's about feeling continually sick and ashamed of ourselves all the time we 'pass' as heterosexual, knowing that our silence – our failure to assert our lesbian identity – contributes to our own oppression, and that of our sisters. It's about never being able to forget that we are 'other', that we don't belong. Heterosexual privilege is about having, and assuming, the right to be more 'normal' in both public and private. (Public not meaning outside your home, but in absolutely all dealings with the everyday world.) This kind of invisible validation is of such great psychological security that it is almost immeasurable, and the stress of living as a lesbian is of never, ever having it. Heterosexual privilege means secondhand access to male power; it is not power in its own right, but nevertheless, it is power over *us*, power which is an automatic benefit of heterosexuality.

Anti-lesbianism manifests itself in the WLM in various forms. We are marginalised in the movement as the loony fringe, while many heterosexual feminists gain credibility for themselves by denying that lesbianism is a crucial part of feminist politics. This process is further reinforced by the way the media, including some self-defined feminists, represent lesbianism as the irrational force of feminism, the only place in the movement, and indeed the world, where man-hating is to be found.

And while other feminists deny us, by disassociating themselves from us, they are still able to cash in on the security and approval both of men themselves and straight society in general. Their politics and their demands are, after all, only 'reasonable'. And we, by implication, are excessive and obsessive. Wherever lesbians are made invisible in feminist writings, discussions and campaigns, we are being undermined by anti-lesbians. Whenever we are accused of 'dominating' just by being present, vocal or hardworking, we are being silenced and oppressed. We are *accused* of having more *time* for feminism and political activity because we are not having sexual relationships with men. It is anti-lesbianism that is going on whenever our commitment to women is dismissed as sexually motivated, or motivated by more 'need' of the movement than that of heterosexual women. All that really means is that we experience oppression more acutely and therefore put more energy into fighting it. We want to turn the assumptions on their heads and ask, *why* allow servicing and/or engaging with men to take away energy and time from political struggle against women's oppression. Heterosexual feminists need to face these questions in a self-critical and searching frame of mind.

We are tired of being characterised as sexual predators on the one hand (a classic old stereotype), while being exploited by heterosexual and 'bisexual' women for a sexual 'experience' on the other. (I tried it, and didn't like it . . . ever heard that one from a heterosexual woman?) We are tired, too, of having lesbian behaviour and culture criticised by heterosexual feminists without their ever trying to understand either lesbian history or the pressures of living as a lesbian, and without their ever having to define as a problem *their* behaviour and sexual culture as heterosexual women.

Having said all that, it is most painfully true that anti-lesbianism has its place among lesbians too, including those with a public voice in the media. This comes, more than anything, from our need to survive, a survival which is sometimes dependent on getting whatever benefits and privileges we can from a system which most of all excludes black and/or working-class lesbians, who are kept furthest away from the centre of white male and heterosexual privilege, proportionately increasing their oppression. It also comes from our internalised self-hatred, our reluctance to be one of those continually described as disgusting, and the inability always to be up-front in a world which hates lesbians. What we are now seeing is an era where many lesbian feminists are prepared to take the brunt of coming out as lesbians, but then refuse to acknowledge lesbianism as a specific area of political struggle and strategy. This is a new development in the marginalisation and silencing of lesbianism. Sometimes this is because lesbians do not want to explore lesbian oppression in too much detail because it is too painful to acknowledge how deeply it affects our lives, heads and confidence. In other circumstances it happens because lesbian feminists do not want to divorce themselves completely from male approval, professional status, heterosexual friends/comrades or any other kind of validation of their politics. So, for them, lesbianism has to mean no more politically than a matter of sexual preference or choice, no more than the old-style gay rights politics of 'we are people too, no different from you, everybody sing along to "Glad to be Gay" '. Significantly, sexual preference politics have gained a certain amount of public credibility in left-wing groups, some of which now have gay (i.e. mainly male) groups within them. Having at last responded to pressure from gay rights activists within their organisations, it now suits them to assign the issue of homosexuality to the private sphere of individual preference. 'Acceptance' of course is only superficial. Everybody knows that we are still just queers really. Nowadays it's politically 'right-on' on the Left and in heterosexually dominated women's CR groups and campaigns to have a couple of token lesbian friends. But they must take an 'equal but different' line, and mustn't insist on their separateness, their oppression.

To varying degrees, and with varying degrees of choice, we all contribute to the invisibility of lesbianism. We do this when we pass as straight, let queer jokes slip by, or fall back on our children or heterosexual pasts to gain respect or credibility, or by failing to give our support and respect to young lesbians and lesbians outside the women's movement. How often have we heard young lesbians' decisions and choices denied as immature or unreliable. How often have we heard non-movement lesbians' style and behaviour criticised by heterosexual *and* lesbian feminists without due respect for their courage, and with no political perspective on their importance to our lesbian history and identity. In doing these things we bolster ourselves at our sisters' expense, and we become out of touch with our vision of lesbian sisterhood.

We are angry about the refusal of heterosexual feminists to take us seriously. But we are also tired of heterosexual feminists listening to what we say about our oppression and then, having listened, counting themselves among the 'sympathetic non-oppressors', going away feeling they have done their bit simply by listening. Heterosexual women cannot fail to be part of our oppression. So long as they remain in relationships with men they are contributing to the *status quo*, and, like it or not, they are a part of it.

We do not want to ask heterosexual women to begin sexual relationships with women if that's not something that comes from their own experiences and feelings. But we would ask heterosexual women who actively wish to support us to begin by looking at themselves. We would like these women to examine their own anti-lesbianism. We would like them to take stock of the privileges they gain from relating sexually to men, and how in doing that they oppress lesbians. We would also like heterosexual women to look for the reasons behind their own inability to love women sexually. Feminism is about caring for and loving women, and so lesbianism is an integral part of that. We would like heterosexual women to accept that if they are *unable* to relate sexually to other women then this is a problem. It can't be explained away by a sexual preference or choice or the right to a self-defined sexuality. All such explanations hide the woman-hating and divisive nature of compulsory heterosexuality. This will involve heterosexual feminists in examining a 'right' to a 'self-defined sexuality' which actively oppresses their lesbian sisters. We are not saying that lesbians are necessarily more feminist than other women. Women care for each other in many different ways, and sexual love is only one of them. We accept that lesbian relationships are not necessarily always caring ones either. But, having said that, we still maintain that the feminism of heterosexual women, necessarily, is problematic so far as their sexuality is concerned.

We would like heterosexual women to understand why lesbians cannot be content with mere statements that they support us, and why we do have such a deep mistrust of them when we know their statements are not backed up by positive actions.

Uncompromising lesbianism is still, as ever, the unacceptable face of women's liberation. For any of us, lesbian or heterosexual, who see feminism as a radical force, this should tell us something about the political potential of lesbianism.

REPUBLICAN WOMEN POWs,
ARMAGH JAIL

Letter to the Women's Movement

First published in *London Women's Liberation Newsletter*, 199

A Chairde,

There are twenty-eight republican POWs on protest for the retention of political status in this gaol. As stated in our appeal to you, there will be a number of us embarking on a hunger strike in the near future. We have been on a 'no wash' protest since 7 February 1980 and conditions in general are deteriorating daily. We are locked twenty-three hours a day in our cells, with nothing to occupy us or provide us with any form of mental stimulation. Our cells are covered in excreta, urine, dust and dirt. We have no sheets, no pillowcases, only old grey blankets which are completely filthy. The windows of our cells are blocked off by large pieces of wood, thus denying us adequate fresh air and daylight. The lights in our cells have to be kept constantly on to enable us to see properly, and because of this glaring electric light, many women suffer from severe headaches. Understandably, we ourselves are filthy. Our bodies are covered, or rather encrusted, with months of dirt and grime. Our hair is caked with dirt and dust and our scalps are a yellowish colour. The skin of our bodies has turned a greyish colour tinged with yellow, thus creating the impression of jaundice, and is so dry that it flakes all over.

Medical facilities are practically non-existent. Some of the medical staff refuse to enter our cells because they can't stand the stench. As is the usual procedure, anything from a minor ailment to a serious one is treated with pain-killers. We seriously question the capabilities of some of the medical staff who beforehand were screws. As far as we can ascertain, these screws have absolutely no medical training. Our menstrual cycle is a time of danger, the risk of infection being high. On occasions, sanitary towels are thrown into us without wrappings, thus absorbing the dust, etc. in our cells. Many women have already developed infections, which obviously through time will only get worse.

Many women have also lost weight. This is due to two factors, one being the totally inadequate diet we are forced to exist on. We are unlocked two at a time to collect our meals, and because of this time-consuming method our meals are virtually cold and uneatable by the time we receive them. The other factor is due to outbreaks of vomiting and diarrhoea. Many of us have suffered and are still suffering from this complaint. Because of the regularity of these attacks, health can only deteriorate further. A recent development has been the arrival of mice. We are infested with them, although at the time of writing they have not entered our cells as yet. One can only hazard a guess at the risk of infection because of these small creatures.

The screws are clad in protective clothing, including masks, and their attitude is both hostile and aggressive. We are subject to physical and verbal abuse not only from female screws but also male screws, who patrol our wing daily, continually peeping into our cells and hurling abuse at us. Many women have suffered injuries at the hands of these screws, whose delight in abusing us can only be termed as sadistic. We are harassed on returning from our monthly visits, whereby six or seven female screws pull us in to search us, and if they feel a sanitary towel they demand to see it. This is yet another degrading tactic employed by the administration here, and scuffles have developed because of this, whereby women have suffered injuries at the hands of these screws.

As stated, conditions deteriorate daily and one never knows what tomorrow will bring. We hope that this general run-down will give you insight into our situation, and we urgently appeal to you once again to raise your voices in the demand for political status before death intervenes.

P.S. This letter was smuggled out, written on a piece of toilet paper.

MICHELINE MASON

LIFE: Whose Right to Choose?

First published in *Spare Rib*, 115, March 1982

I find it difficult to write a 'continuation' of the discussion about the Down's syndrome baby case begun in the last issue.[1] I do not want to discuss the issue. You are speaking about my life. You wish me to discuss whether or not, as a woman born with a 'severe' disability, I think I should have been murdered. It does not sound reactionary to me to hear of people who want to put an end to the killing of babies because they have disabilities. It sounds wonderful.

The Leonard Arthur case and its subsequent publicity in the media was very distressing to me and many of my friends with disabilities. We became afraid to turn on the TV or radio in case we were landed with another dose of 'Should we let them live?' When you already suspect the world would rather you weren't there, this sort of barrage can be most depressing. We felt the overall result was to legitimise and make respectable the most appalling aspects of our oppression. Strangely enough, what cheered me up was the realisation that almost no one I heard had any idea what they were talking about. It is always easier to deal with ignorance than with malevolence.

The medical profession sees the world through the most blinkered eyes. Their discussions about the 'quality of life' left me squirming. They are part of the establishment, dedicated to law, order and the state. They do not like 'misfits' who may not be able to earn their living or look beautiful, who will remind them that they cannot perform miracle cures like Jesus.

Doctors, parents, people in general are notoriously ignorant about disability. Hardly any of my able-bodied friends know what 'spina bifida' or 'Down's syndrome' mean. They, like everyone else, are caught up in the stereotyped images of helpless vegetables needing 24-hours-a-day care, slobbering, agonised, hopeless lumps of human flesh who ruin everybody else's life as well as their own.

In fact, this is hardly ever true. It is people's fears of disability which are the problem.

These fears are fed mercilessly when the possibility of 'choice' arises. I do support the campaign for abortion to be freely available, but I think it very naive to believe that any woman is free to 'choose' whether or not to give birth to, or keep alive, a baby with a disability, given the climate in which she is supposed to make that decision. All the pressure will be in the direction of abortion or killing the baby, when that baby – and not the society in which it and she will have to struggle – is seen as the problem.

> LIFE do not care about the lack of facilities and support that exist for people with disabilities and those who care for them, which must be one of the central questions involved in the decision to allow a severely handicapped baby to die.[2]

It's probably true that LIFE do not concern themselves with facilities for people with disabilities. But, on the other hand, how do you expect things to improve whilst you accept that another simpler solution lies in the murder of the seeming cause of the problem?

There are enough resources to support everyone in a comfortable, fulfilled life, whether they live in London and have spina bifida, or live in Bangladesh and are starving. It is the big illusion of our time that it is the resources that we lack. The problem is that some people control them, misuse them, and deny them to the majority of the rest of the world.

I believe that women are being manipulated into believing that it is in their interests to destroy life because it may cause problems to society, rather than seeing that it is society causing the problems by standing in the way of their right to demand and receive the support they need to raise their children, regardless of their human condition – or even to hand over their children to others who have the personal resources they may feel they do not have.

Murder, masquerading under the euphemism of 'allow to die', can never be an answer to a human problem. What difference is there between this and Nazism? The Nazis started off their concentration-camp techniques on people with mental disabilities, whom they called *unnutze Esser* or 'useless eaters'. Rudolf Hess called this project *Vernichtung Lebersun werten Lebens* ('the destruction of life not worthy of living'). Sounds familiar, doesn't it?

It is quite normal for some children to be born with disabilities. We are part of normal life. Until this simple fact is understood, accepted and reflected in the structures of our society, the arguments about 'quality of life' and so on are utterly misleading.

We will be born, we will suffer, and some will sink and some will triumph. We will not go away. Nor will we stop shouting until the right to choose to live or die is ours, and ours alone.

Notes

1. LIFE brought a case against Dr Leonard Arthur for the attempted murder of a baby suffering from Down's syndrome. He was acquitted.

2. 'Life: a doctor's right to choose', *Spare Rib*, 114.

SANDY THOMPSON AND RUTH WILSON

Working-Class Women's Speakout

First published in *Plymouth Women's Centre Newsletter*, 23, July 1981

It was a great relief to get to talk about how we felt at the four meetings that we had – two where we got together as working-class women to organise what we wanted to say, and two where we 'spoke out' to those women who don't currently define themselves as working-class (w/c).

It was nice to see so many women at the 'speakouts'; shows how people realise how important it is. In the first meeting we found it surprisingly difficult to express how we felt and many women felt as if they were being attacked and/or made to feel guilty. That had certainly not been our intention – we merely wanted to raise the level of awareness and did so successfully, although of course some things remain to be cleared up. The second meeting was easier – we presented a lot of valuable ideas on how things could be improved, both to make w/c women now involved with the women's centre feel more involved and to attract new w/c women. Work has already started on implementing some of these (thanks, Di and Salle).

There seemed to be some confusion in the large meetings about what was meant by working-class. The classic Marxist definition is anybody who sells their labour power for less than the value of the goods they produce. That not only includes all homeworkers and mothers (usually called non-workers) but the vast majority of the population. There are, however, a lot of barriers to people realising how they are oppressed by the class system, and those women who got together before the two speakouts were in the main those who are currently aware of their own oppression and want to explore how that works in the context of the women's centre. It wasn't until a few of us got together and talked about how we felt that we realised there were other women who felt oppressed in the same way. Hopefully more women will be interested in meeting regularly as a working-class women's group because we did find it easier to express how we felt in that group. We also had a lot of fun.

Education was talked about a lot. Many women felt unable to express themselves if they didn't have 'the right words' and felt that many discussions were conducted in a language they didn't understand and which therefore excluded any contribution they might want to make. Those of us who did get an education got it on middle-class terms which denied our experience of life – a real split which worked to make us ashamed of our backgrounds. Those of us who are lesbian as well had that oppression to fight too in our grotty school and work environments.

One of the messages passed on to working-class people is that if only we had been smarter, if we or our parents had worked harder, we could have had all the things that everybody else seemed to have. This shame (it's all our own fault anyway, so what right have we to complain?) is a large part of our oppression and that is why we should be listened to with respect when we explain how we feel – to deny our experience is to rehearse what's been happening to us all our lives. What often happens, though, is that other women feel guilty and try to convince us it's either not important ('Surely we're all women together') or that we're imagining it all ('Surely it's just because you're new, everybody feels like that at first'). Yes, of course there are other factors besides class operating to make women feel uncomfortable at the women's centre, but we must beware of the really strong pull to talk about everything else *but* class because it's difficult to see clearly how it works, where we all fit into the various categories and because it makes almost everybody involved in trying to talk about it feel bad – for us it's the feeling of shame and anger; for others it's mainly guilt; and for everybody there's a feeling of confusion. But it is important because we do need a *real* unity as women and not an apparent unity which survives, however inadvertently, by silencing those women who experience the various forms of oppression under patriarchy. We do need to share our experiences, and hopefully we'll hear 'speakouts' from other groups of women soon.

DENA ATTAR

An Open Letter on Anti-Semitism and Racism

First published in *Trouble and Strife*, Winter 1983

     I wrote the following letter to the *Spare Rib* collective in response to their collection of articles 'Sisterhood . . . is plain sailing', published in issue 132, July 1983.

The feminist movement in Britain is currently facing a crisis over its handling of racism, and of working-class politics. Some women have become almost unbearably angry, while others are feeling insecure and threatened. I believe we must all go through the painful experience of first recognising and confronting racism in others and in ourselves, and then of reassessing our politics. In the midst of guilt, self-doubt, anger and recriminations, women can feel so overwhelmed they don't know where to begin. Radical feminism fifteen years ago was inspired by the insight of women creating the new movement that you start from where you are. That still holds good.

Dear sisters,

I am one woman who wanted to write to you after reading *Spare Rib* 121 – 'Women speak out against Zionism'. I didn't write then, partly because I had no time but mainly because of how I felt after the massacres at Sabra and Chatilla. My sense of shock and grief made me feel that it was just not the right time to take up the separate issue of anti-semitism. But nevertheless I did feel, not just anger and distress, but also real fear about the anti-semitism which was quite evident to me in some of those articles. Other Jewish women I talked to around that time seemed to have the same reaction – were alarmed about what was appearing in *Spare Rib* but didn't want to write to you about it, because they felt they did not want to give even the slightest grounds for anyone to think that they supported Begin's war in Lebanon. In retrospect I think we should all have written, however difficult it was at the time and however much courage it took.

Jan Parker writes in this month's issue (132), 'How anyone can support the genocide of the Palestinians is beyond me.' It's beyond me too, but who is she talking about? No doubt you've had your share of loony extremist letters, but that doesn't seem to be what this debate is about – surely no one is suggesting that that's what you should publish? Of course there are some Jewish women who are right-wing, women whom I couldn't describe as feminist. But they don't represent the rest of us, Jewish feminists who are critical of Zionism and also critical of the anti-semitic articles you've printed. So to suppress letters from Jewish feminists who, by definition I would have thought, are not right-wing or pro-Zionist makes as much sense as suppressing any coverage of the Palestine Liberation Organisation (PLO) on the grounds that Palestinian splinter groups have bombed synagogues in European cities.

Two of you explain that the women of colour decided that *all* of those letters were Zionist and/or racist. You haven't let us see the letters, so I can only take up this point on the basis of what's been said elsewhere, and knowing what I would have written. I don't know how you decided that. But I do know two things – that Jewish and Zionist are not, never have been, interchangeable terms; and that saying 'Zionist' when you mean 'Jewish' has always been the practice of neo-Nazi groups like the National Front. I write this not of course to accuse any one of you of sharing any of that sickening ideology – I know you don't – but to try and explain why we cannot accept that *you* have the right to label us Zionists when we don't call ourselves Zionists. As for the charge of racism, I wish you would explain what you are referring to. My impression, from various things I've read in *Spare Rib* recently, is that the charge that Jewish women are also being racist crops up in two contexts. One is where the writer is assuming that Jews are white and Palestinians are not, the other is where the history of Jewish communities in the Middle East is mentioned.

It seems to me that because of your lack of information about our history you are resorting to stereotypes, and in the process you are creating new myths. One such myth is that Jews were never oppressed in Arab countries, but always co-existed happily with their Moslem neighbours: therefore women who challenge this picture of our recent past are being racist. I can understand why you would like to believe this, and it is true that, compared with what happened in Europe, Jewish communities in the Middle East were relatively secure. But the truth is that they were still an oppressed minority. I am the daughter of an Iraqi Jew. My father used to tell us stories about the persecution of his home community in Mosul – how, on the Day of Atonement when it was customary for the Jews to walk to synagogue barefoot, their Moslem neighbours scattered the road with broken glass. In the fifties his family, and most of the Jews of Mosul, fled/were expelled from Iraq and ended up in Israel.

My relatives in Israel are Arabic-speaking, are mainly poor and ill-educated – the women have large numbers of children and many of them are illiterate. And it is perfectly true that they hate and fear the Palestinians and the Arabs, though they also believe that the Palestinians and Arabs hate them and are out to destroy them. If you say simply, as you have said, that this is just racism, what does that mean? What does it have to do with imperialism and colonialism, when two peoples are so much alike – can you tell an Arabic Jew from a Palestinian or Moslem Arab? – are locked in such bitter conflict? This is a real and not a rhetorical question, because I know that it is to do with imperialism and colonialism, but not in the simplistic way that you make out. Your analysis doesn't go far enough. We need to know and understand more, we need to work out what ways our feminist politics can help us struggle against racism and deal with nationalist politics, but I don't see that it is any help to reduce everything to a formula. And it is worse than useless to try to suppress facts about our experience which don't fit in with what you would like to believe, or like us to believe. None of this is an apology or a justification for the actions and policies of the Israeli state. But if it's true, and when it's relevant, why should it not be told?

We need to do a lot more work together on understanding the mechanisms and the causes of racism. Women of colour and Jewish women – remembering that the groups overlap – should not be fighting each other over these issues when we are each so fearful, insecure and unsupported in relation to the growing reactionary forces around us. But just as it is true that Jewish women must take responsibility for dealing with other kinds of racism besides anti-semitism, so it is true that you, the women of colour, cannot dismiss anti-semitism as 'a white women's issue' and refuse to discuss it. Jew-hating kills Jews just as surely as other forms of racism kill their targets. That knowledge is part of my daily life. I live in York, best known as the city where the entire Jewish community was burnt alive by the good citizens of York in the year 1190. (I do not know what imperialism or colonialism had to do with it – you tell me.) About a year ago, a mere eight hundred years later, they got around to putting up a plaque to commemorate the victims. The man who led the massacre has a whole village named after him. Walking around the town I can see swastikas daubed up any day. I recall when I lived in London reading in the local press about Jewish youths walking home from Yeshiva (an Orthodox religious high-school/college) beaten up by gangs of fascists, about one who was stabbed to death, and about how we could never have anything to do with the kids next door after one of them told my sister, 'Hitler didn't do a good enough job.' Having lived with this fear all my life, it adds to my insecurity when one of you writes, 'There are more important issues to me to fight for WOMEN, such as Paki-bashing, gay-bashing, Irish-bashing and deportations of black women.' Why, I am asking you, do you consider those to be more important rather than of equal importance?

I am also frightened when you write: 'Let me remind you that there has been a black and Third World people's holocaust for centuries and it is still continuing . . .' Why do you see it as a contest, that we cannot pay any attention to each other's histories because in each case our suffering has been so great? What price solidarity then? But I want to point out to you that for me and for all Jews the word 'holocaust' has a very specific meaning, and always has had. It has always been used to refer to the systematic gassing of six million of us by the Nazis, and whenever the word gets extended, the meaning gets changed and its original application is forgotten, my fear and the fear of other Jewish women is that the world is trying to forget, or minimise what happened. The far Right after all spends a lot of its time trying to rewrite history and claims either that there was no holocaust or that it was not really so bad. Can you not accept that we are in no way minimising the crimes against black and Third World people, the enslavement, murder and rape that has gone on for centuries, when we raise the subject of our own recent history?

I believe that one reason why there is such a recoil is just because it is so painful for us, and for you, and we don't become better informed because the facts are unbearable. The row that's going on has reached the depths of bitterness it has because of the extent of our pain. When you say 'it [the holocaust] is still continuing in India, Africa and to native Americans . . .' I don't know what terrible pictures come to your mind. But I know what the word 'holocaust' evokes for me. My parents had a book about the concentration camps, which I looked into once when I was a child and then could never open again, it held such terrors. The description I remember is of the marks scored in the concrete ceilings of the gas chambers, left by Jews in their death agonies scrabbling with their fingers against the concrete in vain hope of escape. That could have been my family, my parents. It was the relatives of many Jewish women here now. That's why we can't talk to each other calmly. But we have to try, we have to reconcile our fights against racism and mine, rather than wasting our time fighting each other and failing to respect each other, or what hope is there for any of us?

Lastly, I want to answer two other points you make. One of you says 'Define my power'. You are not powerless. None of us is completely powerless or how could we hope to struggle for anything? Working on *Spare Rib* you have the power to open up debate, to communicate ideas and information, to change women's politics and encourage them to work for change themselves. If you don't believe that, why are you working on *Spare Rib*? One of you says, 'It is pointless to explain oppression.' I don't agree. We have to, all of us, stand up and make ourselves visible and point out our oppression and keep on pointing it out. That's not to say other women should not also take responsibility for 'doing their home-work'. But if you still think I and women like me are racists and imperialists, where and how do we 'do our homework' if you decide not to talk to us and inform us? I rely on *Spare Rib* as a source of information and political analysis, and if you don't continue to offer it where else do I and other women go? What do you gain by making it harder for us to learn? Some of the things I've written here I've never spoken or written about before – that's one reason why you know as little as you do about the oppression of Jews, because it hasn't been mentioned. I believe now that it's vitally important we start talking to each other about oppression, and listening to each other, but without the spirit of competition there seems to have been so far – in order to learn more, understand better and be better able to resist racism and imperialism and all forms of patriarchal oppression.

To get back to the issue which started all this. I had no objection to *Spare Rib* giving support to the Palestinian people and condemning the invasion of Lebanon. You were right to do that. You were wrong to print articles which were anti-semitic in content, although you obviously did not realise that they were. You were wrong to refuse to publish criticisms of those articles and depict *all* the women who criticised them as Zionist and/or racist. I would like to think that we can begin again, working out how to express support for the Palestinians and analyse the situation in the Middle East without compromising our politics of feminism and anti-racism in any way and without having to distort, minimise or ignore any of the issues affecting us. That means working hard at trusting each other, at developing our own analysis and avoiding glib over-simplifications. I think it also means going back to the politics of experience in the sense of making sure our rhetoric *means* something to us, and isn't just a form of words. I'm thinking here of a woman who wrote to *Spare Rib* saying, 'Feminists must give full support to the Palestinians and the struggle to smash the State of Israel. Anything else is a wet liberal cop-out . . .' I don't know just what she means by full support, and smash the state: does she? Does this mean feminists are expected to support anything done in the name of the Palestinians by any Palestinian group? What about those Palestinian groups, disowned by the PLO, which carried out terrorist attacks on Jewish targets in Vienna and Paris? I am sure the writer would say she doesn't mean us to support those actions. Then what's the point of using that kind of rhetoric? I find it profoundly alienating when I encounter phrases like 'smash the state', familiar from Socialist Workers' Party papers and suchlike, because I don't know what I'm supposed to understand by them. What does it really mean in terms of what we can do now?

I am not prepared to suspend my judgment or shelve my feminism for any cause – I believe we can only give *full* support to women and for the struggle of our liberation, but that we can give critical support, though not mindless automatic responses, when it comes to other liberation struggles.

Roisín asks what support white readers will give the women of colour at *Spare Rib*. Jan says *SR* has been experiencing increasing withdrawal of support from the Women's Liberation Movement. From all your accounts I get the impression of isolation from your readers, almost of being under siege. Well, I hope you do get a lot more support, and I offer my support too, to all of you for what you are attempting, and particularly to the women of colour who are the most isolated. But it cannot be unconditional support that I offer in that I must continue to point out to you where you are putting forward anti-semitic lines or refusing to acknowledge that anti-semitism is an issue. And I hope it doesn't have to happen another time, or that another time you would listen.

In sisterhood
Dena Attar

KAREN WELCH

Racism in the Feminist Movement

First published in *Cardiff Women's Newsletter*, April 1983

As Bell Hooks shows in *Ain't I a Woman?*, feminist analysis of racism is too often simplified to suggest white women are 'good', i.e. non-racist victims, and the white man is bad, i.e. 'racist oppressor'. How can white feminists claim to represent women and expect black women to align themselves with a movement where the members do not choose personally to involve themselves in the politics of racism?

Racism has now been a key issue in the feminist movement for several years. Yet, when Feminist Black Liberation was an issue in the 1960s, white women hastened to define their situation as similar to the black (slavery)/white divide. However, analysis about black women's particular status as doubly oppressed has merely been touched on by white feminist literature. Black women's experience is different from and worse than that of white women. It encompasses racist, sexist, and classist attacks from those in the other (and in each case more privileged) position. Feminism does not support black women if it refuses to pay more than lip-service to these truths. A typically racist attitude from feminists is the way black and working-class women are grouped together so frequently as generally 'oppressed'. *All* white women have a higher status than black women in racist society.

Thus, the symbol of feminism does not signify the strength of all women to black women because it ignores our position. The racism of the movement is constantly obvious in the assumption that black women largely do not have feminist analysis because they are not amalgamated with the feminist movement. The effects of racism (as persistent and more dangerous than those of sexism) cause suffering which is unremitting, yet largely unnoticed, unmentioned and placed as a minor issue amongst our 'sisters' at gatherings such as conferences. Our black brothers have shared a lifetime in Britain of racist attack both blatant and violent or more subtle and unchallenged. We know attacks happen to us individually, day and night, and know no support can be relied upon from white strangers who witness this. We are all wary and aware of being forced on the defensive by white *women* as well as men in this society – but when I and other black women emerge at conferences, etc. we are often assumed to be less (if not anti-) feminist because of the alliance existing, of necessity, with black men. *But what are you doing, sisters?*

Feminists employ the term 'women' to denote all women. Yet women know that as 'mankind' deflects notice from the different position, oppression, even existence, of women, so too does feminist use of 'women' as a blanket term suggest a united group and deflect the different situation of all black women. I do not intend to cover the harm and misuse of imagery which the analogy of women as the equivalents of black people in racist society has caused (and the subsequent confusion of issue) in this article. Instead, I intend to show how white feminists' demands of men can be related to black women's demands of their white sisters.

'I'm not sexist – I'm anti-sexist.'

As if the first statement were equal to the second! I would expect a man who made such a claim to prove the first assertion in his personal actions, reactions, language, etc. Anti-sexism would further denote active political reaction to sexism. The same is true of feminist assertions of non- or anti-racism. Why should black women believe women are not racist merely because they declare so and often seem to think this is enough? Saying this commits feminists personally to take on anti- or at least non-racist behaviour, which includes analysing the racist consciousness this society has developed, unchosen, in us all. Furthermore British feminist literature (like its white US counterpart) has mostly ignored black women and little other anti-racist action is in evidence.

'After the revolution we can sort out a perfect society.'

Women, rightly, have become disillusioned with the male-orientated Left's views that details such as sexism can be sorted out 'later' after larger political issues have been won. In reality, this attitude found women supporting men's issues (usually subordinately). Likewise, white women unconsciously demand that black women cover white (often middle-class) issues for the majority of the time. Awareness of this bias has set a trend for inviting working-class and black women into feminist groups and campaigns. Apart from the patronising equation of one group with the other mentioned earlier, for black women, racist attitudes affect every aspect of life – including white, working-class women's racism. Black 'middle-class' women do *not* have parity with white women in the same position, but there is an insulting lack of analysis around how racism affects general theories of class, particularly with regard to black women. Many feminists seem to perceive these differences as largely about insults and the need for 'equal opportunities' – very much as many men seem to perceive the problem of sexism. What are the issues that support black women's struggles which should justify our participation in and acceptance of the feminist movement at the moment?

'Women just do not organise/participate in our union, party, revolution, etc.'
This surprise, that a group which exists to further women's causes as much as men's *where the issues are the same* does not attract women also, is an attitude which white women often have towards black women joining the movement. Feminism does cover aspects of all women's lives, that is undeniable, and white women are struggling to liberate women generally from various oppressions. However, the assumption that because black women do not involve themselves in the women's movement they are not political about their lives is patronising and racist. It is generally unrecognised that many black women *choose* not to be a part of a movement that ignores an essential oppression in their lives and does not value the very different ways black women live and relate to others which are not known or recognised by the majority of women involved in the feminist movement.

'I want to learn, but I need you to teach me.'
'There are books: you can think, you can raise your consciousness – get on and do it,' is the feminists' firm reply. 'You are in the privileged position: we need to move forwards and to raise our consciousness – and anyway that comment is sheer laziness.' As a walking symbol of 'black women's individual and collective consciousness', at conferences, in groups, on marches, etc., I, like many of my sisters (not all), am prepared to discuss racism with white sisters sometimes, but I am not prepared to be a teacher – I am developing too.

'I acknowledge that sexism exists. But the best thing I can do is what I know about best (i.e. pursue his interests). After all, it is not my fault and I do not contribute to it.'
Of course he contributes to sexism – by his own lack of action: by selfishly pursuing his own interests and, worse, by acknowledging the truth of women's oppression and then ignoring it. The

assumption is: I've looked at the problem, I know it for what it is, and I can now continue as a non-(anti-)sexist man. It is clearly presumptuous to look at such an issue as sexism or racism and then to simplify it to that extent. If seriously considered this must be an issue for on-going debate. With the issue of race (as sex) – guilt for inheriting a superior position in the capitalist hierarchy is worthless and is not required – but your position does not alter if it is disregarded.

'Women organising separately alienates your cause and leaves us out. We want to help you.'
Men can help women by organising about issues of sexism *as well as* women. By helping to change patterns in society they help women and justify women's faith. Few do though – the statement is all. Black women have considered feminism and often rejected it for the same reasons: anti-racist attitudes have been expressed frequently – but seldom acted on, i.e. organised. Instead, the overwhelming impression is that it is black women's problem (this attitude is frequently expressed too). Instead, black women have felt forced to organise separately and white women have allowed this to be enough. Racism seems to be out of fashion at the moment. It is assumed to be known and debate seldom occurs. It is usually one (or two) discussions at the feminist conference – if at all. Or it is a workshop organised for black women to meet at (great – but is this the sum of thinking for the day?) because there is then little space organised for white women to discuss the same points. Hence it is organised to be our problem again.

Black women are angry about their oppression due to sexism but we have also known oppression and hatred from the moment we've mixed with white people (from nursery/primary-school days). Our anger cannot concentrate on one dimension of our oppression – it spans several, and whilst feminist attitudes hold racism secondary it will not express consciousness for black women.

This article has expressed some of the questions which black women must consider when they consider feminism.

An Opinion

First published in *London Women's Liberation Newsletter*, no. 227

Dear Sisters,

On July 24 the Iranian Women's Group had a picket outside the Iranian Embassy. It was the day of the Presidential Elections, and we were protesting against the recent execution of women in Iran, the undemocratic system of the election, the general mass oppression and repression, and the executions by the Islamic government.

The picket was poorly attended, with only six women there; five of them Iranian and one American sister. This was despite the fact that we had put an ad in the *WL Newsletter*; no women came to support us. In this letter I am critical of the sisters who read and subscribe to the *WL Newsletter*, and I want to explain why.

The Iranian Women's Group is a feminist group set up in this country after the revolution. At present we meet monthly in A Woman's Place. We have all the problems that a small women's group has: limited energy and womanpower; the need for better organisation and stronger commitment; added to which a feeling of insecurity as being women in exile. As we only began to organise the picket three weeks ago, we could not publicise it as much as we wanted. However, we did contact the Iranian Left, the two groups that don't have open hostility to us, and invited them to come. At the last minute they considered our slogans to be too democratic, and did not support the picket. An Iranian sister who is also a member of the IMG (International Marxist Group) put an ad in their paper and also invited them to come. We also raised it in the Women Against Imperialism Group. The reason why it was submitted for entry into the *WL Newsletter* calendar was that we assumed that out of 400 London subscribers there would be some women who would be interested enough to come and support us and our demands, which are basically the demands of women's liberation groups in other countries. This is the second time we have had no response from readers of the *WL Newsletter* (we also had a public meeting a couple of months ago). I have a sneaking feeling that feminists in this country do not support women's issues outside England, not beyond Europe anyway. This is disappointing because women beyond Europe also need support and solidarity from us. I know that practical support, pickets and demos in cold rainy British weather are a nuisance, but how can we avoid it?

Five Iranian women and the American sister stood on the picket line bravely for an hour and a half through the drizzle, laughter of the police and mockery of the Embassy staff (well, everybody knows a women's group isn't much of a threat anyway).

A few days later, I am still angry . . . angry with you.

ZEE CLARKE

Black Rebel Sistren

First published in *Southall Black Sisters' Newsletter*

We are black women
We rebel against this system
A system that divides humanity
A system that relies on vanity
So come,
Unite
We sistren.

Black rebel sistren
It is us who are talking
A voice you have not heard for so long
Because mankind has tread us down
Captivity has kept us bound.

The ruling philosophy say
Them with more money
Must have more rights
And they make sure
It is no more
Than a few
European.

Hypocritical section
So small
Control the whole world
The power at their fingertips
Is final
Devastation
They bring with their greed.

Yet they will be hidden in shelters,
It is time we rebel idren
Time fe take a hold on this situation
Time the people took control.

And black women
Take no heed
Of what the man a preach pon we
Him say we can't think for weself
When him don't even start to question.

It's all to fool we
And keep we as his personal slave
Wash, clean, cook and multiply
But no sistren
We na do it
Stand firm
Control
Our own destiny.

Black rebel sistren
It is us who are talking
A voice you have not heard for so long
Because mankind has tread us down
Captivity has kept us bound.

ROISÍN BOYD

Recognising Anti-Irish Racism

First published in *Spare Rib*, no. 133, August 1983

In June 1980 I came to Britain to work. Like thousands of Irish women and men before me I crossed the water for skills and experience (and money) I could never find at home. Though I was coming to work in an 'alternative' job at *Spare Rib* I have a common identity with other emigrants. We are forced to migrate to a country – England – which dominates and colonises our country. When I came to work on *Spare Rib* and in the British women's movement I thought it would be different, that it would be another home, and I would be welcomed. I was wrong. Slowly it sank in. I was supposed to adapt and become part of *their* movement, culture, politics. I was never asked about what was happening in Ireland, whether things were different or the same. It didn't matter. 'But I thought you were just the same as us' – after 800 years of Irish struggle for self-determination and trying to exist separately from England, you think we're the same! Because it is considered 'natural' that we migrate to England, that there are more Irish people living in England than there are in Ireland and almost as many Irish feminists living here as are in Ireland, we are made invisible. Our history and culture, so inextricably tied to the English oppression of Ireland, is whited out. That English feminists have access to resources that are a million miles away from Irish women's reach is not a fluke. We are impoverished because Britain was enriched through colonial power by both our produce, land and people.

The contradiction of my presence on *Spare Rib* as the first and only Irish woman on the collective was always pressing. We talk a lot about power, usually male power, in the Women's Liberation Movement. But seldom is the power some groups of women have in relation to other groups of women acknowledged. Those women who are considered to be *outside* the 'norm' – those who are *not* white English or American – are not allowed to set the terms of reference in which debates and issues are taken up. Black, Third World, Irish and other groups of women are always struggling to have our voices listened to against the prevailing wind of what's perceived to be 'real' feminism. Once when I was explaining why I felt it important that *Spare Rib*, a *British* feminist magazine, support Troops Out, a member of the collective exclaimed, 'I don't know how any feminist could be a Nationalist.'

My feminist credentials were always in doubt because I didn't identify wholeheartedly with the English women's movement. It is made more difficult to challenge this privilege and power because there is a constant refusal to acknowledge that some feminists have more power than others. That English feminists are ignorant of English history in Ireland and of the Irish women's movement's history, is itself power. They can afford to be ignorant. We live with the results of that ignorance every day.

Anti-Irish jokes and remarks aren't only condoned in the British media, comedy shows and the 'straight' world. In the English women's movement it is quite common to mock Irish accents and the way we speak. At a benefit disco organised by Irish women and attended by many English women a 'classic' case of Irish-bashing took place. When an Irish woman was announcing prizewinners from the microphone, an English woman doing the disco took the microphone and said, 'For those of you who don't understand "Irish", I'll read out the numbers.' In fact, the Irish woman was speaking English! Because we use the English language differently we are thought amusing; 'It's so Irish' is a common insult. We don't speak Irish because the English colonisers outlawed its use in Ireland. Today very few people speak it. So it has a particularly cutting edge when we're reproved for talking 'Irish'. Language has been analysed by feminists as a tool used by men to oppress women and obliterate our existence as women. But for many of us the English language also denies our culture and history and it is a constant reminder that we are 'foreigners' in an alien country.

That all women are oppressed is what unites us as a liberation movement, but what divides us is not a recognition that men oppress women but that women from different cultures and class have different and pressing priorities. I can never forget that there is a war going on between Ireland and England and women are suffering from it. Northern Ireland has the highest unemployment rate, the highest poverty, the worst housing and the most women using tranquillisers in Europe. There is an army of occupation on the streets of Ireland. However, when feminists in England speak of supporting liberation struggles abroad they tend to ignore the one in Ireland. It's easier to support struggles not so near to home.

In the many books that have come out recently about the women's peace movement, Ireland is barely mentioned. There is a refusal to admit that a war is going on *now* in the 'United Kingdom'. When it is acknowledged then all the old chestnuts about 'religious' war come out with all the usual racist stereotypes. In a US book, *Women and Men's Wars*, which otherwise has some interesting pieces, the article on the war in Ireland analyses the 'peace women'. Their first march is described as follows: 'Protestants poured out of their houses and embraced the marchers . . . howling extremist Catholic women attacked the marchers, kicking and pulling some to the ground. Three youths dragged one girl around a corner and urinated on her.' The 'natives' depicted as 'savages' by their oppressors is not unusual in colonial situations. But you might expect differently from a feminist book that considers seriously the involvement of women in liberation struggles in Zimbabwe and the Philippines.

Most feminist theory, literature and media is dominated by middle-class American feminist and English academics. Obviously a lot of what is written is relevant to many women but also a lot of it isn't. This is seldom recognised, rather it is seen as the 'real' voice of feminism. Very few books have been published about Irish women's experience because we lack the resources. Feminist presses should make their resources available or consult particular groups of women when they are considering publishing material on their experience.

Irish women in England have organised separately for some years now and this validates our experience here. But although white English feminists are constantly telling various groups of women to articulate their demands these are seldom met when we do. It's not enough either just to tack various groups of women on to *old* theories so that their particular oppression is recognised, or the writer gains credibility.

But the women's liberation movement *is* open to change and the changes that have taken place within the last year on *Spare Rib* have been dramatic. I realise that as a white woman I have privileges and power that women of colour don't have, but our common experience of being marginalised and undermined by the dominant white English culture has created some solidarity between us.

We feel tremendous resistance to change, resistance to challenging the power structure that allows white, middle-class women to dominate, and to deem what's important and what's not important. Until we recognise this structural inequality, as *Spare Rib* has in some way, the Women's Liberation Movement in this country will never be a *really* radical movement because various demands and changing consciousness will only acknowledge *aspects* of women's oppression *within* the racist, imperialist, sexist British state.

GAIL CHESTER

Why the Jewish Question Must be Answered by Feminists

First published in *Catcall*, August 1982; conference paper, first National Jewish Feminist Conference, January 1982

Considering that a large proportion of the Women's Liberation Movement comes from a Jewish background, it is surprising that we have not been more visible as an ethnic minority before now. This could be for many reasons: because of the relative ease with which we can 'pass', people often only know we are Jewish if we tell them; our age-old tendency to fight other people's battles whilst minimising our own oppression – a well-known survival strategy; little conscious commitment in the movement to fight against racism and fascism until relatively recently; or a lack of clarity within ourselves about what being Jewish means. Because of the strength of my Jewish background, these questions and others more related to my personal situation have preoccupied me, shaping my perception of myself as a human being and as a feminist. It is only recently that an atmosphere has been created within the women's liberation movement in which these issues can be raised.

I was brought up in an orthodox Jewish family with liberal political leanings, mainly in north-west London. I rejected the religious aspects of my background when I was eighteen, although I have always remained conscious of my cultural and ethnic heritage. I have been active in the women's liberation movement since 1970, in a variety of consciousness-raising and campaigning activities. In 1979, I joined a consciousness-raising group consisting specifically of Jewish women. The reasons were in many ways similar to why I think it was important that we had the first National Jewish Feminist Conference; for me the one led to the other, wanting to look at some of the insights gained there with a larger group of women.

Meeting together as Jewish feminists has a number of functions: to identify our common experience as Jews, women, and Jewish women, believing in the importance of consciousness-raising for achieving women's liberation; to examine our cultural identity to see if there are any non-patriarchal and positive bits of it we wish to retain; to achieve some measure of solidarity so that when we see anti-semitism around us, in the WLM or elsewhere, we feel strong enough to confront it. It is not about being a religious revivalist movement, above all, it must not be that if it is to be part of a politically radical movement, nor is it about being cosy and safe together against a hostile world, nor is it about trying to perfect the ideologically correct line about Israel.

Joining the consciousness-raising group provided a way of discussing problems in my life associated with growing up Jewish (and especially orthodox) which I didn't feel non-Jewish women could so readily identify with. These ranged from the most immediately personal to the more broadly societal – the pressure to marry (and *only* a Jewish man); the horrors of growing up and being found wanting in the eyes of Jewish boys; how far to try and pass on a Jewish identity to our children, if we dare procreate, on our own or with a non-Jew; feeling answerable to the Jewish community (in whose eyes one is already a pariah because of one's eccentricity); feeling a bit of an outsider in English society, slightly anxious in case one day *they* make us move on again; or feeling disloyal to the memory of our ancestors, if such emotions are not embedded in the psyche, but remain an intellectual response to observable reality. It was good to have a place where one member of the group could discuss her feelings about her rich, property-owning father without worrying about the anti-semitic thoughts other women might be having. I enjoyed being in a group where I didn't feel like the noisiest person and we could discuss these aspects of our self-image without lapsing into mocking stereotypes.

When I joined the CR group, I certainly felt that my attitudes to being Jewish were entirely shaped by the anti-semitism of the society around me (or the fear of it that emanates from the Jewish community), and I still feel more or less the same. If there were no anti-semitism, I would not be forced to experience pride/anxiety/joy/alienation/solidarity/defensiveness/safety/being humiliated/being comfortable/uncomfortable in relation to other Jewish people. We could all just *be*. The feeling of comfort, of instant identification, at times makes me feel uneasy; it proved to be an oversimplification when our CR group split up after 2½ years – on feminist, not Jewish grounds, I think; it continued to worry me in some of the attitudes around planning for the conference.

Nevertheless, I believe we must ask whether Jewish solidarity should be looked at politically as the same phenomenon as black pride. How much solidarity should we seek with other Jews, and for what reasons? How much is necessity rather than choice?

I see the fact that I continue to think of myself as Jewish as being mainly the product of anti-semitism, or the fear of it, but nevertheless I do not hate being Jewish and never have. There are aspects of it which give me great pride. I see being Jewish as very similar to being a woman . . . in an ideal world most of the differences between us and others would be irrelevant. Those differences that exist now are culturally defined and magnified to assume an unnatural importance, but as long as I am endowed with them, why should I do the oppressors' work for them and deny and hate what I am?

So, apart from a shared oppression, are there any cultural forms which unite Jewish people? Well, yes and no. There is the Jewish religion, which most Jews have abandoned, apart from a vestigial honouring of certain rituals, such as the Day of Atonement or at the death of a parent. Then there are the domestic rites which many of us recognise – the cholent[1] and the cheesecake, the manner of making kiddush, the way to behave at barmitzvah parties. But it is quite clear that Jews from Eastern Europe follow one tradition, Sephardis another, while Indian Jews follow a third, and so on. Maybe the Jews of Morocco have more in common culturally with Moroccan Moslems than German Jews. I was reared in the Litvak/Russian/Ashkenazi tradition, the dominant one in Britain today, and feel embarrassed at my ignorance of the others.

Some parts of my Jewish culture seem to be fairly widespread, but are they only Lithuanian – or not universally true, even there? For example, although the men are every bit as patriarchal, they don't seem to go in for much domestic violence, are generally more interested in their kids, and don't get drunk much, except at weddings and on Purim. At Jewish get-togethers, the emphasis is usually on the food rather than the drink. And then there is the famous Jewish family! – but that needs a paper all of its own. With assimilation, these cultural differences diminish. Patriarchs and feminists alike may bemoan their passing, but for different reasons.

While I continued to live in north-west London, my brand of Judaism was so much part of the dominant culture that I never felt at all unusual, all the time I was growing up. But in recent years I sometimes get irritated with being seen as part of an exotic subculture. I don't see this as anti-semitism in the conscious sense, just part of the great British insularity and amazement that someone might come from a different cultural tradition.

When I was in New York and Philadelphia last year, I noticed how much more an accepted part of life it was to be Jewish, how even non-Jews knew about Chanukah, how the price of kosher meat was an item on the main news bulletin, not just tucked away for half an hour early on Sunday morning. It made me feel less extraordinary, without intruding on my privacy. I got a sudden insight into why some people are so keen on Israel. It's that reassuring sense of normality, where you can be in the majority for once, the towns are reasonably small, you bump into your friends and relatives on the street, it has all the advantages of Hendon without the lousy weather.

Part of increasing feminist consciousness about Judaism must be to heighten awareness of anti-semitism. There is gross anti-semitism, which fortunately I have experienced very little of. But there are ways that I feel put down as a Jewish woman. I came up with the following list. It certainly ignores the more blatant examples of conscious and vicious attacks, verbal and physical, but it contains items that non-Jewish people could do something about. Examples of unconscious anti-semitism include:

1. Thinking that everyone celebrates Christmas.
2. Thinking that everyone who is not from the Indian subcontinent must be Christian.
3. Thinking that all Jews are white.
4. Failing to understand why I visit my parents on Jewish New Year and Passover.
5. Wearing a crucifix.[2]
6. Making a fuss if somebody doesn't eat meat or shellfish.
7. Failing to understand why we might have problems relating to Germans.
8. Believing somewhere in your heart that the stereotype of the Jewish mother is exempt from the normal accusations of racism and sexism, because it's a joke – or true.
9. Running the country so that everything happens on Saturday, never on Sunday.
10. Assuming there is only one ideologically correct line about the Middle East.
11. Assuming that if I'm Jewish I will be on the wrong side of it, or the right one.
12. Telling me how much I look like somebody you know. When I meet her, I discover there is not the slightest resemblance, we just both happen to be Jewish.
13. Not appreciating the security problems we had in organising the conference.
14. Always picking Biblical examples from the New Testament.
15. Telling me I don't look English. Demanding to know where

my parents came from. Expressing disbelief when I say 'Shepherd's Bush and Dublin', or else replying, 'Ah yes, I could tell you were Irish by your blue eyes.'

Notes

1. Glossary

Barmitzvah – the ceremony which welcomes boys of thirteen into manhood and full participation in religious ritual.

Chanukah – a celebratory festival which falls near Christmas, commemorating a Jewish victory over the Roman army of occupation.

Cholent – a type of stew which can be left cooking on a low flame throughout the Sabbath, when no work is allowed.

Kiddush – a domestic ritual of sanctification, which incorporates making a blessing over wine.

Kosher – food prepared and meat killed according to Jewish dietary laws.

Purim – another festival of great jollity, which celebrates how Queen Esther saved the Jews of Persia from annihilation.

Sephardi Jews are Jews who lived in Spain and Portugal up until the Spanish Inquisition of 1492 when thousands were tortured and killed while others fled and sought refuge in other countries. A form of the Spanish language (Ladino) has been kept intact until this day, and the Sephardi culture remains distinct from *Ashkenazi* (Yiddish) culture which flourished in Eastern Europe, and from the various *Mizrachi* (Eastern) cultures of the Middle East, Asia and Africa.

2. It is quite clear that a number of the items on my list are not *only* oppressive to Jews, any more than every single item of anti-feminist behaviour is *only* oppressive to women; however, all of them have specific symbolic significance when used against Jewish people. I feel this particularly strongly about the wearing of crucifixes, for a number of reasons: (a) The wearing of any overt, self-chosen symbol means that the wearer wishes to be identified as a member of that group, to distinguish them from members of *other* groups; 'I am *not* a Jew' in this case. (b) The crucifix is a powerful symbol of death. Every time I see one round someone's neck, it reminds me that many Christians not only believe that the Jews killed Jesus, but perpetuate this myth to justify and fuel present-day anti-semitism. (c) It is the most aggressive symbol available in our society to assert a person's inalienable membership of the dominant culture. It is a reactionary reinforcement of that culture, and it perpetually confronts me with the knowledge, that even if I wanted to (which I don't) I can never be part of it.

Postscript

When I wrote this, Israel had not invaded Lebanon and the WLM had not consequently plunged itself into anguish over anti-semitism, anti-zionism and the connections between them. I would not now dare make such an apparently flippant remark about Israel, but I would be censoring myself for the wrong reasons – fear of seeming not right-on, of deviating from the 'party line'.

Jewish feminists have been under pressure in the last eighteen months from those who assume that there is only one correct line on the Middle East and that Jews are bound to be on the wrong side of it, whichever position we choose. The invasion of Lebanon is tragic and devastating, but has it made a greater difference to my life as a British radical than events in El Salvador and Grenada? Daily reality for Jews in this country has not changed; only the pressure to speak out has.

I can't straightforwardly condemn the attitude of Jews who see in Israel merely a sense of personal security, when I know how narrowly many of them escaped the gas chambers, when I see how insubstantial is our own protection from anti-semitism, even in the WLM. At the same time, I despair when a people which has suffered so greatly seems oblivious to the suffering it inflicts on others.

I get no help resolving this dilemma from radicals who clamour for Jews to condemn our fellows, yet make no attempt to understand why Jews feel threatened. How can non-Jews deny the anti-semitism behind this, however unconscious? How can they ignore their own part in perpetuating the feeling that Jews can rely only on each other? When other feminists hold me personally responsible for a terrible war thousands of miles away, I am more tempted to sympathise with those Jews who equate Israel with their home and community – places like Hendon. That is not my position, but I understand it.

Crèches: two letters

First published in *London Women's Liberation Newsletter*, 258

Dear Sisters,

The following is a letter we sent to crèches against sexism explaining why we decided not to use them to run the crèche for our conference on 10 January 1982. We hope this contributes to the debate about conference crèches which started in *WIRES* and the *London Newsletter* a while back.

CAS[1] offered to run the crèche for us long before their treatment of WAVAW, etc. was made public, and we had no reason to turn down their offer. When we heard how they had behaved we discussed at a planning meeting whether we should still go ahead with them. Most of us felt quite strongly that we did want to make demands on men, which includes running crèches, and, after all, they had approached us. However, from their initial contact with us, which came in the form of demands about various aspects of the organisation we must perform, we felt uneasy. It seemed to us that they had been advertising themselves widely as a crèche-running service, which meant doing the *work* beforehand as well as on the day; now it seemed that their willingness to do this would be conditional. We were told on the phone, 'It depends what your project is', which they already knew perfectly well – it was simply to run a national Jewish feminist conference. It felt like they wanted the glory of doing the crèche and the pleasure of being with the children without doing too much surrounding shit work. They also insisted that they could not give us a decision about doing our crèche until after meeting us and seeing the building – even though they had approached us about it in the first place.

After our meeting with them, when we went to look round the building, we decided that a lot of their arrogance sprang from their assumption that they had a monopoly over childcare at conferences (at least in London), so that once again men were back in the position of being able to dictate terms to women. To have asked

291

women to run it at that stage would have been to avoid the issue, and many of us remain committed to asking men to take responsibility for childcare. Meanwhile we found another group of men who were prepared to take the responsibility of organising the crèche for us, but we were/are angry that so much anxiety and energy had to be expended on what should have been a straightforward transaction.

National Jewish Feminist Conference Planning Group

Dear Crèches against Sexism,

We promised to let you know by letter why we decided to turn down your offer of doing the crèche at the Jewish Feminist Conference. Because of the current debate that is going on about whether men should do crèches at all, we want to make it clear that our decision was not based on this as we intend to find other men to do the crèche. It was to do with your attitude to running crèches in general and to our project in particular.

Overall, we felt you were very hostile to us. In general terms this came out in the way you implied more than once that you knew more about running crèches than women – any women. Considering the thousands of years women have been performing the tasks associated with childcare, without getting any recognition or pats on the back, we think this is an insult. This attitude also contributed to the inordinate fuss you made about the unsuitability of the available rooms. Of course, there are bound to be limitations when there is not a purpose-built nursery, but we cannot honestly see how you would have found better accommodation than that provided. It is part of a day centre for disabled people, and thus contains many toilets, sinks, lifts, comfortable chairs, and so on, which will make life pleasanter for everybody attending the conference and using the building. We felt your unhappiness about the accommodation was such that if you came to do the crèche in such circumstances, it would make life more difficult for us all.

We were also very upset about how rude and insensitive you were to the staff who run the day centre. Apart from boring old-fashioned notions of bourgeois politeness, you might have considered that alienating the staff was going to make our task in running the conference more difficult. Even more significantly, as you are supposed to be aware of sexual politics, you were there as our assistants, and we cannot image that a group of women in a similar situation would have presumed to interfere in this way when another group of people were in charge of some organisation.

Finally, in the particular case of our conference, we were very distressed by the anti-semitic comments you made. An important part of our politics as Jewish feminists is to be proud of our Jewish background and to encourage positive images among others, both Jewish and non-Jewish. Not all Jews are rich and privileged, and the day centre is run by Jewish and non-Jewish people who do not need to be patronised.

All the time we were negotiating with you, you created unnecessary organisational difficulties. You behaved throughout as though you were in a position of power over us because we needed you to provide a crèche which you would only do on your terms. This is the same deal men have been offering women since time immemorial – conditional support – and it is not good enough. You are not indispensable, you are supposed to be part of a political movement, and it is only on these terms that we will ask you to run crèches.

Yours sincerely,
National Jewish Feminist Conference Planning Group

Note

1. Crêches Against Sexism.

MARIA K.

No Woman-run Crèche: a letter

First published in *London Women's Liberation Newsletter*, 208

I am horrified to read that there is no woman-run crèche for girls at the forthcoming (1981) Lesbian Conference. My daughter will not go to crèches run by men – *I don't blame her*. My only recourse will therefore be that I have her with me throughout the conference weekend, unless I enlist the (unpaid and over-used) help of my mother (or another woman friend).

Why could we not take up an idea which Leeds feminists (I believe) originally had – that of asking women nursery nurses/ workers to look after our daughters? (Children of both sexes were looked after by women nursery nurses at these conferences, but it's about time we gave our daughters the women-only rights we demand.) We would of course pay these women (if possible, slightly more than they usually earn) and of course make sure we were not inadvertently excluding lesbian or celibate women from the possibility of attending the conference, if they wanted to. Also they would be paid from money paid to conference organisers by *all* women at the conference (and more money from rich(er) women) and not just those who normally live with and/or bring up the children/girls.

I don't want my daughter staying overnight with men – (lots of them) ugh! whether they be anti-sexist or not. (All that means is that those men fuck feminists or that they drain lots of energy and emotional support from us/women/feminists.) I am so angry but also so extremely upset. If we can't ask for and expect to get a woman-run crèche for our daughters at the Lesbian Conference then WHEN ARE WE????!! I admit that my contribution to the planning of this conference has been minimal, if not non-existent (attendance at one planning meeting, a couple of phone calls), but then I don't expect this to be something of concern only to mothers of daughters and/or other lesbians/women who are already concerned with the care of girls. In the present climate of blatant lesbian and woman hatred from within the supposed safety of the

WLM have we been so terrified that we dare not even ask women not going to the conference (and I don't mean male-to-constructed-female transsexuals – *they are men*) to look after *our daughters*.

PIRI MARCUS

Motherhood: a letter

First published in *WIRES*, no. 123, December 1981

Dear women,

I am more and more desperate about and noticing more and more facts about how mothers are oppressed by non-mothers; in other words, biological fathers, other men, and childless women, and obviously feminist and lesbian women without children as well. I don't see the point in analysing here how lots of them make women pregnant, to make children and then degrade and exploit the women or leave them to cope completely alone with the children: everyone knows these facts. But I want to write here about how I continually meet feminist women who oppress me as a mother, and oppress all other mothers, even when they are relating only to one of millions of us.

I am very, very glad that there are women who dare to make a decision not to have children, and I don't want to encourage any woman to have children; I feel sorry because in the past I have encouraged women to make children. But their right not to make children does not necessarily mean that they have the right to continue the discrimination, degradation, hatred, accusations, denial, ignoring, excluding and the hypocritical 'helping' tradition, which historically and in its original interests belonged to men. Now some of the interests of this ugly game have become the interests of 'childless' women too, at least on an immediate level; just as far as it is in their interest not to notice, not to want to imagine, understand or admit the intolerable situation mothers are in.

Mothers need a liberation movement to articulate loudly and challenge and to change their situation radically, and the situation of children. But mothers hardly have the time or energy, or the space and encouragement to organise, write and agitate for alternatives, because they are chained to their kids. And mothers are basically *not allowed* to talk about the intolerability of their situation, because of public ideas like:

– the mother who is not happy and satisfied is a 'bad mother';

– she does not like her children;

– she is not human enough if she does not recognise the beauty of children but instead complains about her life of full-time or almost full-time motherhood;

and beliefs about the responsibility of . . . who? of the mothers, of course, who else could be responsible for 'her' children?

I want to ask: who is, in reality, responsible for the terrible life of mothers? Please, please don't come back with the self-justifying argument that mothers have 'chosen' to become mothers. To begin with, this is a lie, and I doubt whether anyone seriously believes it, except childless people perhaps, because it serves their interests and morally justifies them. Secondly, even if mothers have chosen to have children, why should this 'free choice' mean a lifelong, or almost lifelong punishment, which today practically means killing the mother-person?

There are lots of ways of discouraging mothers from complaining about the present situation of mothering and about the theories and 'science', 'advice' and general attitudes towards – and against – them. The most powerful one is the institutionalisation of either the children she has given birth to, or the children and the mother, or only the mother herself. The mother might be sent to mental hospital, sometimes even to prison; children might be sent to 'children's homes' if the mother 'can't cope'; that is, if she is not fulfilled and satisfied by mothering itself.

Let's look at the Seven Demands of the women's liberation movement. Where and how does it mention the urgency and commitment to change the present circumstances of mothering? All it says is, 'the right to free contraception and abortion' (with which I completely agree) and 'free twenty-four-hour childcare', which does not offer me anything unless I can determine what *kind* of childcare this provides. This is, in my present experience, absolutely unreal, as the people whom I meet who are working in the present official childcare system, which operates for 8 to 10 hours in nurseries, for example, are never prepared to discuss childcare seriously. Who will guarantee that the childcare will not be sexist, racist, patriarchal and oppressive, and who will guarantee that it will be child-respecting? The 'twenty-four-hour childcare' which I suppose the state is supposed to provide is only a *lip-service demand*, I feel. For me it represents, proves in fact, the *total misunderstanding* of the urgent changes mothers *and* children would need, *now, today*.

Instead, I would like to suggest some urgent demands. These could either be included in the Seven Demands, or mothers could make their own manifesto and list of demands. I would demand at least:

1. no event without childcare arrangements by non-mothers (either crèche or babysitting).
2. An end to discrimination against mothers, and the start of positive discrimination (in the feminist movement as well as everywhere else).
3. Make mothers with young children mobile, for example, by arranging transport with those who have cars and have spare seats.
4. An end to educating girls and women for 'compulsory childbirth'.
5. Stop forcing women to be 'happy', 'satisfied' and 'fulfilled' because they have given birth, and are mothering their biological children.
6. End the 'pink' myth, the saintly, heroic and 'human' picture of having children, but instead encourage mothers to talk about their experiences, including the forces which have been and continue to be the cause of the *isolation* of motherhood; encourage and publish accounts of how much children suffer too in the present childraising system. The myth of the saintly mother only conceals the compulsory nature of having and raising children.
7. End the monopoly and 'science' of non-mothers (especially bloody fathers and other men) to talk about and theorise about motherhood, and misrepresent mothers.
8. Do everything against isolating childcare, encourage and help shared childcare, both for parents and non-parents.

GLADYS GOODENOUGH and
ELSIE DOGSBODY

On Bringing Up Boys

First published in *Birmingham Women's Liberation Newsletter*,
3, May 1982

A mother is only brought unlimited satisfaction by . . .
a son; this is altogether the most perfect, the most free from
ambivalence of all human relationships [Sigmund Freud, *New
Introductory Lectures on Psychoanalysis*].

Boy children present many problems to feminist mothers. Given
our particular political beliefs about men (we believe men are the
class enemy of women, and thus that talking to individual men
about sexism is unproductive) how should we bring up our sons?
The irresolvable conflict we feel due to the fact that our boys are
both males (and as such members of the oppressor class) and also
our children, often leads us into situations where we feel we have to
protect them from our feminism. For instance, we don't like to 'talk
anti-men' in front of our boys. Any woman who has felt her young
son stiffen in her lap when other women make disparaging remarks
about men, knows how such remarks leave boy children with an
undefined sense of guilt which they can do nothing about. After all,
they are doomed to be men. As parents we feel it is too cruel to let a
child grow up believing that he has no hope of becoming a good
person because of an accident of birth.

Boys also cause problems when it comes to women-only events;
should we take small boys to women's socials, etc.? How can we let
boys join in when we sing songs celebrating our sisterhood and
rejecting men's oppression? We would agree that boy babies would
cause no difficulty, but this leads into the whole question of when
does a boy become a man? A babe in arms is one thing, but two or
three ten-year-old boys together can give off an air of pre-
adolescent male aggression which we think would be quite
disturbing at a gathering of women and girls. If, however, we ban
boys from women's events, how can we avoid discrimination against

their mothers who, given the perennial problem of finding babysitters, will often be effectively banned themselves if they cannot bring their children with them?

Another point on which we feel a lot of uncertainty concerns the extent to which boys need positive male images to identify with. What do you do when you don't believe there are any positive male images? We are not saying that a boy's development is hindered if he does not grow up with a father; in fact, in our experience little boys are far better-off emulating their mothers than their fathers. Sooner or later, however, all feminist mothers of sons are faced with the hopeful question: 'But not *all* men are sexist, are they mum?' or 'But dad's not like that, is he?' to which we tend to have no answer. On the whole we are not very honest with our children, boys or girls, about their fathers. As regards mothers bringing up children on their own, although we try not to fall into the trap of building up their fathers to the point where our children blame us for the fact that daddy left them, we do not tell them the truth, which is that daddy never really wanted to know them when he lived with us and that once a week is as often as he wants to see them now!

Should we talk to boys about sexism? We have already noted that, by and large, we find it pointless to talk to men about the oppression of women. Yet with our children we have often felt compelled to do so, if only for the sake of our daughters. For example, we have felt obliged to comment on sexism in children's television, comics, etc. when boys and girls are watching together. However, this brings problems: first, it inevitably leads us into a situation where we have to lie about our expectations that our sons will grow up as part of the oppressor class, and thus as our enemies; and secondly, we sometimes feel that by pointing out instances of sexism to boys we end up by showing them their power over women. We feel that they learn this soon enough anyway, without having the process accelerated by us. We believe that as our sons grow up and become increasingly receptive to influences outside their immediate family (which is non-nuclear and one-parent) they quickly learn the advantages of being male and incorporate these into the manipulation of adults which all children practise. Thus we have practically given up talking to our sons about sexism and avoid the subject wherever possible.

One of our main problems which occurs when we are bringing up boys and girls together, is that we would like to reinforce different behaviours in boys and girls. In order to counterbalance the conditioning our daughters get from every source other than us (to be meek, gentle, passive, pretty, weak, etc.) we believe we should actively encourage them to be assertive, to be able to fight when necessary, and to be noisy and uninhibited and confident instead of being quiet and submissive. However, these traits which we foster in our daughters are the very ones we want to discourage in our sons. We feel they already get too much permission to be noisy, aggressive and self-centred. However, trying to achieve this differential treatment without being accused of favouritism is an impossible task. Try to explain positive discrimination to a six-year-old! As mothers we are constantly aware that we ourselves are often part of the negative conditioning forces which surround our daughters. When, under pressure (and single working mothers are always under pressure), we ask our daughters to perform an urgent task because they are invariably quicker, more willing and more efficient than the boys, we know that we are contributing to their oppression. When we tidy up after the boys because we simply have not got the time to call them in and stand over them while they do it themselves, we know that we are consolidating our traditional role as servants of men. On the other hand, when we are accused of favouritism by any of our children we are never sure whether we have gone too far or not far enough in our efforts to achieve equality.

Two further issues which we feel will become more problematic in the future are those of education and sexuality. As our children approach secondary-school age we find ourselves again on the horns of various dilemmas. We feel that it is vital that our daughters go to all-girls' schools but this would mean sending them to selective schools, not comprehensives, which goes right against our general socialist principles on education. Conversely, the last thing we want is for our sons to be exposed to the brutalising, rugger-club atmosphere of an all-boys' school. But how can we justify inflicting our sons on girls at a mixed school? These are problems to which we can find no solution.

With regard to sexuality, we firmly believe that the institution of heterosexuality is inherently oppressive depending as it does on an unequal balance of power between males and females. Thus we have real worries about our children, boys and girls, growing up heterosexual with all that this entails. We do not want our boys to be sexual oppressors and we do not want our daughters to be sexually oppressed. In fact, we don't want any children of ours growing up to be 'men' at all! Again, these are problems to which we can find no solution.

Finally, we appreciate the point that this whole article represents time and energy put into men which might be better channelled into thinking about our daughters. After all, they are the ones who suffer in a world which routinely oppresses women and girls. However, as mothers we do not have the option to withdraw attention from our boy children. We cannot simply put them low down on our list of priorities. We sometimes feel that the thought and worry we put into boys is a painful preparation for the time which seems inevitable when we will have to withdraw from them in a way which we will never have to withdraw from our daughters.

AMANDA CORNU, Sisters Against Disablement

Open Letter to the Organisers of the Lesbian Sex and Sexual Practice Conference, April 1983

First published in *London Women's Liberation Newsletter*, April 1983

Sisters,

Through a contact on the organising committee, I have learnt of the deliberations of your group concerning access for lesbians with disabilities to your conference. From the beginning, she argued that the conference should be totally accessible and that if venues in London were not accessible, that the conference should be postponed and held elsewhere in the country in an accessible venue. She argued for and won the facility of a sign-language interpreter for deaf lesbians, and was able to insist that the agenda give space for lesbians with disabilities to discuss disabled sex and sexual practice.

All these gains however were lost when you selected Kingsway Princeton as the venue of the conference. By advertising your conference as partially accessible you delivered a further insult to lesbians with disabilities.

You do not explain what you mean by 'partially accessible' and only those who know the venue can understand what this might mean to some lesbians with disabilities, and what some of us will and will not be able to do at the conference. I know that there is no wheelchair-accessible toilet, that many of the rooms where the workshops will be held will be on the upper floors, and that the canteen is obstructed by a flight of stairs. By organising in this venue, you are excluding lesbians with disabilities from a choice and freedom of movement at the conference. You will choose which workshops we go to, you will exclude us from socialising over meals with other participators, and you will dictate the amount of time some lesbians with disabilities can stay at the conference because of the lack of an accessible toilet.

What you have demonstrated by doing this is that you don't really want women with disabilities to come to this conference, and by doing this you have sold out on your principles . . . [those who] use conventionally sized toilets will still be able to participate fully in the conference while our sisters who use wheelchairs or are unable to negotiate flights of stairs despite not using a wheelchair, won't. If you had not considered the question of access at all we would have been able to unite all lesbians with disabilities in anger at the way you have organised. But because some of us are still able to participate you are forcing us to collaborate with you as oppressors of women who do use wheelchairs.

Many of us were eager to attend your conference, because we felt the issue of sexual practice for lesbians with disabilities to be extremely important. For too long we have been excluded from the lesbian scene because of the way you organise and communicate. We find it hard enough as people with disabilities to recognise that we have a right to the exploitation of our sexual practice in a world which surrounds disabled people with taboos and myths. As lesbians with disabilities we have not only fought and triumphed over this, but have discovered our sexuality and come out as lesbians in a world which you know does not welcome lesbians. All you have done by this action is make us want to withdraw further into our isolated ghetto, fully aware that even lesbians will collude with the heterosexual world in order to imprison and exclude us.

Sisters, these are bitter words, but we are angry and deeply disillusioned. We ask you as organisers of this conference to think about what we have said in this letter as a valid political argument, and not as something concerning the personal tragedy of a handful of women. We ask that you set aside a room on the ground floor at the conference for women with disabilities to meet and discuss what we want to do at the conference. And we ask you never again to organise anything which excludes and divides women with disabilities in this way.

We ask that all lesbians attending the conference remember that lesbians with disabilities have been excluded, to show your anger, disgust and your solidarity by supporting us in whatever action we decide to take on Saturday, to respect the space that we will take for ourselves in order to discuss our action, and if finally that means that we ask you too to leave the conference, to do so.

With disappointment and anger,

Lesbian Members of Sisters Against Disablement

Acknowledgements

The editors would like to thank all the women's liberation publications which responded quickly to our requests for copies of their publications and who were so helpful and co-operative throughout the process of putting this book together.

We have listed below only those publications from which we have extracted articles or letters; there are many more weekly and monthly publications available. For further information on these, or for details of local women's groups working on specific issues, contact WIRES, PO Box 162, Sheffield 1 IUD; telephone (0742) 755290.

When writing to any of these publications please send a stamped addressed envelope – they don't have any money either!

Birmingham Women's Liberation Newsletter No fixed address, contact WIRES for up to date information. Irregular.

Breaking Chains C/o Abortion Law Reform Association, 88a Islington High Street, London N1. Bi-monthly. 20p. Subscription £6 annually.

Cardiff Women's Newsletter No current address now available.

Catcall 37 Wortley Road, London E6. Irregular. A non-sectarian forum for discussion, theory, and the exchange of ideas by and for women in the women's liberation movement. 30p. Subscriptions minimum £1. Women only.

FAST C/o PO Box 336, Manchester M60 2BS. Irregular. FAST stands for Feminists Against Sexual Terrorism and is for feminists interested in working against male violence against women, in all its forms. Women only. Each issue is produced by a different group. Three issues for £1.75 including p&p. Sold mostly on subscription and at some selected bookshops.

Feminist Review 11 Carleton Gardens, Brecknock Road, London N19 5AQ. Published three times annually. A journal aimed at developing the theory of the women's liberation movement, produced by a collective based in London. Subscriptions: individuals £7.00; institutions £19.00.

Hull Women's Newsletter C/o The Womens Centre, 40 Middleton St., Spring Bank, Hull. Every three months. 20p.

Irregular Periods Bradford Women's Newsletter, c/o 85 Beamsley Road, Shipley. Monthly. 30p. Women only.

Leeds Women's Newsletter C/o Corner Bookshop, 162 Woodhouse Lane, Leeds 2. Monthly. For women living in Leeds.20p for low/unwaged, 50p for waged. Women only.

Link 16 St John Street, London EC1M 4Y. Published quarterly. The Communist Party women's journal. 40p.

London Lesbian Newsletter C/o 66 Marchmont Street, London WC1. Monthly. By lesbians for all lesbians. 20p. Distribution in the London area only.

London Women's Liberation Newsletter A Woman's Place, Hungerford House, Victoria Embankment, London WC2. Weekly newsletter. 25p. Subscription £13 annually, subscriptions for shorter periods available on application.

Lysistrata 7 Florence Road, Brighton, Sussex. Newsletter for the Brighton women's liberation peace movement. Write for details.

Manchester Women's Liberation Newsletter 18 Hawarden Avenue, 36 Whitechapel Street, Manchester M20 0TX. Monthly. Local women's liberation newsletter. On open sale in some bookshops but intended for women only. 15p. Subscription £3.50 for ten issues.

Manchester Women's Paper 58 Central Road, West Didsbury, Manchester M20 92B. Irregular. Local newsletter available at some women's events, alternative bookshops and the local drapery store. 20p.

Merseyside Women's Paper 18 Hawarden Avenue, Liverpool 17. Quarterly. Local paper for women in Merseyside. Available from alternative bookshops, newsagents or by subscription. £2 for five issues, 25p per single copy.

Outwrite Women's Paper Oxford House, Derbyshire Street, London E2. An anti-racist, anti-imperialist feminist newspaper. 30p. Subscription rates £3 (poor/unwaged), £4 ordinary rate. Write for free copy.

Plymouth Women's Centre Newsletter Peacock Lane, Plymouth. Irregular. 10p. Subscription £2.60. Women only.

Revolutionary and Radical Feminist Newsletter (Rev/Rad newsletter) 17 Kensington Terrace, Leeds 6. Irregular. 50p. Subscription £1.50 for three copies. Available on tape for blind women. Women only.

Scarlet Women 5 Washington Terrace, North Shields, Tyne & Wear, NE30 2HE. Irregular. Socialist feminist newsletter, each issue containing several articles, with different viewpoints, on a specific topic. Usually 60p, depending on size.

Sheffield Women's Paper C/o Common Ground, 87 The Wicker, Sheffield 3. Irregular. 30p. Articles, news items and many, very funny, cartoons. Women only.

Shocking Pink C/o Cromer Street Women's Centre, 90 Cromer Street, London WC1. Irregular. Feminist magazine produced by young women for young women. Write for details.

Southall Black Sisters Newsletter C/o 86 Northcote Avenue, Southall. Irregular. Write for further details. Women only.

Spare Rib 27 Clerkenwell Close, London EC1R OAT. A monthly women's liberation magazine. 70p. Subscription £9 annually, write for details of six month subscription, overseas rates and special institution rates. Tape subscription for blind women £6 annually.

Speakout C/o Black Women's Centre, 41 Stockwell Green, London SW9. Irregular. 30p + large SAE.

Spinster 40 St Lawrence Terrace, London, W10. Quarterly. Radical feminist publication of theory and creative work with an emphasis on the work of lesbians. 75p. Available by mail order.

Trouble and Strife 30 Brudenell Avenue, Leeds 6. A radical feminist magazine. Published three times annually. £1.50 per copy.

WIRES PO Box 162, Sheffield 1 IUD. Irregular. (National Newsletter of the women's liberation movement.) May be moving soon; post will be forwarded. Phone (0742) 755290 for details. Women only.

York Feminist News Shelf 17, c/o 73 Walmgate, York. Irregular. Three or four times yearly. Local newsletter. 20p. Women only.

We have also extracted pieces from the three general publications listed below and thank them for their co-opereation:

City Limits 313 Upper Street, London N1. Weekly 'what's-on' magazine for the London area only. 60p.

Marxism Today 16 St John Street, London EC1M 4AY. Monthly theoretical journal of the Communist Party. 60p. Subscriptions £7.20 annually for individuals, £9.60 institutions.

New Society 30 Southampton Street, London WC2. A weekly magazine of social science, social policy and social reportage. 70p.